Mystic by Default

Mystic by Default

James Swartz

ShiningWorld.com

Third edition

Printed in the United States of America in 2019

ISBN-13: 978-0-9674444-0-6

ISBN-10: 0-9674444-0-3

Second edition

Printed in the United States of America in 2012

ISBN-13: 978-0-9674444-9-9

ISBN-10: 0-9674444-9-7

First edition

Printed in the United States of America in 2012

ISBN-13: 978-0-9674444-2-0

ISBN-10: 0-9674444-2-X

Cover photo courtesy James Swartz

Cover and book design by Robert Grey

Contents

Chapter I
The Land *of* Light

Home Is Where the Heart Is

As THE DECREPIT boat chugged past rusting geriatric tankers listlessly anchored in the harbor, and the city appeared like a phantom out of the choking noon-day haze, my mind was overtaken by fantasies gleaned from years of reading Victorian fiction: snake charmers, *fakirs*, bejeweled *swamis*, white slavers, dancing girls, Mogul invaders, cartels of master criminals and swindlers presiding over myriad forms of corruption, alleys teeming with brown-skinned brigands, an opium den on every other corner, emaciated unfortunates expiring in the streets. Even recently-acquired spiritual fantasies were swallowed by the torpid atmosphere.

The pristine high from the trip across the Indian Ocean from Mombasa refused to stick around in the gargantuan metropolis. I had worked my way halfway around the world, suffered endless indignities and three close calls with death in the last two months for this?

We docked next to the Gate of India, a tribute to the glory of the Raj. Once an impressive monument, it was now in a state of hopeless neglect. Its journey from pride to poverty had transformed it into a haven for hawkers, thieves and pickpockets, a venue for promenading crowds and a playground for countless rats that went boldly about their business in the light of day.

With effort, however, I conjured an image of the Viceroy, dressed to the nines, attended by his guard, a company of spit-shined equestrian troops and a brass band standing beneath its generous arch welcoming dignitaries from England, perhaps the Queen or the foreign minister disembarking from an elegant wooden schooner, her starched white sails fluttering in the breeze. One would not expect Mother India to take pride in a symbol of her enslavement, although Calcutta's Victoria Memorial still retains most of its grandeur, but at least it had not been razed to the ground in a fit of revolutionary fervor at the time of Independence. Instead, it suffered the fate of most Indian real estate: it was permitted to slowly crumble into the earth, victim of Kala, Time, the great devourer.

Leaving the sleepy harbor and entering the warren of fetid streets along the waterfront, I tuned into the heart and pulse of the city, my senses overwhelmed by a tremendous roar, the blending of countless vibrations into an overpowering, shaking riot of energy – ten million souls desperately scratching and clawing to survive. Although a shadow of its present self, contrary to my first impression the Bombay of the late sixties was a dynamic, exciting and cosmopolitan city. Unlike our great cities, however, the sun shone year-round and the streets at three in the morning were remarkably safe.

Ambling leisurely along, eyes peeled for proper accommodations, I was accosted by an army of touts and vendors presenting me with fabulous deals. A small, mustachioed, immaculately dressed man enthusiastically offered to shine my shoes for a rupee, about eight cents. When I pointed to my skimpy rubber sandals, he seemed unimpressed.

"Very good shine, *sahib*. I do best work!"

For "pipty annas," four cents, a skinny, one-eyed, turbaned Rajasthani offered to clean my ears with a long-hooked, needle-like metal pick to which a small wad of cotton was attached.

A young boy with a big smile, eager to book my trip to Srinagar, Kashmir, informed me I would be the honored guest of his uncle, a very famous man, on an old houseboat built during the waning days of the Raj. He proudly presented a worn and dirty photo of a hippie smoking a chillum on the verandah of a ramshackle boat on Dal Lake, the hint of snow-capped mountains, which I took to be the Himalayas, in the distance. "Paradise," he said, obviously coached by Western travelers. "Only two thousand rupees!"

I walked on, the price cascading with every step.

"Okay, last price, one thousand rupees!" Then, "Five hundred rupees, last price. With breakfast!"

A noseless, fingerless, lion-faced leper hobbling on a rag-encrusted homemade crutch aggressively thrust a cracked, bleeding, scabrous, putrefying stub in my face, demanding *baksheesh*.

An amputee stuffed into a small wooden box-like cart lifted legless stubs in the air, crying pitifully from his station under a huge banyan tree near a reeking public latrine and next to a small shrine to the monkey god, "*Baksheesh, sahib! Baksheesh!*"

Demanding five rupees, a king's ransom, a barefoot rheumy-eyed young girl, not more than five years old, dressed in rags and full of chutzpah, darted through the chaotic traffic carrying her snot-nosed, thumb-sucking baby brother, naked except for a string around his extended belly to which was affixed a small cylindrical copper amulet containing a holy *mantra* to ward off the evil eye. When I mimicked her pathetic stomach-to-mouth gestures, she broke out laughing and wandered off singing a film song after protracted negotiations yielded half a rupee.

A small boy, immaculately dressed in white with gentle, light-filled eyes hoisted a large brass platter sporting an artfully constructed altar garlanded with fresh jasmine on which was enthroned a picture of the great god Rama, pride of the race of solar kings, the orange monkey god Hanuman genuflecting before him. A wafer of camphor, the size of a communion host, burned in a pile of sacred ash next to a smattering of small odd-shaped aluminum coins. Silently, he vibed a rupee from my pocket.

A stooped, graying Muslim woman presented a much-folded paper written with the help of a foreigner and attesting to her impoverished state. It informed prospective donors that she had been given a small plot of land by a generous *zamindar*, a landlord. To top it off, by the grace of Allah, the reader was to be allowed the honor of contributing ten thousand rupees, a princely sum in those days, toward the construction of a retirement bungalow.

They were unlike Western street people. Apart from demands for money, no one had a bone to pick or an agenda born of low self-esteem. I was not expected to feel guilty for our disparate fates; *karma* was *karma* – mine to be rich, theirs to be poor. I soon realized that, needy as they were, the extraordinary whining, crying, grimacing and moaning were simply high art. The second I passed by, lives resumed without so much as a by-your-leave. Life was a *lila*, a divine play, and on both sides of the equation, beggars and beggees, we were cast to be supremely indifferent, gods sporting on earth. In a couple of days I became invisible. The word was out; he knows what's up.

In the real estate trade it's sometimes said that home buyers decide to buy within the first ten minutes of seeing the property. I wasn't buying a house, but in the first two hours of my arrival I bought a home, a culture and an idea that would serve the rest of my life, one I only dimly grasped as I wandered around gawking at the fascinating multi-cultural city: the Dharavi slum nestled in the shade of multimillion-dollar high-rises, a quarter of a million people living in less than a square mile, elegant Indo-Saracen architecture, riotous bazaars, colonial mansions, pompously imperial buildings of the Raj, the steamy red-light district, thousands of temples, shrines and mosques. And above all, incessant humanity – frenetic ants animated by the unforgiving tropical sun.

Over the years I have met dozens who did not survive the first twenty-four hours, jetting off to less challenging destinations a day after touching down, but

I found India hopelessly charming from the start. Like Africa, it was home to many cultures, but unlike Africa, it was a civilization, held together for thousands of years by an endlessly unfolding spiritual mystery.

I had come home.

Initially unsure of how to handle the poverty and motivated by compassion on one hand and guilt on the other, I often gave more than necessary. The magnitude of the problem, however, produced a strange indifference. A standard comment on the subject was, "Ten minutes on the streets of Bombay would bankrupt even Lakshmi, the goddess of wealth." Many beggars were professionals, members of families with generations of experience in the trade. Parents sold their children for a pittance only to have them scarred and brutally deformed to render them particularly valuable. After much thought, I budgeted a fixed sum every day, like a tithe.

During my search for a hotel I stopped at a restaurant for lunch and struck up a conversation with a businessman.

"Who takes care of them? They have to eat," I asked wolfing down my sumptuous lunch.

"We do, of course," he said. "Everybody gives a little something, but nothing changes. We have few resources and a large population. The government discourages giving, so foreigners won't get a bad impression, but it is nonsense. You don't need beggars to see that we are a poor country."

Lunch consisted of buttered *naan*, tasty flat bread smothered in *ghee* and baked in a *tandoor*, an earthen oven. It was accompanied by a fiery, soupy spinach dish and a sweet mango *lassi*, a delicious yoghurt drink similar to a milkshake. My tongue still smarting from the cayenne, I stepped into the baking afternoon, looked down the block and spied a faded green hotel that brought to mind New Orleans French Quarter antebellum times. Given a second-storey room at the top of a creaking staircase, I sat in a rickety white wicker chair digesting my meal, smoking hash and watching the passing show.

Mother would have labeled the Carleton seedy, and soft focus was indeed preferable. However, even four-star hotels, such as they are, sport medieval kitchens, soiled carpets, smudged walls, leaky plumbing and incompetent help. How amazing that a country that developed a grand civilization well before the time of Christ, famed for spirituality, mathematics, arts, letters and sciences, could not, over the course of millennia, fathom the concept of building maintenance. Obviously-worshipped icons of Vishnu, the cosmic preserver, adorned every other home and business, yet concerning real estate, the god seemed hopelessly indifferent.

The clientele, like the hotel in Khartoum, represented a motley diaspora of ne'er-do-wells, romantics and desperados strewn like seeds in the wind from the four corners of the earth. Druggies were well represented but the vibes were not, in the argot of the times, "heavy." Something about India, even in the depths of her archaic miseries, keeps her from heaviness. Unlike their armored, tech-savvy, mobile Darth-Vaderesque U.S. counterparts, city cops, for example, in deference to the weather, are clad in khaki shorts, scout caps and sandals. They sparingly use the *lathi*, a thin, long cane stick, on miscreants of all ilk as they leisurely wander the streets extracting bribes from all and sundry.

Even crooks believe in God and propitiate the deities with lavish devotion. A *swami* informed me that the immense wealth collected at Tirupathi, said to be the richest temple in India and perhaps the world, the temple of choice for those wishing to expiate sins associated with black money, ill-gotten wealth. Devotees appear daily in their tens of thousands and suffer interminable waits in the sweltering heat, only to fling their bodies at the feet of a miraculous boon-granting granite icon, Venkateswara.

India's version of *Time* magazine recently reported that in a precinct in Bihar, a rural area in eastern India famed for criminal activity and near the spot where Buddha attained enlightenment, women in the last month of pregnancy committed crimes requiring a month in lock-up so the baby would be born in jail. When queried about the reason, the mothers said that since the child would be a career criminal and spend much of its life behind bars, it was important that it feel comfortable there from the start.

After pondering my first few hours in the Land of Light, I took a siesta, and as the roiling sun calmed to a simmer about four in the afternoon, wandered through the neighborhood. I ended up sipping a fresh mango shake in a juice shop catering to hippies while a pet monkey dressed in a red skirt and chained to a tree branch masturbated in sync to The Rolling Stones' (*I Can't Get No) Satisfaction* blaring from a battered tape deck.

Darshan

From a nine-to-five point of view my travels might seem exciting, funny, romantic, exotic and maybe even slightly glamorous. But real life, the inner journey, with the exception of the recent epiphanies, was a titanic struggle. More often than not, after a day on the street I returned to my hotel to sit up half the night tormented by fears and desires too numerous to mention.

I cannot begin to count the times I blew into town hoping to meet a glorious destiny, only to encounter my own very limited self sitting in the corner of a crummy vermin-infested café in an overpopulated third-world country, sipping bitter tea and resentfully observing thoughts, as dark as the natives, marching across my consciousness.

Although I wanted to believe that my suffering was profoundly romantic, it was hopelessly banal. I experienced homesickness, longed for the touch of a woman, worried over dwindling resources, struggled with my addictions and suffered the gratuitous vanity that my greatness had yet to receive its due from an indifferent and capricious world.

Superficially I was as strong, confident and clever as I could hope to be, but I questioned everything, a practice not conducive to happiness. I was quickly coming to the conclusion that the puzzle of my being would not be solved by lonely introspection or a life of adventurous distractions. I needed help.

I would think through every doubt from a dozen different angles, yet the riddle would not yield. There I was. There was the world. Getting the two to interact and produce lasting fulfillment seemed impossible. At times I thought I was quite mad. What, except weak genes, could explain why a nice middle-class boy from a good family with all the right stuff apparently preferred to sit in a juice shop in Bombay watching a masturbating monkey instead of taking his rightful place in society, as Mother so quaintly put it?

In terms of interest in what counted in the world – security, gainful employment and family – I was light years from reality. I was not rejecting that – or perhaps I was – as much as I failed to see its long-term relevance. You got all the stuff, you did all those things, but what was the point if they slipped you into the inviting warm earth with a big existential question mark on your worn-out face? There had to be a better reason why we were encased in these strange, meaty, waste-producing tubes.

After wandering the streets for a couple of hours I went back to the hotel and picked up Mr. Patel's book, the *Bhagavad Gita*, suddenly realizing that the war forming the centerpiece of this great spiritual work was not an outer war but a symbol of the conflict between the dark and light forces within the mind. Krishna said the answer was to know oneself as the self. I had had my glimpses, tasted the peace and joy, but how could I establish myself beyond the dualities and become a man of steady wisdom?

I prayed for enlightenment.

The next day, sitting in the juice shop reading a book on Hinduism, a handsome young man in an immaculate white *kurta* with a red *tilak* on his forehead sat down at my table uninvited. Having experienced every possible permutation-combination of human hustle, before and after the epiphany in the post office, I rarely put up with the natives unless I was hopelessly lonely or bored. If you're a female they want sex or money, not necessarily in that order. If you're a male they want money, except in Muslim countries. No matter how innocent it all seems ("Come home and meet the family; let's go the park and see the sights"), in the end it always boils down to: "Please help with my son's education and marry my daughter so she can get her green card and smuggle the lot of us into the U.S. Okay, maybe that is a lot to ask of our ten-minute acquaintance, but at least send me a transistor radio or a hair dryer when you get back." One fellow requested that I bring a refrigerator when I returned to India. "It's a small thing, no?" he asked.

I ignored him, going deeper into my reading, scanning occasionally to pick up his vibes, waiting for the inevitable interruption. But he sat sipping his juice as if I didn't exist. As time passed, my wall of cynicism dissolved and I began to feel positively happy. To my surprise I realized that the energy was coming from him!

I observed him carefully, a detective looking for something that might provide an opening, when he said, "What is your native place?"

"America, U.S.A. And you?"

"Just here."

"What do you do?" I asked.

"I'm a student."

"Oh, what do you study?"

"The *Vedas*," he replied.

"This is very interesting," I replied. "I'm just now reading the *Bhagavad Gita*. I think it comes from the *Vedas*."

"No, not exactly," he said, "it's a *Purana*, but the ideas come from the *Vedas*."

"But you must have a job. You can't just study holy books."

"No, I don't have a job. My father wants me to learn our ancient culture, so he supports me."

"Do you practice meditation?"

"Yes."

"And what do you experience?"

"Peace."

"What meditation do you do?"

"I listen to the words of my *guru*."

"So how does that work?" I asked eagerly.

"He just talks and I listen. Then something happens and I experience peace."

"Are you in meditation now? I can feel some good energy coming from you," I asked.

He seemed surprised.

"Yes. I came from *satsang* with Maharaj."

"Maharaj?"

"My *guru*."

"What's it mean?"

"It means 'great king.'"

"So how is he a king?"

"He rules over his own mind."

"How do you know that?"

"Because he is at peace. I become peaceful in his presence."

"And what's *satsang*?"

"When you sit with a *mahatma* and you experience something."

"Are you a *mahatma*?" I asked innocently.

He laughed. "No, I'm just his devotee."

I couldn't explain why, but I knew exactly what he was talking about. "Will you take me to the Maharaj?" I asked.

"Yes, we will go. No expectations. Not everybody experiences something."

"That's okay," I said. "I'd just like to see what these *mahatmas* look like. I came to India to find God. I've had experiences and read books, but I'm still in the dark. Maybe your Maharaj can help."

"Maybe," he smiled, getting up to leave. "My name is Ravi. I will meet you here tomorrow at nine."

"So what happens at these *satsangs*?" I asked as we left the juice shop and made our way through the crowded streets.

"We sit. Sometimes there is a question and Maharaj talks. Don't say anything unless he asks you a question. To experience the self, silence is best."

"But I thought you said that you experienced it when he was talking."

"I do, but I also experience it when he isn't saying anything."

"I don't get it," I replied. "How can you experience something when nobody is saying anything?"

"Too many questions," he said. "Just you see."

The next morning we arrived at a storefront on a busy street. In an atmosphere of total silence we deposited our sandals on a landing at the top of a flight of stairs and entered a room where about ten people were sitting on the floor in front of a small, clean-shaven man. I don't know what I expected, but he seemed quite ordinary, like the thousands of men we had passed in the street.

We sat for a long time, the sounds of the city melting into the silence like ice in hot water. I felt agitated, tortured by many questions.

Toward the end, the Maharaj spoke to Ravi, who turned and said to me, "Maharaj wants to know where is your native place."

"The U.S.A.," I replied.

"And why have you come?"

"I want to know God," I said.

Maharaj says, "Who wants to know God?"

"I do," I replied, thinking they didn't hear properly.

"Who are you?"

"You mean you want to know my name?" I asked.

"No. You. Who are you?"

"You want to know what I do?" I replied.

"No, not what you do. Who you are."

"Well, I don't know," I said, irritated at the question. "I've never thought about it."

He repeated the conversation to the Maharaj, who looked directly into me and said in English, "You are God."

Suddenly my mind went blank and I could barely make out his body, which seemed to be a one-dimensional cut-out superimposed in the center of a limitless radiant light! He answered my question in the only way possible – by an experience of the self.

I felt someone gently shaking my shoulder and suddenly became aware of the world. The room was empty.

"The *satsang's* over," said Ravi. "Shall we take juice?"

I got up, nearly unable to stand. Everything was fresh and new, bathed in a subtle light. As we slipped on our sandals Ravi said, "The Maharaj says that perhaps you will find what you are seeking in Rishikesh."

As we sipped our mango shakes he said, "You are very blessed. Many people wait for years to have such an experience. It is good *karma* from previous lives."

"But why did he tell me I would find what I was seeking in Rishikesh?" I asked. "Why shouldn't I go back to see him again?"

"So many questions," he said affectionately. "In India we do not question the *guru*. He knows things that we don't."

"Maybe, but why look for a *guru* if he can do this for me," I said, referring to the blissful feeling that was still very much with me. "Why should I go all the way to Rishikesh?"

9

"You are a funny man," he said. "I think the Americans believe everything is logical, but life is not logical. You have to let go. It is not up to you."

Ravi was right. I thought too much.

Robbed of my ego and intoxicated by a wondrous sense of well-being, I wandered the city for several timeless days watching events melt effortlessly into each other in an unending flow. The Maharaj had shown me the door to Bharat, the Land of Light and the spiritual name of India. Oddly, I did not feel compelled to see him again, though I thought of him often. It was his will.

Three days later, I boarded the train for Delhi and the Himalayas. Two years later I would discover I had stumbled on one of India's great *mahatmas*, Nisargadatta Maharaj, a man of the highest realization, who lived an ordinary life in the heart of Bombay.

City of Saints

Today Delhi, like all major Indian cities, is drowning in a flood of country migrants who have exchanged the grinding poverty of the hinterlands for the grinding poverty of an ugly, polluted city. The situation is out of hand. India's population increases by over twenty million a year.

When I arrived in 1969, however, New Delhi, the area built by the British as the seat of government, was still livable and almost enjoyable. I took a clean, safe room in Madame Colaco's Guest House near Jantar Mantar, a sixteenth-century astronomical observatory with building-sized instruments constructed by a Rajput king, and breakfasted at the Imperial for the daily price of my room, two dollars.

The Imperial conjured up memories of the Raj: the turbaned, white-jacketed waiters attended an elegant clientele seated in wicker chairs at tables set with starched white linen napkins and polished silver, resting under the shade of striped canopies, all carefully positioned on the close-cropped grass of manicured gardens. The air was reasonably clean and the sounds of the morning traffic did not scale the tall, whitewashed, bougainvillea-covered walls to disturb the tranquility of the patrician patrons as it does today. Even the touts and vendors hanging out near the front gates had a bit of class.

After breakfast, I networked with travelers and picked up information on the libertine hot spots: Goa, Kulu-Manali and Kovalam beach. Certainly God was great, but I thought it prudent to be prepared should the God-quest not pan out. After lunch at Nirula's, I popped over to Old Delhi in a cycle rickshaw for a taste of the exotic – Chandi Chowk, the riotous bazaar, the snake charmers and magicians on the lawn in front of the Red Fort, Himayun's bat-infested tomb, Qtab Minar and Raj Ghat on the Yamuna where Mahatma Ghandi, the father of the nation, was cremated.

But the world, which seemed far away and unreal, failed to enthrall me. So, burdened with the belief that rubbing elbows with the teeming masses of the Asian subcontinent was an indispensable step on the road to enlightenment, I caught the pigs-and-chickens bus to Rishikesh, suffering conditions that would have made the Black Hole of Calcutta seem spacious. Why I was willing to endure rock-hard seats, puking babies and screechy Hindi film music blaring from the world's most primitive audio technology to garner another useless credential for my traveler's résumé, I still cannot fathom.

The shady road to the foothills of the Himalayas, where the Ganges enters the plains, proceeds through endless cane fields broken by small towns and villages, where peasants pass a medieval existence in mud-walled, thatched-roofed hovels clustered around a central well.

As the bus careened along the potholed road, which it shared with pigs, chickens, goats, ox carts, trucks, bicycles and countless pedestrians, its horn sending out intermittent blips of energy like bat radar, I glimpsed an old man sitting on a rope bed smoking a hubbly-bubbly, a woman drawing water from the well, small children knocking about in the dust making mischief and lean men scratching the red soil with primitive wooden plows pulled by teams of lethargic oxen. It seemed idyllic from the bus, but share a few days of these lives of quiet desperation and you will be quickly disabused of romantic notions. Ignorance, poverty, superstition and disease abound. What passes for peace is simply torpor.

About ten miles from Rishikesh I noticed a billboard saying, "Welcome to the City of Saints." The town, a noisy, dirty, crowded, unesthetic agglomeration of commercial establishments and residential dwellings, was far from celestial. Cranky from the ride, I fought my way through the rickshaw *wallas* and hotel touts, and walked downtown where I found a decent restaurant. The proprietor, Subash, served a nice meal and sat down to talk.

"I saw a sign on the road from Haridwar saying Rishikesh was the 'City of Saints.' It doesn't look all that holy to me," I said.

"Which *ashram* are you looking for?" he asked.

"I don't know," I replied, "it doesn't matter. This is my first time to India."

"Well, you have to be careful," he said. "These *yogis* are not always too scrupulous."

"What do you mean?"

"Just because one fellow wears the orange cloth, has a long beard and a wild look in his eye doesn't mean that he's a saint. Most of these *sadhus* are useless, lazy fellows on the lookout for money or drugs, drop-outs, I think you call them."

"But I thought they took vows not to have money, sex, drugs, all that."

"They do, but not many stick to it. Some good ones are there, but most are just parasites."

"Parasites?"

"They live off the society and don't put anything back. And they're now going for the foreigners since The Beatles came."

"The Beatles came here?"

"Yes, they came to see the Maharishi, who is now a famous *guru*. They put him on the map. He goes all around the world now, making lots of money. Before, he was just a little *guru*. Now he's too big to even visit."

"So what happened to The Beatles?"

"Nothing. They came, spent a few weeks and left, like most of the hippies. But now many people in your country know about Rishikesh and *yoga*. New ones come every day looking for peace of mind, like you. And the *sadhus* are doing good business."

"But I thought this spirituality was free," I said naively.

"Nothing's free in this life. You may not have to pay money straightaway, but you will pay sooner or later. We call it *karma*."

"They really are dishonest?" I said incredulously.

"I'll tell you a story," he said warming to his subject.

"About two years ago a European woman, Swiss, I think, came from Delhi. She'd inherited some big money and was looking for peace. She got off the train, and one taxi *walla*, a glib fellow, saw her looking confused about where to go. He offered to take her around, show her the *ashrams* at no charge. He drove her around a bit and found out her story. So on the way up the river to the *ashrams* he said he was an honest *guru* who didn't want money like the rest of them, that he worked for his living and gave his money to *sadhus* who were looking for God.

"The woman thought it was *karma*. How could it be only a coincidence that she had come looking for peace and God had sent her straight to this humble *yogi*?" he said with a grin.

"The fellow suggested that she put up in a local hotel and he would teach her some *yoga*."

He paused, sipped on his tea, and smiled.

"So what happened?" I asked.

"He taught her some *yoga*, all right. He told her his path was *tantra*, sex *yoga*, and that the fastest way to get to God was to sleep with an enlightened *tantrik*. She was lonely and middle-aged, and he wasn't a bad-looking fellow, so they took up with each other. He told her all sorts of things; the story is common knowledge around town. He's a shameless fellow. And she believed it all. Before long she was talking about building him an *ashram*. But he wanted to see Europe, so he got her to marry him and take him to Switzerland! Just a taxi *walla*, mind you. And in the end he got all sorts of money and left her and lives not far from here in a big house with a nice young wife. So you have to be careful."

"I don't think these *yogis* will want to sleep with me," I said. "And my money is running out."

He laughed.

"No, I don't think so. You look like a smart man."

"I was a businessman in my country," I replied. "I know the whole game, but I'm serious about this God business. I met a *mahatma* in Bombay who said to come to Rishikesh. I think he must have known that something good would happen here."

"I don't mean to discourage you," the proprietor said. "There are also good *yogis*. Go to Shivananda Ashram. Swami Chidananda is an honest man."

"What about you?" I asked. "Do you have a *guru*?"

"Yes," he said. "See that picture on the wall behind the counter? That's my *guru*, Neem Karoli Baba. One of your famous men, Richard Alpert [now Baba Ram Dass], a Harvard professor, came here and gave him some LSD."

"What happened?" I inquired eagerly.

"Nothing. Nothing at all. The Maharaj took it and just sat there. Your professor couldn't believe it. He was expecting him to get high but it didn't work."

The memory of the trip with my friend George in the Riff Mountains came to mind. "I think I know what you mean," I said. "He was already higher than the LSD."

"Yes," he replied, looking at me with interest.

"Where's he from?" I said. "Maybe I could see him."

"You could," he said, "but he's in Almora, near Nainital, many hours from here in the Himalayas.

"Why is he a *guru*?" I said, somewhat surprised by his bulk and lack of grooming. He didn't seem at all mystical, but he had a fabulous smile.

"He is a real *mahatma*," Subash said. "He has great *siddhis*."

"*Siddhis?*"

"Powers. He is known as the Steam Engine Guru because one day he stopped a train with the power of his mind. The wheels on the engine were going around but the train wouldn't move until he released it."

"Do you believe that?" I said.

"Yes. Many such things happen here. It was witnessed by many people. But it does not matter, because he is an incarnation of love. He has changed my life completely. Before I met him I was very unhappy. Now I have no problems. Even business is good."

So where are the *ashrams?*" I said.

"Just keep on this road. In about a mile you'll see the Shivananda Ashram. I hope you find what you're seeking."

I walked up the dusty road, full of anticipation, thinking about the conversation. Traffic died at the edge of town and only a couple of *tongas*, colorfully decorated horse-drawn carriages with big wooden wheels carrying brightly-clad women, passed by. The sight of the Ganges and the mountains pulled me out of my thoughts.

I observed four stocky men and a boy with oriental features, whom I judged to be Nepali or Tibetan construction workers wearing vests, colorful hats and work pants, carrying the tools of their trade – picks, sledgehammers and shovels – driving several small, worn-out, knock-kneed mules laden with heavy boulders and sand from the river.

A well-dressed family of Hindu pilgrims walked silently along, the wife dutifully bringing up the rear, followed by three well-behaved children. Two dignified, clean-shaven, saffron-robed monks with begging bowls and staffs emerged from a path on the hillside and joined the flow.

Today the road to the Shivananda Ashram is a dusty, ugly corridor of makeshift businesses exploiting the boom. Sadly, the *tongas* are gone and the once-pleasant walk is now a torture best endured crammed in the back of a soulless motor rickshaw, hands over ears to block the incessant cacophony of horns, the grinding of gears and the roar of dozens of two-stroke engines.

The City of Saints has been discovered. A jet boat of American design rushes mindlessly up and down the river, marring the timeless serenity, desecrating Hinduism's most sacred symbol. At four hundred fifty rupees a head, a considerable sum by Indian standards in those pre-boom days, raft after raft of Delhi yuppies sail past *sadhus* and pilgrims bathing in the river.

When the river and the mountains came into view, a thrill of recognition lifted my mind and I sensed that I was about to make a giant step on my journey home. I suppose I shouldn't make so much of it since it was what any pilgrim must feel approaching the primary symbol of his or her religion for the first time: Lourdes, the Mount of Olives, the Kabbah or Swedagon Pagoda. But I wasn't consciously religious and my knowledge of God was rudimentary, to say the least. Still, the experience is as clear today, forty years later, as it was then.

A large cluster of unesthetic buildings clinging to the banks of the Ganges, the Shivananda Ashram, appeared. Across the slate-blue, placid river on the right I noticed a string of temples and *ashrams* stretching half a mile downstream above the *ghats*. A dream I had in Montana two years before flashed in my mind; it was becoming reality. A wave of sweet, warm, tingly energy arose from the base of the spine, irradiating my cells with ecstasy, intensifying my already-heightened state. I followed a path down the boulder-strewn sandy banks of the river where an open longboat with wooden benches was about to embark for a large complex of buildings and temples on the other shore.

Like a small dinghy in a hurricane, the mind burst its moorings in a storm of inner energy, obliterating the past. I saw myself from far away, walking eagerly into a crowd of brightly-dressed Rajasthanis, weathered low-caste working people from India's western desert, caught in the excitement of a once-in-a-lifetime pilgrimage, waiting for the boat to leave for the other shore.

In those days the average daily wage was about ten rupees, roughly seventy-five cents, a sum that served to feed and clothe a family of four or five. Thirty years of backbreaking work might permit a family to accumulate enough to justify a week-long pilgrimage to the Ganges. From infancy, tales of the exploits of the gods and goddesses, of whom Ganga is one of the most revered, recounted by the village Brahmin and enacted in colorful rituals large and small throughout the year, capture the imagination of the masses.

Recently the *Ramayana* – an epic poem presenting Vedic culture's loftiest ideas in the form of a story of one of India's best-loved gods, Rama, a warrior king whose faithful wife was abducted by a wicked demon king – was converted into a forty-episode drama for television. During weekly screenings, the whole country, roughly a billion souls, ground to a halt, rendering the purchase of even the most rudimentary goods virtually impossible. Myth – psychic fact – is alive and well in India, reaching deep into the soul to touch the essential, the hidden current of meaning, in every Hindu.

Led by the children, the group waded eagerly into the river chanting *mantras*, garlanding the placid surface with marigold leis, anointing themselves with its healing waters, tossing coins for good luck.

I looked upriver as an orange-clad monk and his disciple emerged from the warren of *ashram* buildings. After gazing at the river for a few moments, their elegant forms silhouetted against the mountains, the senior monk turned to speak to his disciple and I saw – or think I saw – a stream of timeless love pour from heart to heart, an event so meaningful it brought tears to my eyes and awakened the pure light within, which, like the sun reflecting off the river, refracted off the flow of my thoughts and reawakened my mind to my ultimate purpose. It was the moment that, as the Buddhists say, I entered the stream and dove wholeheartedly into the culture that would mold and shape my aspirations.

The boat pulled up at the dock and we entered, every hand clutching an offering: a flower, coins, small balls of *chapati* dough. As we pulled away from the shore, the turbaned leader chanted to the river goddess and everyone chimed in.

"Jai! Jai! Gange! Jaya Hare Gange!" Victory to Ganga, the Holy Mother.

A large school of silvery carp, some nearly a meter long, appeared alongside the boat, swimming effortlessly in the current, begging shamelessly for the dough. Glistening coins sank into the swift green depths as small leaf rafts with flower offerings were set lovingly on the glassy surface.

Ascending the *ghats*, I wandered downstream through Swarg Ashram, entranced by the bizarre religious statuary lining the walk. First, I noticed a small ecstatic blue boy playing a flute and dancing on one of a multi-headed cobra's hoods, the god Krishna, whom I would eventually come to love and adore. Next, I spied a potbellied elephant god, Ganesh, with four arms and one tusk, symbolizing non-duality, near an indifferent white *yogi*, Shiva, the Ganges streaming from his matted locks, a cobra coiled around his neck. A bit further on, I came upon an elegantly dressed goddess, Saraswati, playing the *sitar*, and just beyond her there was a flying monkey with a crazy grin, Hanuman, carrying what appeared to be a forested mountain in one hand.

The last in the line, set back a few meters from the edge of the flood plain in an area called Muni Ke Reti, the place where sages revel, I discovered an *ashram* called Veda Niketan, Home of Knowledge. Knowing what I know now, I wouldn't call it a proper *ashram*, but it was right for me at the time.

Twenty or thirty sun-drenched rooms on ground level clustered around a courtyard. To impress visitors and ensnare the odd rupee, a sheet metal tank encased in wire mesh had been constructed near the entrance in which was to be seen a floating stone! A poorly lettered sign proclaimed the miracle. How this extraordinary phenomenon, a porous lava rock with a suspicious resemblance to a sponge, related to the awesome spiritual power of the resident *swami* was not apparent, but the mind was free to draw conclusions. Since his spiritual might seemed to be mainly involved in keeping the rock afloat and bona fide Indian devotees were much in absence, the *ashram* had become a budget hotel for Westerners who ended up in Rishikesh awed by the magic of the Himalayas and the lure of enlightenment.

My first task was to find *gurus*, which to the untrained eye seemed as innumerable as stones in the Ganges. But, as Subash had warned, more than one clever long-haired fellow with the gift of gab and less-than-carefully-examined intentions had donned orange robes, tacked *ananda* – bliss – to the end of an already-unpronounceable Sanskrit name and set out to trap the unsuspecting spiritual seeker.

Shiv Kumar, a high school drop-out, might morph overnight into His Holiness the Great Blissful Lord of Yoga. A ready supply of superstitious Indians with great reverence for the *guru*-disciple institution, and an equally gullible pool of foreigners streaming into Rishikesh since The Beatles took up with the Maharishi, made the *guru* business an attractive proposition. I quickly learned to spot the phonies: worldly men seeking name and fame, drop-outs, neurotics playing God, the crazies, deadbeats and dopers.

I wondered if the tranquil atmosphere was responsible for the many composed and indifferent half-naked men with glowing eyes wandering the banks of the Ganges. Perhaps it was the other way around: the feeling of great peace emanating from the *sadhus* blessed the cows, rocks, trees and flowers. Theirs was a strange religion indeed: no one seemed even vaguely interested in shoving his concept of God down my throat. I had to figure it out on my own.

Dogma apparently had little to do with it. It all seemed to be in the living. And the principle, as far as I could see, was "keep it simple." If you don't want anything, you don't have to get it. Having lies in being, not getting. If you have nothing, you have nothing to lose. I was familiar with the concept. It was time to make it real.

Armed with a rudimentary but reasonably accurate version of the theory of enlightenment, as I understood it – God hides within, covered by conditioning; remove the conditioning and God is revealed – I set out to purify mind and body. I vowed to avoid dope, Western clothing, tea, coffee, sweets, fried foods and sex. On the positive side, I enthusiastically pursued a rudimentary program of prayer, meditation, scriptural study and *yoga*. It was ironic indeed that only two years before I had been hobnobbing with a Mafia Don beside his swimming pool in his mansion on the slopes of Diamond Head in Hawaii.

The Serpent Power

Although I had a dim appreciation of the impermanence of existence, India was the nail in the coffin of my belief that the world of the senses was capable of delivering happiness. Although I could not have known it at the time, I was walking into another dream, confirming the fact that I was not satisfied with myself as I was and buying into one of the world's most attractive and useful deceptions – religion. But it turned out to be the appropriate course because it led me to freedom. After forty years of unbroken bliss, fullness beyond measure, I can categorically state that embracing religion was perhaps the wisest choice I ever made. Why it happened can only be attributed to the divine logic that was obviously shaping my destiny.

Because I was flying blind, I simply aped what I saw. I threw out the hippie rags and donned *yogi* garb: the *dhoti, kurta, tusli mala* and *tilak*. I ate like a bird, gazed intently at the setting sun and the tip of my nose – which someone said was meditation – and sang devotional Sanskrit chants for hours a day.

One day I learned of a *yoga* center near Lakshman Jhula, a small town about a mile above Rishikesh. I walked upriver along a shady path lined with huge mango trees and headed up a trail on the side of the mountain that entered an open field in front of a small cluster of white buildings. In the center of the field a group of about twenty squeaky-clean young Westerners, mainly women, were clustered attentively around a handsome thirty-something *yogi* sitting in a wicker easy chair giving a talk in passable English. When the talk ended he invited me to stay.

His *yoga* was called *kundalini*, the serpent power. Without putting too fine a point on it, the theory states that human spirituality is a dormant and hidden energy, coiled like a serpent in a *chakra*, or psychic center, at the base of the spine. Through a series of esoteric practices the energy can be awakened. When it is awakened it uncoils and journeys up the spine, leaving the body through the top of the head and reuniting with the cosmic spiritual energy. This fusion of the individual and the universal is meant to be enlightenment.

I set out enthusiastically to get fit for the great event, like an athlete preparing for the Olympics. I was told the energy was fussy and would not become activated in a polluted body, so I was enjoined to swallow yards of wet salty cotton gauze and retrieve it inch by inch once the impurities from my stomach had been absorbed. I also ingested and expelled gallons of saltwater a day, poured herbal concoctions in one nostril and out the other, ate spoonfuls of strange herbs and cayenne pepper, brushed my teeth with black powder and a stick, contorted my limbs into pretzel-like shapes, fasted, deprived myself of sleep and bathed in the icy river at the ungodly hour of 4:00 a.m.

Evidently the path was fraught with all manner of dangers, but I suffered nothing more than nausea and fatigue. During his discipleship the *yogi's* attempt to purify the bladder by sucking water through a glass catheter inserted in his penis caused the catheter to break. He had good *karma*, however, because after medical attention his plumbing still worked. Several of the "surrendered" female devotees, such as they were, reported that his prowess was second to none.

In spite of my enthusiasm and dedication nothing mystical happened, yet I continued to swallow the doctrine along with various bizarre concoctions. *Kundalini yoga* is based on scientific principles, but it was not designed to serve the needs of neurotic meatballs like me from consumer societies in search of instant *nirvana*.

In Vedic times young men with spiritual inclinations were placed in forest academies under the care of dispassionate *mahatmas* who patiently trained them in the spiritual arts for many years, imparting more and more profound disciplines as they matured, so that when the awakening came the divine energy would function through a truly beautiful instrument. I believe the recent fascination with *kundalini* is fueled more by its exotic, romantic, esthetic mythos than by a disinterested understanding of the requisite qualifications and the complex factors involved.

I went to the *guru* to find out why it was not working. I think I believed that enlightenment was a tricky game of skill and the body a clever puzzle, a bit like the wooden Chinese ball that falls into many pieces with the application of subtle pressure on an unlikely part. After much fiddling, you make the right moves in the right sequence and, presto chango, out pops the prize – enlightenment!

He suggested corrections and sent me back to the mines to continue my labors. In the meantime we became friendly during daily walks along the Ganges banks. I am not sure what he saw in me, because we had nothing in common. Perhaps he envied the uninhibited and unapologetic way I pursued life. Because their society is so highly structured, Indians have a gargantuan longing to be free. In fact the most common word for enlightenment, the obsession of Vedic culture, is *moksa*, freedom. Though he was supposedly inwardly free, I must have seemed much more outwardly free. Perhaps that was not his reason at all, because inward freedom renders any circumstance conducive. I later learned that he was very ambitious: he just wanted an invitation to the States. Evidently he eventually got what he wanted and predictably ended up in one of the tawdry sex and money scandals that regularly seem to afflict India's export *gurus*.

Still, after several months nothing of note had happened and I began to question the whole idea. Minus the drug-induced spirituality, which I can't take credit for, I had garnered quite a few transcendental experiences for my spiritual résumé before I arrived in India. Then the *maharaj* in Bombay revealed the Divine to me in the twinkling of an eye, and the day I entered the stream was a gift straight from God. I began to wonder why I should work so hard for something that seemed to come frequently without conscious effort. Perhaps all this spiritual work was interfering with my enlightenment.

So I made an issue of it, saying, "This isn't working, Yogaji. Please give me something else. What does how much mucus I can coax out of the body have to do with enlightenment? It doesn't make sense. What did your *guru* give you?"

"It's not like that. You have to work hard and have faith," he replied. "It will come at the right time. You're not ready yet."

"Well, I've invested a lot of time and energy in this project, and since it's not working, I think I'll leave," I said.

To my surprise he did an abrupt about-face and said, "Well, you have been working hard and maybe you are ready for the next step. I'm going to give you the practice my *guru* gave me."

So I quit the swallow-and-vomit drill and began a complex practice of muscular contractions, breath control and *mantra*. The work required intense concentration, and the *ashram* with all its distractions was unsuitable, so I moved upriver in search of a cave on the banks of the Ganges.

Carrying a blanket and a cooking pot, I came upon a huge rock in the middle of a sandy beach. During runoff the river had gouged a large hole under the rock, a perfect cave, suitable for sitting in the shade midday and sleeping out of the elements during the night.

At the end of the first week I realized I had a roommate, a three-foot cobra that came and went through a hole in the back, sleeping during the day in a well-concealed crevice. Because our schedules did not overlap and animals rarely attack without provocation, I decided not to move. Instead, I took its presence as a positive omen.

The cobra is the primary symbol of *kundalini yoga* and the vehicle of Shiva, the great Lord of Yoga, from whose matted locks the Ganges is said to flow. And snakes, according to the *yogi*, represented the latent electricity of consciousness and have carried the spiritual projection for ages. Everyday naked ash-smeared *naga babas* (snake daddies), devotees of Shiva with matted locks, passed the cave on their way to Kailash, the Himalaya's holiest peak, source of the Ganges and the abode of Shiva. So I imagined I was enjoying the protection of the god.

A couple of days after I discovered the snake, a small scorpion stung me on the little toe of the left foot. The toe immediately swelled and sent shooting pains into the foot, which ballooned until the skin was painfully tight. Immobilizing the ankle next, the swelling moved up the calf toward the knee, and my leg became so stiff I couldn't properly bend it. When the poison reached the heart, I set out to find a doctor, hobbling toward Rishikesh three miles downriver.

I had scarcely covered a hundred meters when I heard twigs snapping and rocks sliding on the side of the mountain, suggesting that a fairly large animal, perhaps a tiger, was making its way downhill in my direction. Driven by the pain, I pressed on, certain to encounter the beast in minutes. I managed another thirty or forty meters when suddenly a tall, naked *naga baba*, his eyes glowing like hot coals, burst from the jungle in front of me! Carrying an iron trident decorated with amulets in one hand and a bundle of old manuscripts wrapped in strips of orange cloth in the other, he stopped directly in front of me.

He looked down at my leg and made a small gesture, which I took to be an imitation of a scorpion stinging. I nodded. Placing the bundle on the path in front of me, he untied one of the cloth strips, walked to the edge of the path, tore the strip into three pieces, tied them in a neat row on the branch of a nearby bush and resumed his place in front of me.

After a moment of intense silence I heard a low rhythmic rumbling coming from the region of his solar plexus, vibrations so subtle I couldn't make out the words, although they were most certainly Sanskrit. Hardly twenty seconds passed when the pains in the chest stopped. He continued chanting and I felt a distinct lessening of leg pain. A few seconds later, my knee returned to its normal state.

The energy emanating from him was so powerful my mind became luminously still and I could actually see the subtle form of the poison as the *mantra* chased it down the leg. Next, the ankle returned to its normal state and the poison, chased by the *mantra*, retreated to the point where the stinger had broken the skin. Then it left the toe like the spirit leaves the body at death and dissolved into space.

The chant stopped and the *sadhu*, without the slightest change of expression, walked over to the bush, retrieved his strips, tied them back together, bound his manuscripts, nodded slightly and walked back into the jungle! When I examined the toe the skin was unbroken.

I returned to my cave and resumed the practices, which were generating inexplicably high feelings and crystal-clear insights into the nature of the mind and reality. Often I felt as if I didn't have a body at all. Overcome by a deep, nearly unbearable current of bliss, I was unable to practice for two days, sitting motionless instead for hours on end. I twice heard celestial music and on one occasion smelled an otherworldly fragrance so pure it nearly took my breath away. For several hours one morning I heard a deep humming coming from inner space, which *yoga* texts call *nada brahman,* the universal sound that creates the world.

Sitting on the sand one evening shortly after sunset, I was overcome by a terribly dark energy, as if the weight of the whole world were pressing down on me. Unable to sit, I lay on my back with outstretched limbs, staring into the sky in which a few stars were appearing. Observing an ominous black cloud form out of nowhere and fill the dome of the sky, I wondered if it was out there in the real sky or a vision taking place in the inner spiritual sky, but it really didn't matter, because it was unbearably real. As I watched, terrified, the cloud formed into the goddess Kali, who was endowed with such radiance that I couldn't look on her for more than a few seconds before I lost consciousness.

The next day, sitting on the sand in front of the cave in a state of awe and wonder, marveling at the experience of the goddess, I observed the orange-clad corpse of a *sadhu* floating slowly past, a crow sitting on the chest picking at the decomposing flesh. I took it as a symbol of life's impermanence and vowed to redouble my efforts.

Almost six weeks to the day after I moved into the cave, I was sitting on the riverbank in the half-lotus pose, chanting a *mantra,* when my body became so light I wondered if I was going to levitate. I was again magically endowed with a kind of x-ray vision that permitted me to observe life on the cellular level. The spaces between the cells began to grow and grow until the body ballooned to an enormous size and quickly surpassed the size of the Himalayas and then the earth, which was receding into the distance. It expanded to the limits of the cosmos and dissolved, and I could see galaxies without number spinning in eternity as my real self appeared as limitless radiance pervading an awesome emptiness!

I got up and headed downriver toward the *ashram* to express my gratitude to the *yogi,* walking but not walking, carrying an exhilarating current of divine electricity. Like a lightning bolt, it struck a villager coming along the path, causing him to fall to the ground in full prostration, his arms stretched toward me. Another villager, petrified by fear, huddled in a crevice on the mountainside as

I passed. The normally voluble vendors in Lakshman Jhula became silent and every eye turned in my direction. Several members of a group of pilgrims coming to worship at the temple made the gesture *namaste* and said, "Ram, Ram," in such a way I knew the *shakti* had awakened the vision of the self in them. Continuing under the shade of the mangos lining the path, I passed two sleeping *sadhus*, a blind beggar and his wife chanting devotional songs to Krishna, and a naked *yogi* lying on a bed of nails.

Yogaji and his devotees were sitting in the garden almost exactly as they had been the day I arrived. The feeling that this would be our last meeting floated through my consciousness. Turning my attention on my *guru*, I received a rude shock. Like the devotees, he too was locked in the sleep of worldly consciousness! Everyone started to react to the energy, and the *yogi*, fearful but remarkably collected, dismissed the *satsang* and turned toward me.

"I think it's time for you to leave," he said coolly, "I've given you everything I can."

I smiled, nodded, picked up my pack and walked off without a thought, as if my whole life there had been a dream.

For three days I wandered in God as God. The experience was similar to LSD in that I found every mundane detail of every object, superimposed on the blissful radiance of the self, intensely absorbing. Every thought and feeling was exactly equal, the mind a placid lake. There were no highs and lows, no goods and bads, rights and wrongs. I might equally appreciate the tiny veins in a small leaf as the cacophonous tones of the film music blaring from the tea stalls. Each happening in the realm of the senses made me realize yet again that life was little more than a silly comic strip pasted on the eternal reality, an experience Hindus call *Maya*, the grand cosmic Illusion.

Then, after three wonder-filled days, as unpredictably as it had come, the divine experience slowly dovetailed into everyday reality, consigning me once again to life in the shadows. The loss of my own child could not have touched me so deeply. Thinking I had attained my heart's desire, I wound up with nothing but the cruel memory of three days of transcendent bliss.

I considered returning to the cave to try again, but knew better. It had been a gift, not the result of my actions, although somehow my actions had invoked it. But why had it ended? Could it have been His will? What had I failed to learn?

Sitting on a rock beside the path leading up the mountain to one of India's myriad temples, tormented with doubt, my heart an open wound, I heard the sound of voices tinkling like sweet bells in the distance and spied a bent old woman slowly leading a blind man in my direction. As they passed she paused for a moment, turned, looked deeply into me and sent a ray of love that pierced my heart. Suddenly the self reawakened and my perception rearranged itself, negating the world.

It was back!

This time I experienced sinking into a vast and secure darkness, a tumbling and floating in an ocean of peace and bliss so sweet I lost consciousness. Not that I lost consciousness – I was completely awake and totally aware – but the world as I knew it was gone.

When the senses re-emerged the sun was charting a descending path in the sky. The leaves of the trees, pregnant with life, seemed ready to explode with life and every stone in the dry creek bed was glowing with awareness.

Evidently a part of me died during that experience because the veil of separation lifted and life went on automatic pilot. A person took me to a music teacher who gave me a harmonium and lessons in devotional chanting. When I felt like communicating people appeared out of the blue, the divine spark passing into them as we spoke. A deep sexual longing caused a lovely young woman living in the *ashram*, who had heretofore ignored me completely, to come to my room on a pretext and offer herself. My visa about to expire, I was led to a bribable official who brought the papers, his girlfriend and a picnic lunch the following Sunday.

Chapter II

The Disease *of* Ignorance

As I was wondering why I had been blessed with the good fortune that brought me to this point, the mind skipped back to two years earlier. I was working late, doctoring the books, when the phone rang.

"How much?" I shouted. I could not believe she was still holding out. "Look, Charlie," I said sucking in my rage like a fat man his gut in the presence of a babe, "This won't do. That…" I was about to say, "bitch," preceded by a string of unflattering adjectives, but thought better of it. Everything was going wrong and I needed more trouble like England needs more rain. Furthermore, I didn't want him to know how deeply involved I was. Five years of hard work and lots of money were about to go sloshing down the drain.

On the other hand, since I had no friends who would listen to me whine, I didn't want to miss the opportunity, so I let my wrath escape in constipated little dabs.

"She's been jerking my chain for the last six months. I've had it up to here!" I said, gesticulating wildly, my voice rising again.

"Please be reasonable, James," he answered.

I hated that calm, lawyeresque voice. It reminded me of Mother, the judge. And the shrink they sent me to when the university gave me the boot. What was his name? Patton, Peyton, Penton, something like that. I'll never forget him. After six months of poking around in my childhood, like a proctologist checking the prostate, constantly asking how I felt about things… Puddy! Walt Puddy. That's it! What a name; we made some typically sophomoric jokes about that one. In case you don't know, in those days the "pud" was one of a thousand names for you know what. I am sure the language has moved on; I have no idea what they call it now.

Anyhow, I was tired of the long drives – Spokane was one hundred ten miles away, and I was bored living at home. Come to think of it, it wasn't actually too bad. Dad, God rest his soul, gave me a 1957 Lincoln he'd picked up from a doctor's widow. It was the kind with the gas cap inside the tail light; you pushed a little round red reflective button outlined in chrome and the tail light popped up! We didn't worry about gas; it was the 1950s. Dad was a great finagler. He got it wholesale for twelve cents a gallon and put in a tank under the driveway so we could pump it ourselves.

Monstrous sharklike fins shooting out the back and tons of chrome. What a machine! The ladies loved it and the cops didn't bother it; they must have thought it belonged to some rich stiff. It ruined me for what was to come: the soulless, tight-assed, computer-controlled, environmentally sensitive Japanese rigs with plastic bumpers zipping all over the highways like water spiders.

The doctor special-ordered it for ten grand, a fortune in those days. It had power seats, power steering, power antenna, power radio dialing, power everything. I could make it from Lewiston to Spokane in an hour-and-a-half. That may not seem like a big deal these days, considering the state of automobile technology and the new highway, but you have to know that the figure included the Lewiston hill, a seven-percent grade with ten miles of hairpin switchbacks, which in an ordinary rig took a good thirty or forty minutes. That sucker was heavy, hugged the road liked a baby monkey hugs its mom and whipped around those tight curves at fifty like nobody's business. When I hit the prairie I let it rip, tearing through the quaint little farm towns in the Palouse like a demon, raising a cloud of dust you could see for miles.

Actually, the biweekly visits to the shrink weren't so bad. After my fifty minutes I would saunter down to skid row, quaff a few brews, play pool and rub elbows with some pretty seedy characters.

Anyhow, I was getting fed up with the endless chit-chat. I felt one of my impulses coming on. The impulses landed me on that silly couch in the first place. The present one was about to get me off.

I was trying to be on my best behavior until they shipped me off to the next Waspy institution. I was in disgrace for getting kicked out of a very prestigious school for reasons we won't mention.

"You have all the gifts, James," Mom, who had character and ambition, used to say, making me feel guilty as hell. "With the right opportunities you'll be somebody. And we're here to see you have the opportunities."

I asked the shrink point-blank what was wrong with me.

He did a double take, regained his composure, packed in a nice tidy little pinch of sweet tobacco, fired up his beloved meerschaum, which he fondled obscenely when he was not smoking, and swiveled the armchair around to gaze profoundly out the window at Spokane's skyline, which was dominated by the Ridpath Hotel, a 1930s fantasy of Moorish opulence.

I thought he was just being dramatic, carrying his donnish, avuncular, Ivy League persona to the max, but I was wrong. He was actually getting ready to be real after all those months. He sat lost in thought for eternal minutes, swiveled back, took a tasty little drag, looked me right in the eye and in a brand-new voice, one which I have since come to recognize as truth, said, "Well, James, at worst you are slightly maladjusted." Another long pause. "But, considering the times, I would say it is a good sign."

That blew me away.

All along I was thinking that maybe everybody, Mom and the attenuated queue of officialdom that seemed to have been sent to Earth primarily to torment me since day one, were right; maybe there was something seriously wrong with me. But the good doctor didn't seem to think so. I heartily concurred. He probably didn't realize it, but he'd just given me license to continue my long slide into the pit.

Seriously though, something was wrong; he just did not know what it was. Or if he knew, he couldn't say. He was a well-meaning, liberal intellectual who thought the world of Dr. Spock and couldn't very well call me a nasty little devil and lay on a few well-deserved whacks; it wouldn't have been scientific and may have permanently damaged my tender psyche. You'd think a guy getting fifty bucks an hour, a lot of money in those days, would have been able to figure out that my morals were shot because I didn't know who I was. But even if he had, how would he have gone about clueing me in?

I had to keep falling.

Sorry, I am getting off-track, wandering around in antiquity. It's like that when you look back; the thoughts branch uncontrollably as the mind hunts the kernel, the event meant to burst radiantly out of the gloom of the past and illumine the present.

Where was I? Oh, yes, grousing about the way so-called professionals speak. I didn't need a lawyer because I was in hot water, at least not yet, but I needed one because I couldn't talk to Magdalena about money. We did okay with the small talk: sales, designs, inventory, all the nuts-and-bolts stuff, but when it came to the subject of how much I was worth, the conversation invariably turned nasty.

Anyway, I stuffed my anger because I needed him and because he wasn't a bad guy. He took his biweekly trouncing on the courts like a champ, and I often thought that if I wasn't who I was, maybe in a more perfect world we might even be buddies, slop some suds and chase a little tail, something like that, not that I'm into that sort of stuff these days.

I apologized and took my side of the conversation to the level of a righteous whine, "But Christ, Charlie! It's worth twice that. I busted ass to build it up to this level."

"That may be true, but it's only worth what she's willing to pay. She's got you by the short hairs. We've been through this before. She has voting control of the stock. This is as good as you're going to get."

That pissed me off and I decided to play my ace.

"Wrong, Charlie." I upped the price.

"Christ, James, are you nuts? Here's a solid offer. She thinks she's being taken to the cleaners as it is and you want another fifty grand. You should accept her offer. You know how long it would take me to get together that kind of money?"

"You're a lawyer. I own forty-nine percent of a successful corporation. But that's another issue. She'll go for it."

"You sound pretty cocky, James. Is there something I don't know?"

"That's right, Charlie. Tell her this isn't going to court."

"We've been through that too. If you don't go for this offer, it will end up in court. What you got?"

"I haven't been completely straight with you, Charlie."

"Wait a minute, James. Think twice about this. If it's seriously illegal you're putting me in a bind. I can't represent you if you're into something heavy."

"How'd you like an expenses-paid, two-week vacation for you and Pam in Tahiti? Golf, scuba diving, breakfast in bed, the works."

"Is this a bribe, James?"

"Let's say you're a stand-up guy, a great lawyer and a buddy. I'd just like to show my appreciation."

"This must be bad. I'm not sure I want to hear it," he replied without conviction.

"You want to hear it, Charlie. If you don't like it, tell me to take a hike. I'll dig up someone else."

"Jesus, James, take it easy. Okay, why will she go for this offer when she's already screaming bloody murder?"

"Because I've got the second set of books."

"You mean…"

"That's right. After you guys get through with us and the IRS shows up, and I have a word with a few key people, there won't be much of a corporation to run. The books are worth the extra money. That's the deal."

"God, James, not only are you bribing me, you're blackmailing her, not to mention cheating the government. I don't like it. It's wrong."

But I could tell by his tone that he was intrigued, which confirmed my hypothesis that most people are bored to death and are constantly hoping for a titillating, off-color little something to come along and brighten up their shallow, virtuous lives.

"Wrong or not, it's what's happening. She broke her promise and this is the only way to fix it."

"We've got a fighting chance of getting the court to see it our way. I told you that."

"A fighting chance with five years of my life! That's not good enough. I've got insurance and it's time to file the claim."

I could sense him getting upset, so I tried to appeal to his higher side.

"Don't think I wouldn't like to handle it honorably, Charlie, sit down on the patio and discuss it politely over tea. I come from a good family. I'm no crook. But this is the only way. I don't have it in writing and there's just too much water under the bridge."

"In fact blackmail is eminently reasonable," I thought to myself. "I should just push her off a North Shore cliff after one of our famous champagne picnics. 'Just a little closer, sweetheart. Beautiful, isn't it? Can you see the bottom down where the surf's crashing into the shore, squirting up out of that rock like a big whale's spout? Yes, it is a long drop. Here, take my hand. Go ahead, lean out, I've got you.'"

That would have been a civilized response, as Mom used to say, to her perfidy.

"She'll go for it," I continued. "Face is important to Asians. We've a great reputation and if the word gets out we're scamming Uncle Sam a lot of those big accounts will head south. Plus the business is on fire. You've seen the figures. She'll have it all back in no time."

"You've sure got chutzpah," he said.

"I didn't get where I am being faint of heart, but if it makes you feel better, I don't enjoy this any more than you do."

I think that did it. I meant it. I was sick and tired of the whole mess. It was eating up every minute of my time and I wasn't sleeping well. My gut was hanging over my belt; I was smoking a couple of packs of non-filter Camels a day and socking away a lot of booze. Success was not working.

"Okay, James, I'll tell her," he said,

I felt like kissing him.

"Remember, first class. You coming to the club Saturday? I got a new racquet. I'll cream you."

"I don't know, Charlie. It depends on how I feel then. I don't feel like socializing that much. We're down to the short strokes on this one and I'm almost out of a job."

I sounded confident but hung up wondering if I had done the right thing involving him. If things headed south he might spill the beans.

Until this point nobody knew what was going on and the corporation was just one big happy family. I wanted to tell her myself. We were still on speaking terms, but as I said, everything went wrong when the money issue came up in her presence.

I nearly ran down a pedestrian on the way out of the parking garage when my mind flipped into fantasy mode and I saw her shapely nude body, which I had loved to distraction for the last five years, splayed out on the Sahara, a rough wooden stake driven violently through the heart, a small erotic rivulet of blood tricking from the wound, gumming up the sand, an unpleasant image, no doubt, but it did make me feel better.

Driving up the strip, I felt like crying. I know, men don't cry. At least in those days they didn't. Now, I'm told, it is all the rage; it shows you're sensitive and have feelings. Women are meant to love it.

I hate self-pity. But I'd made a royal mess of things and life seemed ever so much more important then than it does now, so I found myself choking back a string of aching dry sobs trying to work to the surface like rotten farts oozing through a plugged and putrefying colon. Though I tried, not thinking about her was impossible, like the fellow who went to the *guru* for a secret *mantra*. After the instructions had been given, the *guru* said, "Oh, by the way, the *mantra* won't work if you think of pink elephants before you chant." She was stuck in my mind and the only way to obliterate her was to get high.

I parked near Diamond Head, shut off the engine and reached for a joint. I didn't include dope on the list of poisons above, because at the time I thought it was the heaven-sent remedy for my problems. Before long I would figure out I didn't have problems.

I was the problem.

I remember feeling grateful as I rolled the joint, wondering how I'd survived without it so long.

The first time I was turned on flashed through my mind.

I'd just come back to Manila from Zamboanga after a buying trip, island-hopping in dilapidated DC-10s left over from the war, landing on potholed runways so skimpy the wings narrowly missed coconut palms lining the sides, occasionally swerving to avoid the hulking black shapes of water buffaloes wandering lethargically across the pocked tarmac.

What a fop I was! Sporting a Panama hat, Barong Tagalog and silk slacks, I swaggered through fetid tropical towns spreading greenbacks around local markets like a whore sharing the clap at a convention of traveling salesmen, twirling an inlaid baton purchased from an antique shop in Rangoon, which was probably scavenged from a British officer who made the supreme sacrifice in the Burmese campaign. Ridiculous as I was, I don't regret one day spent sitting on screened verandahs in the heat of the day, drinking San Miguel and nibbling *balut*, hard-boiled embryonic duck with tiny bones and fledgling feathers, making deals with Chinese traders.

I unpacked, went for a swim and was lounging by the pool, drinking gin and tonic and reading Conrad, when Emy appeared, setting the old hormones vibrating. She was so deliciously Filipina, a marvelous combination of compliant Malay inscrutability and Spanish passion. She made me ache all over, but putting the moves on her was verboten because she was the daughter of Ninoy, our number one supplier. Sex was sex and business was business, although I certainly hadn't followed that rule with Magdalena.

"Hi, James!" she said, enthusiastically dragging a chaise lounge across the tiles, indifferently depositing her luscious form. "Where have you been? I haven't seen you for a couple of weeks."

"Buying trip. Mindanao. I didn't know you were keeping track," I replied, wondering what she wanted.

"Of course I keep track. Dad talks about you all the time. He thinks you're great."

I was too vain not to be flattered. And I wasn't sure how much of my bullshit Ninoy had swallowed.

"What about you? What do you think?"

"Oh, you're okay. You think you're pretty hot, but you're not a bad guy. You must be smart to have so much money at twenty-five."

In spite of her statement I got the impression she didn't think much of money. Still, I liked her sassy style, her command of English.

"Just luck," I said. "What's in the bag?"

She leaned over and reached for a large raffia bag decorated with straw flowers, her generous breasts nearly falling from a rumpled, partially unbuttoned blouse. She had the right stuff but her hair was a mess and her bikini mismatched, which takes some doing. What did she have against bras and tight skirts, lipstick, perfume and parlored hair? Magdalena would have never left so much unprotected in public.

Emy made me feel like a veritable dinosaur at the age of twenty-six. I was imprisoned in the 1950s, and here it was 1967. How much like Dad I'd become, hopelessly straight and out of it.

She must have picked up her style at Berkeley, where she went to school. Things had changed since I dropped out in 1962 and run off with Magdalena. I was so crazy in love and ready for adventure that when she gave me the ticket and a huge wad of hundred-dollar bills six months before graduation I went straight to my apartment, picked up a couple of novels and a change of clothes and walked out without closing the door. I was never coming back. People were crazy in those days, and I was one of them. I wasn't psychedelic-crazy, at least not yet, but I was crazy. Something was in the air.

Ironically, I recall wondering if Emy believed in free love, if she was part of the developing drug subculture that was giving the readers of *Time* magazine such a start.

She took a record from the bag and handed it to me.

"The who?" I said, unable to make out the weird wavy lettering on the cover.

"Not The Who," she said, "The Beatles, a group from England."

I wondered why these popular groups took such strange names. I hated popular music. Yes, I'd been a big fan when I was a teenager growing up in Idaho, kept up with the Top Forty, danced to Fats Domino and Elvis at the Youth Activities Center, but lost interest and got into classical music as I got more intellectual.

"They're very psychedelic," Emy continued.

"Very psychedelic? What do you mean?"

"Turned on, man. Out there. You get high and everything's different," she replied smiling enigmatically.

Undoubtedly amused, I was so out of it she was anticipating turning me on, wondering how it would turn out. Perhaps she was thinking I would have a bummer and freak out, or worse, not feel a thing. I must have seemed pretty dead. On the other hand, she might have been visualizing me morphing into a wild-eyed hippie, tearing off my clothes, streaking around the pool, fucking her silly.

"What's it like?" I said.

She didn't answer but got up and walked through the open sliding glass door to the apartment.

"How do you turn this on?" she called.

I got up and went in, miffed she had presumed to enter uninvited. I was used to manners.

Nonetheless, I stuffed my feelings inside and helped her with the stereo. The sparks flew when our bodies brushed as I fiddled with the knobs a second before the treacly strains of *Strawberry Fields,* a far cry from my beloved Mozart, suddenly oozed from the large black speakers.

She flopped down on the couch, one shapely leg thrown casually over the armrest, the other on the coffee table. I could see the peach fuzz on her inner thigh.

"You have to be high," she said, picking up where we'd left off outside.

I didn't get it.

"Psychedelic, man! High! When you're high you'll know what 'out there' means," she replied, taking a small bottle of dark brown liquid and a couple of strange little cigarettes from her bag.

I didn't like being put on hold and called "man," but sat down next to her anyway. I was capable of serious repression and mind-boggling hypocrisy when it seemed I was about to get laid.

"What's that?"

"Codeine," she replied.

"And those?"

"Dope, man, marijuana, the nasty killer weed. You want to get high?" she said, snuggling up against me.

A wave of tingly energy swept over me, the thrill of the forbidden.

"What about Ninoy?" I said.

"What about Ninoy?"

"If he finds us sitting here like this it will mess up the whole business thing."

"Sitting here like what?"

She must have known what I meant. We were lounging around on the couch half naked in the most compromising position about to do you-know-what and she's pretending everything is very normal.

"Like, well… I mean… like… here we are sitting around in our swimsuits on the couch about to do something illegal. What if Ninoy came looking for you?"

"This will be good for you. Think of it as medicine."

"Medicine? Are you nuts! What does medicine have to do with it?"

"You're uptight. This will cure you."

My desire to punch her did not seem appropriate. There she was: totally unconcerned, sexy as hell, her pert nipples quivering with excitement. I felt I could act out any fantasy.

"What do you mean, uptight?" It was the first time I'd heard the word.

"Worried, man. Worried. Angry. You're like an old man, like Ninoy. What's to worry about? You've got it made, hanging around over here, taking it easy, making scads of money, messing around with the local girls."

"I'm not messing around," I lied. "I have a girlfriend in Hawaii."

"You mean Magdalena?" she said, laughing dismissively.

I felt a strange mixture of incredulity and rage. How did she know Magdalena? Still, I kept my cool. I could almost taste her full pouty lips, feel the warmth of her body.

"You know Magdalena?"

"Of course. They're one of the richest families here. Everyone knows everything: her mad brother, Manuel, Imelda the ice queen, Juan Ponce who made all the money off the Americans. They're famous. I even heard about your accident, sneaking out of the hospital."

I felt totally embarrassed. How did anyone know about the accident? There were so many thoughts buzzing in my mind I didn't know where to start, so I decided to concentrate on Ninoy.

"Does Ninoy know you take that stuff?"

"You think I'm stupid? You know how they are here. I don't tell them anything."

"Aren't you worried they'll find out?"

"What are they going to do, put me in jail? Come on, James. Take it easy. It's only dope."

"You must think I'm pretty screwed up."

"Let's not get into it. What do you say? You want to get high?"

"What's it like?"

"That's not the right answer, man."

"I just want to know what to expect, that's all."

"Take it easy," she said, caressing my neck. It's no big deal. You want to go to the movies?"

"I just want to know what to expect, that's all."

"You think it's life-threatening?" she asked, a mischievous grin appearing on her pretty face. "It's fun. You'll love it. I'll be there too."

I was about to ask where "there" was, but realized I'd have to take the plunge.

"You'll dig it, believe me. You're ready."

She handed me the joint and I took a couple of deep drags. They burned hotter than my Camels.

Then the bottle of codeine.

"That's cough syrup."

"So?"

"So, I don't have a cold."

"I know you don't have a cold, James."

"So what's it for?"

"It's a narcotic, works great with the dope and cools the throat. It's your medicine, what the doctor ordered. Take a big swig. It will make you better."

"You're having a very nice time teasing me, aren't you? Am I really that bad?"

"You're fine, James. Absolutely fine. But there's something important you don't know, something you can't buy."

She leaned over and kissed me on the neck. I wanted to respond, but the thought of Magdalena stuck in my mind. I seemed to be paralyzed from the waist down.

"What's the matter, James? Don't you want to kiss me?"

"It's Magdalena, Emy. I can't stop thinking of her."

"Do you love her?"

"I thought I did, but if it's love, why does it hurt so much?"

I could not believe I said that. It just flowed out on its own. I always made things out to be copacetic, even when they stunk.

She snuggled closer and handed me the joint. I took a couple of serious drags and handed it back. I can't be sure, because my mind was starting to change, but think I heard her say, "It's only love if you know it's love. I'm not looking for a boyfriend. I just like you. Don't worry about Ninoy. It's okay." Something like that.

It seemed as if she were speaking in an underwater dream, but it didn't matter, because I could hear the sweetness in her voice oozing through time and space, ringing clear in my mind. It seemed terribly real, more important than anything I'd heard for a long time.

Somewhere along the line I seemed to have forgotten about love.

The thought of Magdalena disappeared, and Manila, which was starting to grate after all those months, seemed like home. I couldn't remember why I'd come and it didn't matter. Everything in the room, the table and chairs, the carpet and my books were glowing and changing, radiating an unearthly light. Her words "far out" came floating back, making perfect sense. The music, which

I hadn't liked straight, seemed terribly appropriate stoned, the lyric, "Sergeant Pepper's Lonely Hearts Club Band," irresistibly funny and ironic. I felt giddy, silly and oddly happy.

We kissed, her tongue eagerly exploring my mouth, sending waves of pleasure southward, relaxing the paralysis in my lower extremities.

"Well, what's this?" she said, lightly groping my crotch.

"That's the Willie," I replied.

"It seems pretty uptight. Perhaps it needs to smoke some dope, drink some codeine, learn to take it easy."

"I don't think it's ready. Maybe later. Let's just let it be."

From that point on I can't remember what we said, because we were well out of the world of words. I do recall sliding, tumbling and free-falling down a long, dark, comforting tunnel, Alice on her way to Wonderland. I watched my unforgiving thoughts and feelings slipping away and the years of pain, my life with Magdalena, disappear into nothingness. Floating in an endless sea of warm, intoxicating bliss, vaguely conscious of two bodies rubbing lovingly above, the explosion came as a complete surprise and blew me away like a small cloud dissolving in a clear sky.

"So tell me about the broken leg," said Emy, after we came down a bit.

"I thought you'd heard it all on the grapevine. Besides, I don't come out looking very good."

"I don't care how you look. I'm only interested in who you are."

"Who I am? I'm me, James."

"I know that, James, but who's that?"

"I don't get it. It's me."

"Let's not get into it now, okay? Tell me about the accident."

"But what are you saying, who I really am?"

"It's not important, James."

"But I want to know."

"Okay, James. The truth. I want to know the truth."

"The truth?" I replied.

It seemed to be a novel concept.

"How it really is with you. How you see it."

"See what?"

"See what happened. See yourself. See the world, other people."

"I don't get it. What are you saying?"

"Tell you what, James," she said, kissing my neck. "Let's have another smoke and forget this conversation, the whole broken-leg story. You turn me on."

"An offer I can't refuse," I replied, still wondering what she meant about who I was. So we toked up and went at it again. And as we lay there spooning, sweaty and exhausted, the story just spilled out.

"It was a big-money day at the shops and I was feeling fantastic. I collected the receipts, which filled a couple of shopping bags, mostly tens and twenties, and showed up at her place about eight with a bottle of champagne and a box of chocolates. Charles was working late as usual and the kids were tucked in for the night. She was lounging around in sexy lingerie, reading."

"So how did you feel screwing a married woman?" Emy asked.

"How did I feel? Okay, I guess. Well, not good, actually. I had to skulk around a bit. But you have to see it from her point of view. She gets the kids to school and has the whole day off till after four. And she's not into cleaning, decorating and fussing with the yard. In fact she could use a few housekeeping lessons. Anyway, he comes home for dinner at six and is back at the lab by seven, seven-thirty, every day, like a robot. What kind of a life is that?

"To top it off, she claimed he was not a qualified operator. His idea was once a week between eight and nine on Saturday morning. At exactly nine he'd get up, or a little before if the plumbing worked sooner, put on his running shoes and go out for a long jog. That was it. No foreplay, no afterplay, nothing but the in-and-out and then off to the races. The first day we met we made love nine times.

"So Charles was supposed to come home about eleven, eleven-thirty. We'd been carrying on like that for three years and he evidently didn't suspect a thing, or didn't want to, even though there were a few close calls, like the night I spent two hours lying on top of twenty pairs of high-heeled shoes in the closet until he quit reading and fell asleep. Anyhow, we were in bed when I heard the tires of his Porsche squeal into the drive. That gave me less than two minutes to grab my clothes and jump out the window.

"I was really bombed. Without thinking, I hopped on one of the kid's bikes and pedaled madly into the street and into the path of an oncoming car. Before I knew it I was flying through the air upside down, watching the taillights recede into the night. Another car squealed to a stop within inches and in a matter of minutes a crowd of neighbors gathered. Someone went off to call the ambulance. I couldn't see anyone's face, must have been shock, but I heard Charles' voice clear as a bell above the hushed mumbling of the onlookers: 'Serves the fucker right!'"

"So you couldn't stay anymore and came over here."

"It's not forever. It will all go back to normal before long."

"How can you be sure?"

"Magdalena's arranging for me to marry her aunt who wants a green card. In a couple of months we'll tie the knot and go back to Honolulu. The aunt gets a job and Charles forgives me and everything will be just fine."

"You're incredible," she said.

"Why?"

"You didn't learn anything out of all this."

"What's to learn? It was just a bit of bad luck. Things will go back to normal in no time."

"That's what I mean."

"What do you mean?"

"That's normal? You think Magdalena loves you?"

"Sure, she's fixing up this thing with Corazon so we can be together."

"God, James, you are thick. The way for her to fix things up is to either dump you or Charles. A phony marriage is no fix. It's just more lies. She doesn't care about you. She cares about having her cake and eating it too. You think you know people, but you don't. She'll dump you when she's finished with you."

"No way. She needs me."

"Needs are not love, James.

"What do you mean?"

"Needs are needs, love's love. If she loved you, you wouldn't be holing up here."

I was starting to get her drift.

I don't remember how that conversation came out. The point is that Emy introduced me to dope and got me thinking in another direction. When it was time to go back to our lives I made a fool of myself. I asked her to marry me.

"God, James, you're serious, aren't you!"

"Of course. I love you, Emy."

"I love you too, but that doesn't mean we have to get married. I don't want to get married, to you or anyone else."

"But Emy, we'd be great together. When you love someone it makes sense to get married."

"Not anymore, James. That's the straight world. There's a whole new thing going on. Love is free. You've been stuck in that relationship with Magdalena, doing business for the last five years. There's a revolution going on. People are trying to figure things out. I'm going back and finish my masters degree, and you're going back to Hawaii. Falling in love and getting married isn't where it's at."

And that was that.

Magdalena said the deal with the aunt was straightforward: I would marry her, there would be a generous deposit in my account. We would get another slave to work in the factory or the shops and Charles would relax. So we went through the ceremony with all the relatives gathered around, followed by an extravagant dinner in a fancy hotel. Imelda, her mom, who was now my sister-in-law, seemed to think we needed a honeymoon just for show and sent us off in a chauffeured Mercedes to Baguio, a beautiful mountain resort in northern Luzon. I figured they were showing gratitude for sneaking another Filipino into the U.S. They put us up in a first-class hotel, and on the wedding night the bride, who was in her mid-thirties and well-endowed, appeared in a sheer negligee expecting me to consummate the marriage.

"But I can't," I said. "We don't love each other."

"I love you," she said.

"How can you love me? We don't even know each other."

"But you are very nice when we meet, and now we are married, I love you."

A unique view, I thought. "But I love Magdalena. You know that."

"Magdalena's married. She loves Charles."

"Magdalena loves me. She's arranging this marriage to fool Charles so we can be together. You know that."

She looked as if her first-born had just been run over by a truck. Someone had neglected to tell the poor woman the whole thing was a sham. Or tell me it was not. Maybe they figured I would go for her and that would get me out of their hair. She figured she had just landed a young, rich American.

It was pretty dicey for a few minutes. Visions of her running out into the night and hurling herself off a cliff played in my mind.

I don't know where it came from, it certainly wasn't typical, but I felt genuinely sorry for her. After a long heart-to-heart talk I had a friend for life. I fell asleep about four and awoke an hour later, first light streaming in, to find her snuggled close.

"James," she whispered, "Make love with me."

"But Corazon..."

"Please, James. I won't say a word. Let's pretend we're really married, just for tonight."

The way she said it, the childlike purity in her voice, the idea so romantic it drove me wild... I couldn't resist. As I lay there afterwards I remember thinking that I loved the wrong kind of woman, that even if she did spill the beans it would serve Magdalena and her mother right. A couple of days later we returned to Manila. I called Magdalena, who said the coast was clear.

I should have been overjoyed, but Emy had pricked my fantasy love-balloon and a small hole had opened in my mind through which thought after thought drained down into a dark and vast cavern of self-loathing.

Oddly, I had the sense that I was only returning to see her face. Since I left, almost a year before, whenever I thought of her I'd have a perfect picture of everything: her lovely long hair, her shapely limbs, her sweet breasts. But the face was missing! No matter how hard I tried to conjure it up I couldn't get a picture, not even an eye, a lip, an ear or a nose. It was profoundly troubling.

You need the face.

I wanted her in the story as a real person but, like the missing face, I couldn't remember one thing she said that would give me a hint how she really thought or felt about things, not even enough to come up with a decent inference. Either she was nothing more than her lies or I was in complete denial.

So I came back stateside, a crack of self-awareness opening up within, to witness the last gasps of the dying animal that was our love. That's where this whole story started, wasn't it? I was fumbling through the jockey box looking for a match to fire up a joint and get over the rage that surfaced when Charlie informed me of her insulting offer.

I couldn't find one, which further pissed me off, so I got out and walked through the park to the beach, turning toward Diamond Head, away from the bright lights of the strip.

I hadn't gone a hundred yards when I came across a figure covered by a shawl, sitting cross-legged beneath a tree. The small feet, which is all I could see, made me think it was a woman, but it had to be a pretty crazy or self-confident woman what with all the weird people, sex perverts and the like, hanging around Waikiki.

It was a strange phenomenon, a shrouded human pyramid sitting there still as death. I wanted to go over, lift the shawl and have a peek, but that would have been intrusive, so I wandered up the beach into the night, trying to cap my rage and keep the thoughts from falling into the black hole.

I walked a little more and sat down on the cool sand, looking out at the ocean, reassured by the rhythmic pounding of the breakers, charmed by the profound tranquility of the night, observing the unforgiving thoughts dissolve in the silence. A mile away, the strip, cranking itself up for another fun-filled evening, moments before so real and immediate, seemed far away, lost in darkness like the stars. And Diamond Head, which all these years was nothing more to me than an image on a post card even though I lived on its slopes on the Kahala side, suddenly came alive, looming majestically behind, a reassuring sacred presence. The feeling that I was supposed to be there flickered through my consciousness.

Then, just when I seemed to have calmed down, I was overcome with great convulsive sobs of grief, as if I had drunk too much of life's toxic poison and was having a hearty, well-deserved puke. At the very peak, when I honestly wished I had never been born, I noticed a woman, her figure silhouetted against the city lights, coming my way. I tried to get a handle on my grief, but it was no use. As she passed she turned and looked, breaking her stride just a bit, as if she was thinking of coming over and offering me something. I strained through the tears to see her face but it was impossible.

And then she was gone.

Wave upon wave of grief washed over the beaches of my soul, obliterating the past, wiping away all traces of resentment and rancor, transforming five years' passion, excitement and turmoil into a pointless fantasy, seemingly dreamt by a stranger. The sobbing subsided as mysteriously as it had begun and I felt purified by an inner tropical rain, like the day about six months before when I nearly ran into a little old man at the post office, just before the relationship with Magdalena really hit the skids.

I'm getting ahead of myself as usual. Let's see, where was I? Oh, yes, Corazon and I had a very short honeymoon, such as it was, in Baguio, and then we returned to Manila. She had to wait for the visa but I caught a flight for Honolulu.

As I was clearing customs I looked through the windows to see Magdalena and Charles on the other side! Since his angry last words were still fresh in my mind, I had no idea how to react, yet there he was smiling, with Magdalena, dressed to the nines, draped on his arm like a bolt of expensive silk fabric in a display window. Maybe he was saying, "See, the best man finally won."

I decided to act as if nothing had happened. We shook hands and started right in with the small talk. I had them laughing in a matter of minutes, but it was all nerves since I had no idea what was happening. In the car, Charles, sounding suspiciously as if he had been coached, invited me to live in the mother-in-law apartment in the basement of their new home on Black Point Road, "A nice little love nest for you and Corazon," he said. I could see Magdalena had been hard at work spinning our next big lie, felt a twinge of guilt and wished I hadn't given in on my wedding night, such as it was.

"Well, that might not be a bad idea," I replied. "Why don't I have a look and see if it's suitable."

Charles went upstairs to fix drinks, and Magdalena led me to the apartment. I couldn't wait to get my hands on her.

"Not now, James," she said furtively as I embraced her. "You'll mess up my make-up." She was one of Elizabeth Arden's best accounts.

"So what's this all about?"

"I want you here."

"But what about Charles? What's going on?"

"Don't worry about Charles. It was his idea."

"So what did you have to do to bring him around?" I said.

"You sound positively jealous."

I could see she loved it. "Oh, I get it. He thinks he can keep an eye on me if I'm here, right?"

"Something like that. He wasn't as upset as you think. Tell him you'll take it."

"Okay, but what about Corazon? I can't live here with her."

"Why not? It would be perfect."

I was hoping for irony, but she meant it. We were obviously burdened with conflicting views on the meaning of the word "perfect."

"Perfect? But what about us?"

"Don't worry, everything will work out."

I wasn't convinced, especially when she didn't respond to my second kiss. Emy's words, "She'll dump you when she's finished with you," popped into my mind.

After dinner we sat on the lanai and had a couple of drinks. She disappeared for a few minutes and when she returned in a low-cut cotton shift I realized she'd gone from a 32B to a 36C since I left! She looked absolutely fabulous, but why had she not told me? Was it meant to be a surprise or did she do it for Charles? Or even more likely, someone else?

Tortured with lust and jet lag, I managed to get to sleep just before sunrise. I awoke much later in the middle of a dream in which a voracious Magdalena with monstrous breasts was coming down on me, only to discover it wasn't a dream.

"How do you like them?" she said once she finished.

"Where's Charles?"

"At the lab, where else? Don't worry. Everything's fine. What do you think?"

"Great!"

I lied. They were stunning from a distance, with clothing on, but they didn't fit the form of her slim body. They looked exactly like add-ons, and they didn't feel right either, although I gave them the attention they demanded. Passion always trumps esthetics.

I seemed to have recently been endowed with precognitive powers because I also saw that within ten years she would undoubtedly become one of those tummy-tucked, nose-jobbed, middle-aged, middle-brow mavens one sees in the society page at gala benefit concerts, clutching a champagne glass and mugging a horsey smile for the camera. Everything was right except the color of her skin. Evidently they can even manage that nowadays – bleaching, peeling, whatever.

"So what did you tell Charles? He's been pretty decent, considering."

"I told him nothing happened. He didn't see anything. I told him you came over drunk with the money and walked out the back door just as he arrived."

"So why let me think he knew?"

"He was suspicious. I thought it best if you were gone till he calmed down. We went through this before with William."

"Don't you think it's time you left him?"

"I have to wait until the kids are older."

"Sure, but this isn't doing them any good, is it?"

"What are you saying?"

"I'm saying that seeing us together can't be building a very good image of holy matrimony in their impressionable young minds, can it?

"They don't know what's going on and they love their father."

"Sure, but what kind of a father is he? I'm more of a father than he is. I spend time with them, trundle them around. The guy is never here. He spends a couple of hours with them Sunday afternoons. What kind of a father is that?"

"He's a good father. He loves them."

"Fathers who love their kids spend time with their kids. He's more interested in the life cycles of nematodes than human beings, including you."

"I find this subject very tedious, James. We've been through it many times. I'm not getting divorced. Catholics take marriage seriously."

"So this is a serious marriage? What about me? How do I fit in?"

"Will you stop, James? You're not here one day and we're arguing."

"Jesus, Magdalena, you sent me off for nine months to that Godforsaken island and when I come back nothing's changed. It was hell over there without you."

"Oh, I imagine you had a good time. There are many willing young girls. What did you do with your time?"

"Worked my butt off, read, went to the movies. You think I'd touch one of those girls? I love you, Magdalena. I can't get you out of my mind. I thought of you all day, every day, longed to be with you. I can't believe you'd think I'd do such a thing. I've never touched another woman since the day we met! I'm amazed you even had the thought."

"What about Corazon? Mother said you had a honeymoon at Baguio."

"That's bullshit!"

"Stop shouting, James. I find profanity very upsetting."

"Okay. But you know what that was all about. That was to save face with the relatives. They had to think it was the real thing, didn't they? We were only there one day."

"You mean you didn't touch her?"

"And one more thing, Magdalena – one small detail," I said changing the topic. "Somebody forgot to tell her it wasn't the real thing. I wonder who that was."

"Well, I couldn't very well tell Mama, could I, since I'm a married woman?"

"She knows what's going on. We've stayed with her several times. How could she not know? Every servant in the house knew, which means the whole of the Philippines knows."

"This is all very unpleasant, James. I have these new breasts just for you and the moment you get back you're suggesting I lied. It's a very complicated situation and I didn't know what to say. "

About two o'clock the tennis instructor called.

"What's that about? You, playing tennis?"

"I'm working out these days, have to stay in shape," she said in her most businesslike tone.

I laughed. "Stay in shape? The only exercise you get is the old in-and-out. God, you even hate the walk to the mailbox. Who is this bozo?"

"Nobody, James, just my tennis coach."

Truly, the woman had a pathological aversion to exercise. To reduce her hips, which were absolutely perfect but which she found grossly overweight, she spent hours in bed reading the literary magazines connected to an electronic briefcase outfitted with wires and lubricated flat rubber pads strapped to the offending flesh and allowed to vibrate at any one of a dozen settings.

"I'll play with you. I'm good, state runner-up champ in 1958."

"He's a pro, James."

"At what?"

"You have nothing to worry about, James, it's all very legitimate."

I wanted to believe her, so I let it slide but the thought that she was up to something wouldn't go away. So a couple of days before Corazon showed up with her green card I surreptitiously followed her to the country club.

The instructor, a tall, good-looking, tanned, preppy type with thinning hair and a snazzy tennis outfit, furtively stroked her hand, nudged her shapely brown legs with his hairy, muscular calves, gazed love-struck into her eyes, and like a heathen, snapped his fingers at the waiter to refill her glass as they sat on the patio under a blue and white striped umbrella drinking what appeared to be gin and tonic. And wonder of wonders, no vertical tennis got played that day. Instead, her white convertible followed his Cadillac to a classy apartment near the beach. I am certain nothing happened. They just went up to see his etchings. She was an ardent art lover and, by her own admission, a good Catholic.

Okay, I was jealous, a detestable emotion. But I could not enjoy it since I had more or less lost the moral high ground, such as it was, what with Emy and Corazon and a small army of bar girls.

Admittedly, I am a slow learner, but seeing her enthusiastically disappear through the chrome and glass doors of that luxury apartment building permanently altered my view of adultery as a viable lifestyle. Perhaps I am vain, but I suddenly felt marginally superior. That I was a skunk was undeniable, but at least I was having doubts. The juvenile way she sucked up his seductions and eagerly bird-dogged him to the rendezvous made me realize she was never going to wake up.

The entry of the tennis coach into my tawdry little drama meant events were reaching critical mass. When Corazon arrived they achieved meltdown.

To keep Charles calm, Cory had to stay with me, which naturally caused Magdalena to think twice about the perfect arrangement.

In the best of all possible worlds the aunt is a gawky, homely, graying spinster, the ideal baby-sitter. But Corazon, who was scarcely five years Magdalena's senior, was a babe. What Magdalena owed to science and silicone, Corazon owed directly to God. And, unfortunately as far as Magdalena was concerned, a Spaniard must have scaled the family tree a few generations back because Corazon's features were a tad finer and her skin marginally lighter than Magdalena's. A Westerner wouldn't have noticed, but Filipinos, who calculate skin tones in miniscule fractions, would. And finally, even though she didn't know I'd had my way with Cory, on some level she knew.

It started with an argument over business late one evening.

"We're expanding to the Mainland," she said, "I bought a five-year lease on a storefront on Telegraph. I knew you wouldn't mind."

I did mind. "You what? Berkeley? My God, I can't imagine anything worse. If you'd said Palm Springs, sure, but Berkeley? Who's going to buy this stuff there? It's all hippies, druggies and revolutionaries. Look what's going on there. You read the papers. Christ, Magdalena, why didn't you ask me?"

"You were in the Philippines. I don't like your tone of voice. Please don't talk to me like that!"

"We talked on the phone, why didn't you tell me?"

"It's nothing, just another store."

"Nothing? What do you mean, just another store? You've got to think these things through. What do you think is going on? You think it's magic? We put a lot of research into the other stores and even then we made mistakes. What are you thinking?"

"I want a store in Berkeley."

I stormed out before I said anything I would regret just as Charles turned into the drive.

Corazon was sitting on the couch in her dressing gown with her hair down, watching a rerun of *Have Gun – Will Travel*. I found her simple enjoyment of the corny serial very appealing and joined her for the finale where the hero, a renegade bounty hunter, says goodbye to a good-hearted lady of the night. When they kissed tenderly she started to cry, so I put my arm around her and gave her a not altogether disinterested hug. She turned toward me, her dressing gown fell open, and the rest is history.

About two, still carrying on like a mink in heat, I lost concentration when I thought I heard someone on the stairway, but Corazon, whose mind was fully absorbed, managed to get it back on track. However, as the big moment approached I found myself thinking increasingly about Magdalena and, to put it indelicately, began to lose interest in what I was doing in direct proportion to an increased suspicion that someone was in the room.

I have been particularly frank about my character flaws so far, so it is probably not necessary to provide any more information about them. And, although it does add a bit of excitement to my tale, there is more drama to come. On the outside chance that some of the principals involved are still alive forty years on, it would be bad form to remind them of what happened should they stumble across this tale. Therefore I have chosen not to the chronicle the rest of the evening's events. The net result was that I moved out and Cory stayed, and nobody mentioned that night again. Our negotiations about the sale of my share of the business were proving difficult because it seems Magdalena did not really want me out of her hair for reasons that are not clear to me. Perhaps she did love me, or thought she loved me in some twisted, unfathomable way.

In the meantime, faced with the loss of a successful business and the woman who had been the center of my life, I struggled to find the real me hidden beneath layers of lies.

It wasn't easy.

Sex and booze were, so I drank and sought love wherever I could and sank deeper and deeper into despair. One night on the way home after a night of heavy drinking I staggered into a new nightclub where I was amazed to find dozens of gorgeous women lounging around socializing with the patrons. Spying an unattended blond in a tight silver lamé evening dress, sitting at the bar sipping a martini, I moved in, bought the obligatory drinks and convinced her to come home for the night, pulling over in a nearby park on the way to get things started. However, a few exploratory gropes revealed my she to be a he! I am told that sort of thing is commonplace nowadays, but it pushed me over the edge. I'm lucky no one was around because I pulled the poor fellow out of the car and beat him to a pulp. The deceit. I couldn't handle the deceit.

Any armchair psychologist could see I was really assaulting myself.

Since I am not an accomplished writer and cannot describe my feeling of self-loathing well, you will have to take it on faith that I finally hit bottom, my consciousness peppered with thoughts of suicide. Then, on a lovely tropical morning after a drunken and debauched night with a woman whose husband was out of town, I was sluggishly lumbering through the International Market Place on my way to the post office, the pavement glistening from a light morning shower, the sun playing hide-and-seek with big billowy clouds as the plumerias sprayed their erotic fragrance and gentle trade winds rattled the palm fronds. I noticed a jaunty old man, a vacationer or pensioner come to Hawaii to idly pass the sunset years, appropriately attired in Bermuda shorts, aloha shirt, tennies and a straw hat, perusing his mail as he ambled my way. As he got closer I realized we were on a collision course and sent a message to my feet to move left, but nothing happened! Panic stricken, I tried to move out of the way a second time, but the body wouldn't respond!

I had completely lost control.

A couple of seconds before impact the bodies stopped face to face and I heard a sweet voice speaking through me.

"Excuse me, sir, may I ask you a question?" it said. Someone else had taken over! Since I had no idea what The Voice was about to say, I tried to apologize, but the words wouldn't come. I wasn't connected at the mouth either!

The old man looked up, unaware of my distress, a kind smile on his wrinkled face. "Yeah, sure, sonny, shoot."

Then The Voice, flowing like nectar from a deep place within, resumed, "Out of curiosity, sir, how old do you think I am?"

Since I already knew the answer and didn't have the slightest interest in the opinion of the doddering old codger, I was completely flabbergasted.

Certain that I was going mad, I ran frantically around inside my mind looking for the control panel, but reality, which had a mind of its own, was completely uninterested.

The old man stepped back, pulled on his pipe, gave me the once-over, and judiciously replied, "Well, sonny, I'd say you're forty-three."

A long history of untruth meant I could spot a lie a mile away; he was deliberately underestimating my age to spare my feelings.

"Well, yes, thank you very much," The Voice said sweetly.

"Don't mention it, sonny," he said, proceeding on his way.

I seriously considered the possibility I was losing my mind, but the experience was permeated with such a sense of clarity, I didn't indulge my fear. And then I regained control and proceeded toward my mailbox, the mind settling on the concerns of the day.

But as I entered the foyer I lost it again! Instead of proceeding into the post office proper as programmed, the body confidently turned left, entered the men's room and parked itself in front of a big mirror over the washbasins, eyes glued straight ahead, feet welded to the floor.

"Oh, no, not again! Am I flipping out?" I thought anxiously.

But I wasn't going mad. I was having a good look, courtesy of God, at what I had become. I don't know how long I stood there, unable to move a muscle – perhaps a full five minutes – aware but unaware of the stares of the men coming and going, the flushing toilets and the irritating flicker of the neon light over the mirror. But it didn't matter, because a brand-new world had miraculously opened up, an inner world illumined by a powerful light in whose presence I saw every last bit of the sin and corruption that I was. The moment of truth in the post office lifted a monstrous weight, like Saul's epiphany on the road to Damascus. Though I still looked a wreck, overweight and run-down, my face etched with deep pain lines, I felt young again, inspired by the conviction that I might find an exit from my dark labyrinth.

And for the first time in my twenty-six years I realized there was a compassionate God.

fallen Yogi

What an amazing trip it had been: the worldly success at such a tender age, the sufferings of an ignoble love, the vision of God in the post office in Waikiki of all places, the drug-fueled hippie extravaganza, the dangerous trip through Africa, falling in love with India, meeting the *kundalini yogi*, and now, at the tender age of twenty-eight, enlightenment! Now, it seemed, I would have to figure out what to do with my life.

Seduced by my good fortune, I let my practices lapse. What was the point, I thought, of working to get something I already had? Unfortunately, I had no way of knowing that my ego had merely been momentarily suppressed by the experience of the Divine, and that it was patiently waiting in the wings for its cue to return to center stage. The desire to see more of India set in, and feeling secure in my inner state, I caught the bus for Kulu, deeper in the Himalayas.

Undoubtedly much of the obscene development characterizing many of India's hill stations has defaced the Kulu Valley's pristine beauty, but at the time the long, narrow valley squeezed between the high Himalayan foothills was a relative paradise. The steep mountains were covered with interesting vegetation, including massive bamboo groves, and the valley was planted with fruit trees, mainly apple. The unpolluted glacier-fed Beas River, more of a stream by our standards, flowed merrily around huge boulders on which were carved *mantras*. The most common, *om mani padme hum*, paid tribute to the "jewel in the lotus" – enlightenment.

I stopped at the upper end of the valley near a hot spring in a village called Manali, checked into the local hippie hotel and was shown a room next to Jack, a friend from San Francisco with whom I had spent many happy days in Morocco! More good *karma*.

Reasoning that converting him to God would be an uphill struggle, in the name of old times I started smoking chillums of hand-rubbed resin from the marijuana that grew abundantly on the hillsides, tripping on acid and squandering my spiritual capital on the trite libertine activities of hippiedom.

One afternoon, high on acid, I came face to face with a huge Bengal tiger in a bamboo grove high on the mountainside. Fortunately, I was stoned and crazy enough not to run or exhibit fear. I met its stare and successfully performed my "psychic swell," which evidently convinced the beast that I was much bigger than I appeared. Perhaps it had eaten recently. After several eternal minutes it nonchalantly wandered off up the hillside, further proof, I thought, of the wondrous power of enlightenment.

But the memory of my Rishikesh experiences mocked the petty chemical highs and I quickly grew bored. My longing for God returned with a vengeance, and vowing to regain my spiritual state, I departed for Benaras, where I was led to believe *yogis* and *gurus* literally grew on trees. Jack headed north to Maz-i-Sharif in northern Afghanistan, reputedly the source of the world's best dope.

Benaras *Ghats*

The Ganges scribes a gentle arc as it phlegmatically creeps past the *ghats* on the last leg of its hot and dusty journey across the plains to Calcutta and the Bay of Bengal. The city's mystique derives not so much from its great antiquity or the river itself, which, as famous rivers go, is physically undistinguished, or from the extraordinary architecture, massive stone walls, elegant temples and palaces lining the *ghats*, but an inescapable feeling that countless minds over infinite time have come here seeking relief from the inexorable sufferings of existence, found peace, and left vibrations that hover about her crowded banks, charging the atmosphere with holiness. One senses that Ganga, whose mythic life mingles with humans, gods and the Absolute, has ministered well from her inexhaustible source.

Unlike her clear, cold, drinkable currents at Rishikesh, by the time she reaches the Ten Horse Sacrifice Ghat she has become, by our standards, hopelessly polluted. But only infidels see it. In a land where *yogis* stop trains with the power of their minds and serpent bites are healed with mumbled *mantras*, faith will not permit the senses their reality, the mind its doubt. No earthly water this, but purifying nectar of the gods, boundlessly gushing from the omniscient head of Shiva, patron of the *ghats*.

In addition to its obvious antiquity and association with the Ganges, the *ghats* serve as a vast open-air crematorium where funeral pyres burn incessantly, consuming precious wood and the worn-out bodies of the faithful. The smell of incense and the sound of cymbals, drums and chanting fill the air as processions wind their way through the byzantine maze of streets, rushing lucky souls to their release. Wrapped in a sheet and immersed in the dull brown water to become food for happy porpoises, only holy men and lepers escape the fire. Hindus, of which there are more than a billion, believe that death here permits the soul to step forever off the apparently endless cycle of births and deaths.

One senses the irrational – the darkness – too. A passage from my diary, penned on a subsequent visit when I was confined to my hotel for three days while Hindus and Muslims slaughtered each other in the streets, reads:

"I am awakened from a fitful sleep by chanting from a nearby temple – devotees trying to hold back the madness. Dozens of stray dogs, like tuning forks, reverberate the terror with ancient howls and mindless barking. Racing across the sky, the moon plays hide-and-seek with eerie clouds as malevolent young Hindus and Muslims roam the streets, seeking victims for their slaughter. Temple speakers – gritty low-tech atavisms from the pre-electronic dawn, great black flower-like horns blaring distorted feeling – lend mechanical reality to a fluid night of violence.

"Weird.

"In the *Puranas*, India's mythological literature, this weirdness is portrayed as an insatiable giant, a great warrior possessing the knowledge of good and evil, whose days and nights are measured in eons. Named Kumbakarana, the hidden or unseen cause, he is all-powerful, his intentions unfathomable. A shark's fin cuts circles in the surface of the ocean and the swimmer is filled with terror, not of the visible fin but of the occult malevolent intelligence to which it is connected – like tonight's terror impersonally stripping lives as an elephant strips the leaves of a tree.

"We have our symbols of the weird power of the underworld too – Moby Dick, Darth Vader and King Kong. Reacting to our ignorance of his true self, a misunderstood Kong roams labyrinthine darkened streets and alleys abducting fair damsels, smashing buildings, running amok. Consumed by his angry relationship with his dark self, Ahab, lashed to the side of the whale, drowns in an ocean of fate. These symbols touch the depths because the giant sleeps in each of us, the boy who murders his parents, the father who molests his daughter, the dictator that murders tens of thousands of his own people.

"Ironically, today was dedicated to Saraswati, patroness of arts and letters and higher wisdom. For several weeks artisans have been constructing straw-and-plaster statues of her lovely form, which they sell to all and sundry, particularly young men, who, primed with testosterone, religious fervor and rice wine, work themselves into a cathartic frenzy as they chant and dance through the streets carrying the goddess on their shoulders to the Ganges, her final resting place.

"Tonight I watch the celebrations with interest from the comfort of a rickshaw. My driver, a Hindu, said several Muslims had just been killed, recounting the details with relish. It was okay, he said, because the perpetrators were only students, who could not be counted on to know better, and the victims, only Muslims, who undoubtedly deserved it.

"As we inch along I become aware of the many police, who instill fear, not because of black uniforms, shining weaponry and crackling walkie-talkies like ours, but because of the weakness that causes them to respond, not to policy, but to the promptings of the monster. How effortlessly they lose themselves in weirdness, wading enthusiastically into the fray with sticks, sweat and muscle, Uncle Joe killing with a stick.

"Coming to an intersection, the rickshaw *walla* stops and orders me to step down even though I am still a mile from home. Deprived of the height, I feel vulnerable. I cover my head with my shawl and blend into the crowd.

"A car hits a dog. Howling, it scampers down a darkened alley.

"The pace accelerates.

"A boy trips and falls on a fat lady who screams, upping the energy.

"Awakened to the inner world, I see hidden wraithlike selves, haunting and sinister, distorted by the terror and detached from bodies, streaming to safety. And in the heart of hearts I see Kali, a necklace of bloody skulls bouncing on her breast, brandishing myriad weapons in arms fluttering fast like humming-bird wings, madly dancing on the burning *ghat*, her monotonous foot-beats pounding the giant to consciousness.

"Oddly, in small pockets, life goes on. My favorite café in the bazaar is still open. I forget the night and enter. The waiter brings a steaming chocolaty cup of coffee, but before I take a single sip a terrifying silence descends, freezing life for an eternal moment. A baby cries, breaking the silence. Then hell breaks loose as shop doors clang shut and thousands rush wildly through the muddy narrow streets and alleys. I am safe in the eye of the storm but I do not tarry.

"Concealed beneath my shawl I cautiously pick my way through the night, furtive like a spy, but unafraid. How alert I have become, awakened by the all-pervasive fear, seeing everything, feeling the protection of awareness."

Bad *Karma*

I left Kulu to get back on track, but *karma* caught me up in Benaras. After hanging out on the *ghats* for a couple of days I began to lose energy, and within a week my skin developed a sickly, yellow tint. My appetite disappeared and I spent the next nine days flat on my back in my room. I had contacted hepatitis, probably from swapping spit with Lucy, one of the fun-loving chicks in Manali.

The doctor prescribed serious rest, so with great sadness I decided to return to the States. Lacking the energy to make a reservation, I showed up at the station and boarded the train, but the conductor refused to seat me and I was forced to sit for fourteen hours in the aisle near the toilets. I recall looking out the window as the train moved northward about sunset, the sky filled with flying saucers!

I took a room in a seedy hotel in Delhi, wired for money and lay around wasting away. By this time my skin, nails, hair and eyes were bright yellow. When the money arrived I bought a ticket for Lahore, Pakistan, first stop on the overland route. At the border I discovered that my traveler's checks, which I thought had been carefully concealed with my documents in a leather body pouch, were missing! Fortunately, I found about thirty dollars worth of rupees in a pair of pants in my luggage, enough to get to Lahore and collect a refund. American Express needed to wire Delhi to confirm the numbers, but a week later when it had still not arrived, I realized I was being ripped off. I talked to the big man in the office, but he was in on it too. I was down to my last few rupees.

The embassy wanted to send me home on the plane, but for unknown reasons I refused. I could have wired for more money, but did not, again for unknown reasons. Perhaps the answer lay in a passport-sized photograph that I had taken one day when I was waiting for my money. Many years later I found it tucked away in the back of a copy of the *Bhagavad Gita*. When I looked at it I saw the face of a very arrogant young man and understood why I needed to go through the nightmare that lay ahead.

One night in an unprovoked fit of rage I kicked the sink off the wall and collapsed on the floor of the toilet. The management threw me out into the street to fend for myself. Delirious, I aimlessly wandered the streets and woke up in the morning on a *charpoy*, a low rope bed, in a commercial section of town.

Too sick to move, I slowly watched life ebb from me. When I left their offerings of food untouched, the locals gave up and kept their distance. In those days, and to some extent today, death in the streets was a natural occurrence. Perhaps they took me as a drug casualty, of which there were many, a junkie run out of luck. My impending demise didn't matter to them, and surprisingly, it no longer mattered to me. Why should it? I was nobody. I had been of no use to anyone but myself.

Then one day the thread, some say silver cord, connecting me to the body snapped and I traded one life for another, returning to what I had always been, a limitless, silent, conscious presence transcending the body. For what was probably no more than twenty minutes but seemed eons, I hovered over the wasted yellow packet of flesh like a super-conscious ghost.

A complete non-entity in life, I became a celebrity in death. A crowd gathered, fascinated by the radiant aura surrounding the body, and, as befits a solemn occasion, remained subdued, communicating in muted tones and whispers. Back home I would have been scooped off the street in a matter of minutes, wired to a machine and shocked silly until I came back to life or permanently died. The Eastern mind appreciates death in ways materialists cannot imagine.

As I hovered motionless over the body the crowd grew, reached critical mass and spilled over into the street. At that moment a late-model, black Mercedes Benz pulled up. The driver, dressed in an immaculate white suit and turban, got out and opened the back door for a man of medium height, attired in an impeccably tailored Western suit. The crowd parted like the Red Sea as he approached. The man bent over, looked hard and fast into my face and deftly kicked me in the side to see if I were alive. Because there was no reaction, he kicked again.

He squatted to get closer and the Voice of God speaking through him said, "I can see by the way you bear your suffering you are a refined man. By the will of Allah you will come with me. I will nurse you back to health."

I re-entered the body. From that time on I was blessed with nearly perfect dispassion.

He motioned to his driver, who stepped forward, picked me up and put me in the back seat. We wound through the city streets and out into the country until a stately Raj-era villa at the end of a long tree-lined drive came into view.

The car pulled up and a servant approached. My host gave instructions while the servant helped me up a flight of stairs to the roof, where a four-poster canopy bed was set up under an awning beneath the overarching branches of several very tall trees. Sitting on a marble-top commode next to the bed was a Victorian English ceramic washbasin and pitcher. And next to the stand was a small man with kind eyes, Akhmed, the oldest servant in the house, who would attend me around the clock.

Khalil was a Western-educated businessman from an old aristocratic family, a man who, in a worldly sense, lacked nothing. At the same time, he had an interest in mysticism and was, in spite of a taste for good food and beautiful women, a deeply religious man. He was the owner of the hotel whose manager had thrown me out.

I remained in his care for about three weeks, I believe, during which we talked on a wide range of subjects. On Thursday afternoons when his mistress came I went to the movies at one of the family cinemas. The stay broke the back of the disease, my energy returned and I began to eat regular, if somewhat small, meals. The convalescence gave me a good opportunity to reflect on my life so far.

Chapter III

A Dangerous Path *to* Freedom

IN INDIA A *dwija* is a person who is "twice born," once physically and once spiritually. My first birth was in Butte, Montana, in 1941. My second birth was the moment of truth in the post office at Waikiki, Honolulu, Hawaii, in 1966. Or perhaps it was 1967.

Although I knew that Magdalena had made a mistake taking a lease on a storefront on Telegraph Avenue right in the middle of the People's Park revolution, I decided to try to make it work.

No longer a proper university town crowded with frat rats and cutesy co-eds in pleated skirts and bobby socks who would eventually end up in suburbia with two bratty kids named Bill and Pete, Berkeley was inundated with long-haired flower children who would eventually end up in suburbia with two bratty kids named Shanti and Moonblossom. Psychedelia was in full swing: Haight Ashbury, flower power, the Black and White Panthers, The Beatles, free love and free speech. The town even had a new moniker – The People's Republic of Berserkley.

I deplaned at San Francisco International, rented a car and pulled into a Denny's at Daly City for a burger and a coffee to go. On the way up the on-ramp to the Bayshore I spied a hippie sporting waist-length hair, torn bell-bottoms and a Day-Glo orange shirt, with his thumb out. I hated hippies and I never picked up hitchhikers, so I was surprised when the car, like the body two weeks before in the post office, unilaterally pulled over and stopped.

"Where you headed?" I said, rolling down the window.

"Berkeley, man," he replied.

"Get in, I'll take you," I said.

"Out of sight, man! Far out!"

"So what do you do?" I said as we entered the stream of traffic.

"Do, man?" He seemed confused. "What do I do?" he repeated, apparently trying to come to terms with a difficult question. "I get high, man. What do you do?"

I missed the irony and eagerly launched into an embellished thumbnail sketch of my life, expecting him to be suitably impressed.

But when I asked what he thought, he said, "Not much."

"I tell my life's story and you say, 'Not much.' How many guys my age have what I've got? Shit, I make more in a day than you make in a year."

"So? You may have a lot of stuff, but you're still one uptight bozo."

There was that word again.

"Uptight! What do you mean, uptight!" I shouted.

"Take it easy, man," he replied.

My rage inexplicably drained. The whole improbable scene, fat business-man and scruffy hippie, suddenly seemed cartoon-like and far away, as if it was happening to a stranger.

The Voice from the post office, speaking through me, said, "Sorry. I don't know what got into me. Go ahead and tell me what you really think."

In one of those moments when life plays the shrink better than any one-hundred-dollar-an-hour PhD, he turned, looked me in the eye and said, "Well, man, I'd say you were one of the most fucked-up human beings I've ever met."

A wave of anger arose and miraculously subsided before I could utter a word. A powerful silence filled the car and I realized my companion was seeing what I had seen in the restroom two weeks before. Was I so obviously messed up?

The thought that I had made a terrible mistake a long time ago, maybe before I was born, came. But what was it? Where had I gone wrong? What kind of punishment was in store? I felt a panic coming on, but it was vacuumed by the silence before it could take root. Then The Voice, whose presence filled the car, as if it already knew the answer, replied, "Well, all right, then what do you think I should do about it?"

The hippie, who seemed to be in league with The Voice, shrugged, glanced sideways, reached in his pocket, extracted and uncapped a vial, and handed me two round orange pills.

"Try these. They might help."

"What are they?" I asked, examining the small tablets nestling in my palm as the car sped past Candlestick Park.

Holding them gave me a wild, almost sexual, feeling. They seemed alive, perhaps radioactive. Short wavy lines emanated from them. For a moment the car seemed to be stationary and the skyline speeding by.

When he said "Orange Sunshine" my body tingled and the hairs on the back of my neck stood up as if I was listening to a sublime piece of music.

"What's that?" I said.

"Acid, man. LSD. Good stuff."

"What's it feel like?" I said. Since my affair with Emy and the experiment with pot I had read a number of articles about the dangers of psychedelics. That it was forbidden was not a problem; I had pushed against the grain all my life.

"Out of sight, man!" he replied.

I had a vague idea what he meant.

"I did pot in the Philippines," I said. "Is it like that?"

"Pot's okay, man, but it's kid stuff. This will blow your mind. And it needs to be blown, believe me."

"But isn't it dangerous?" I asked. "They say you can freak out – whatever that means. I read about this girl who stepped off the tenth floor of an apartment building, thinking she could walk on air. They scraped her off the pavement."

"If you're scared, don't take it. I've had a couple of bummers, but it's no big deal. It's only the mind. The stuff wears off in a few hours and everything is back to normal."

I didn't know exactly what he meant, but felt reassured. I was attracted. The perfumed excitement and glamor of the high life could no longer mask the unmistakable stench of suffering.

I opened my hand and looked at the Orange Sunshine again. "What the hell," I thought. "Probably nothing will happen – just a couple of stupid pills." Uncapping the warm, watery coffee sitting on the dash, I washed them down on the spot.

"Far out!" the hippie said enthusiastically.

Within minutes I was overcome with unexplained euphoria. As the car exited the Treasure Island tunnel, I started to change. My companion, all smiles, got off somewhere in Berkeley.

"Happy trails," he said, giving the peace sign.

The car, driving itself, headed for the hills like an animal sprung from a trap. The road and the world, including my body and the automobile, now perfectly synchronized, were expanding and contracting in unison like a giant lung breathing in and out, shrinking and swelling, irresistibly and awesomely alive. My body was shaking with pure joy and I heard myself laughing uncontrollably, not the polished business laugh, but a hearty cascading of uncontrollable mirth.

The hippie was not kidding! Pot was kid's stuff.

Thought lines, like puppet strings running from my crystal palace, merged into the nervous system, instructing the body to move! Thinking across the ever-expanding body-mind gulf, I directed the machine toward an unknown destiny. Before long, however, I realized I would soon be incapable of driving.

Noticing a gravel turnout near the crest of the hills, I reined in the beast, over-running the perimeter and landing in a field. So much was going on I couldn't remember how to put it in reverse, so I left it where it was, up to the bumper in thick grass, and deplaned, a traveler from a distant galaxy stepping for the first time onto the surface of an ecstatic vibrating Earth.

Oaks and madrones danced, their branches swaying, striving to touch the sky like the tentacles of gigantic sea anemones. Earth and sky melted erotically into each other, lovers tenderly sharing a passionate moment. Transfixed by the ineffable beauty of a world endlessly creating and destroying itself before my inner eye, I wandered down a small gully and sat on a rock under an ancient oak whose wrinkled, gnarly, hieroglyphic skin seemed to form, dissolve and reform the rune seen within. I looked through the body's translucent shell and saw an infinitely expanding, self-generating radiant light of indescribable purity pour-ing the sweet ecstasy of life into each and every cell.

For the first time, I noticed that everything here had a purpose, objects nestling into one another like pieces in a puzzle. I saw everything as a living whole, vibrating to a wondrous, all-pervading sound that was spontaneously arising from the emptiness between the atoms. Though inseparable from this indefinable sound, every blade of grass and humble pebble, containing univers-es within itself, unself-consciously displayed its uniqueness. My fractured and lonely life suddenly seemed meaningful, fitting as it did snugly into the total, a guileless child nestled in its mother's arms.

As I gulped fresh air with the relish my former self had guzzled cham-pagne, the healing draughts flooded my worn and damaged body, shocking it to life. I ran down the grassy gully and gracefully leapt over a barbed wire fence.

Until that leap, which seemed a symbol of something profound, the trip was ordered and purposeful, an ever-expanding spiral of unbelievable expe-riences strung one after another, lustrous pearls on a string, way stations at which my soul briefly stopped, took instruction and then moved on. But as I approached the brow of the hills, the warm summer sun a ripe golden fruit slowly dropping into the graceful mouth of the Golden Gate, and the Bay Area spread before me, everything ceased to move and the bundle of ignorance that I was dissolved into Light.

Not that I did not exist. But I ceased to exist as a fat, rich, unhappy busi-nessman. That person, a sort of distorting and concretizing lens, had somehow fallen from the camera and shattered into bits, left behind on the other side of the fence. And the I, the real I, a limitless vision hidden within the body, appar-ently asleep for centuries, began seeing things as they actually were.

Transfixed, frail and delicate as a spring flower, stunned by the intricate beauty of the creation, I realized there were two parallel realities: the eternally living reality of God and the frozen world of conditioned perceptions, LSD just one of many possible tunnels between the two. These strange little orange pills were not creating their own reality. They were showing me Reality, sprucing up the view with a bit of wavy chemical weirdness.

Meanwhile back in the trip, the sun — its rays pulsating atoms of light — raced toward an ocean swelling to receive it as gulls labored through the supercharged evening sky, leaving trails, feathery footprints, in the air. I looked into the body and saw the whole nervous system circulating an unbroken carousel of light, the synapses — microcosmic exploding stars — glowing bright as the energy leaped from terminal to terminal.

Journeying into finer and finer worlds, I experienced a tremendous rush, which I would later recognize as love, when I came upon the place within where God dwells, giving and taking life. Overcome with a feeling of deep sanctity, tears of repentance dripping from the sides of my eyes, I fell to my knees to thank the Great Spirit as day turned to night in an awesome and unforgettable display of transcendental beauty.

Consciousness of my former life returned and for a moment I wondered how I could reclaim it, but something told me not to worry. Sure enough, when the time was right, the body, marvelously wise, turned and walked up the hill, every sense heightened, taking in and processing stimuli, driven by a precise impersonal memory. The car was as I left it, one door hanging carelessly open.

The attaché case on the back seat, cigarettes and the Denny's hamburger still sitting on the dash seemed like archaeological objects. I examined them with interest. I reached for a cigarette and lit up. As the fire seared the lungs and the toxic sludge dumped into the blood stream the mind slowed, the high began to fade and I was unceremoniously sucked back into the meat tube. A wave of nausea, which seemed to symbolize my whole life, overcame me and I hurled the cigarette out the window, the end of an eight-year habit. In a few minutes the smoke purified and the high returned.

I started the engine and pulled out onto the road, which was shrinking up into a constipated little mass and spronging out again like a rubber band. A muscle car came into view, snorting and pawing its way up the hill, vibing like an angry buffalo. X-raying the occupants, teenagers chock-full of testosterone on the way to the woods to guzzle brew and rub genitals, I vibed power and the beast shrank meekly away, giving me a wide berth. I whipped down the road enjoying life in microseconds, the machine an extension of the mind, thought taking form.

It happened to park itself on Telegraph about a block from my old haunt, the Mediterraneum, and before I realized what was happening I found myself sitting at my old table, wondering if anyone could tell I was stoned.

Ordering had gone off without a hitch. When asked what I wanted, "cappuccino" had come out as usual. When I opened my wallet the bills had been alive, glowing and changing like radium. Wading through the patron's mind stuff had been a bit of a chore, but I had acquitted myself well, arriving at the table, an island in a storm, without incident. I felt protected by an invisible energy bubble, like an exotic plant growing in a hermetically-sealed vessel.

My wild eyes reflected from the window and I noticed my tie was missing. That seemed right. I straightened the collar of my sport jacket and ran a comb through electric hair, floating two inches above my skull.

No one seemed to be paying the slightest attention, yet a persistent feeling of transparency, as if anyone could tune in, kept arising as the café filled with a motley crew of featherless bipeds.

At some point I realized I was sharing a table with a glowing hippie.

"Tom. Tom Williams," he said nonchalantly. "S'appening, bro?"

I tried to interpret the lingo. How could I know "s'appening, bro?" was a contraction for "what is happening, brother?"

"Oh, too high to talk, eh? What you on?" he said conspiratorially, making me a little paranoid.

"Getting a little paranoid, eh?" Tom said. "First trip?"

I nodded.

"First trip and a bit freaked out, eh? Know the feeling. Don't worry about me. It's no biggie. Just thought you might like to score some Purple Owls."

"Purple Owls? Score?" I asked.

"Owsleys, man. Acid, man. What you on?"

"I don't know… Orange, Orange something, I think."

"Sunshine, man. Sunshine. Not bad stuff, but you need some for next time."

In my state there did not seem to be a next time. Things came when needed and were not needed till they came. And oddly, a vague feeling the trip was going to last forever kept passing through my mind.

"What you thinking about, man? We're only talking two bucks. Two lousy bucks a hit." He went into his spiel. "Purple Owsleys, the finest acid ever made. Great dope, man, great dope. Pure. Really pure. Better than Sandoz. Since this is your first time, three for five bucks. Judging from that watch, five is peanuts to you."

I reached for my wallet.

"Hey, man, be cool! Not here. Come on up the block and we'll do business. I go out first and you come on in a couple of minutes. Meet you down the block."

We met down the block.

"Hey, man, you don't know nothing, do you?" he said in a kind voice. "Here, gimme the five. Here's your stuff. Sit down, man," he said motioning to a nearby stoop. "Let's toke up. I got to tell you some things."

We sat down and Tom fumbled through his pockets looking for his Rizla papers.

"Hey, man, why don't you run over to that liquor store and pick up a bottle of Ripple while I fix up this here doobie. It sure puts a nice head on you."

Grimacing at the thought of Ripple, I walked to the liquor store, and returned with a bottle of Mumm's Extra Dry.

"Hey, man, what's this stuff? This looks like bullshit, man. Wow, twelve bucks! What we got here, liquid gold?"

"Beats the hell out of Ripple," I said mimicking his style.

"Hey, man, I like you. You got class. Who are you anyway?"

"Nobody, just a fat businessman," I replied. "I can't stand bad wine."

"I'm just like you, only dope-wise. Can't stand bad dope. Think I'm turning you onto some ragweed, some cheap homegrown shit, eh?" he asked rhetorically. "No way, man. No way. I got class too. Know what this is?" he said, flourishing a fat joint.

"Nope. What?"

"Acapulco Gold, man, best fucking grass they make, 'cept maybe Panama Red." He fired up, took a deep drag, his eyes bugging out, and passed it to me.

I took a couple of drags.

"No way, man" he said. "No way. You're wasting that shit. Got to smoke it like this."

He demonstrated.

I did not care. My mind suddenly went into a wild tailspin, a riot of lights and colors blowing off in the brain, so beautiful it took my breath away, my own private Fourth of July.

"Here, man, take a swig of this," said Tom, who seemed to know just what was happening, handing me the bottle. "Kind of mellows things out a bit."

I followed instructions. The lights were on, no doubt, but the champagne strung them out, softened them up a bit, making them eminently viewable. "Wow!" I said. "Unbelievable!"

"Far out, man!" said the dealer, picking up on my excitement. "You look like a real jerk, but you're a real head, ain't you now?"

I heard myself laughing from a million miles away.

***

I woke up the following morning in a motel somewhere in the flats on a sunny warm California day. Though the universe was not expanding and contracting with the cosmic breath, birds no longer left trails across the sky, and the riot of color that had gone off in my head had played out, I noticed that this morning after was not even vaguely like my usual mornings after. Every object in the room exhibited profound integrity, an is-ness difficult to describe. The most insignificant things, like the toothbrush, door hinge or my fingernails seemed ever so real, lights unto themselves.

A bright young man, instead of a debauched, cynical, geriatric adult, stared at me from the mirror. I smiled and noticed I liked myself for a change. When I turned on the radio, the lyrics, "Be who you are," accompanied by a saccharine psychedelic instrumental, played over and over, etching the *mantra* in my brain. Emerging from the shower I seemed lighter, as if I had washed off a bit of my cruddy old self. I opened the suitcase, but the clothing seemed to belong to a stranger. Significantly, I couldn't find my watch, a five-hundred-dollar Omega, but it didn't matter. I managed to force it all on, but was unable to don the tie, which seemed vaguely sinister, more a dog collar than an adornment, a perfect symbol of my enslavement, the jewel in the crown of the capitalist uniform.

I walked up the block to a mom-and-pop café and ordered a hearty breakfast. When it arrived I took one look and nearly vomited, leaving it untouched. For the life of me I couldn't figure out why for twenty-some years I'd enjoyed consuming dead pigs and slimy eggs from chicken rectums. And when I finally found my latest stock in the newspaper, at the bottom of a long column, its two-point drop didn't faze me in the slightest.

As the café filled I studied the patrons. The middle-aged woman at the corner table by the window, surgically slicing her sausage, her napkin neatly folded in her lap, seemed interesting. I wondered what she did and why she was eating alone. She wasn't bad looking, still had her shape and seemed intelligent. I thought of Mother and wondered if I should tell her about the trip just to wind

63

her up. I could just imagine her face when I said, "Oh, by the way, Mom, I've been doing a bit of LSD lately." Of course it wouldn't fly, because I was already in the doghouse. She was still mortified I had lied about leaving school and running off with a married woman. I didn't know how to fix it. The acid must have done something to my feelings because she seemed more like a real person than a mom. For a moment I experienced something akin to remorse. How I had disappointed her and messed everything up.

My attention wandered back to the paper and I noticed an article about the Haight-Ashbury that informed the concerned reader that psychedelia was a dangerous movement threatening "life as we know it." Sounds promising, I thought. Life as I knew it had been hell for a long time – since the broken leg when I was hit by a car trying to escape Charles on that fateful night – and before.

Mecca was only twenty minutes away, so I decided to skip work. I paid the bill, drove across the Bay Bridge, took the Fell Street exit, and parked along the Park Panhandle behind a rundown, riotously painted school bus, home of a band of itinerant flower children. Entering the Haight, a foreign country, I was serenaded by heretofore incomprehensible, now hauntingly familiar, psychedelic tunes blaring from multicolored Victorian flats.

Suddenly everything turned weird and wavy, and I was back on a scaled-down version of the trip. The smell of pot oozed from windows adorned with Indian tie-dyes, peace signs, pictures of the nasty killer weed and psychedelic posters advertising a plethora of acid-rock bands. Nearly everyone I passed was loaded.

Haight Street was alive with funky humanity. The shops, most of which catered to freaks, were filled with lava lamps, multi-faceted mirrored balls, beads, tie-dyes, strobe lights, glow lights, grow lights, Day-Glo posters and scads of paraphernalia: rolling papers, roach clips, hash pipes and hubbly-bubblies. The stoops were packed with bearded, peace-signed, stoned hippies openly peddling acid, grass, peyote, mescaline and magic mushrooms. Scantily-clad, glassy-eyed, disheveled, malodorous, hirsute teenage runaways shamelessly fondled each other in broad daylight. A snappy Beatles lyric pounded from an oversize speaker wired to the back of a beat-up, multi-colored, Day-Glo Volkswagen, "No one will be watching us, why don't we do it in the road?"

For a moment I feared becoming one of them, but the way they looked at me, glancing contemptuously at my narcy black shoes, short hair and tailored suit told me I was "straight," an uptight, capitalistic, plastic person. In short, the enemy. I would have to do something about that, I reasoned.

Madame Zora

Until that defining moment in the post office and my first trip, which was really part of the same change, life had been so painfully full of me and my impulses that I had no idea of the vast inner world of the mind and the limitless Spirit beyond. And even though most of my thoughts were still angry and unforgiving, storm troopers goose-stepping through my consciousness, others, a growing minority, were ironic and detached, floating lazily by like puffy summer clouds. Some hidden part of me was coming forward, a spring crocus breaking through earth's crust, lighting up winter's bleak leavings with freshness and color.

Anyhow, when I got the business up and running, I went back to Hawaii. It was difficult to keep my attention on the inner world with all its promise; the thoughts kept leaking into the black hole called Magdalena. I should have gone straight home from the airport, but the apartment reminded me of Magdalena and my lousy life. I was tired of thinking about her, so I stopped off at Forbidden City, a strip club on the downtown end of Kalakaua, the main drag. It was almost empty except for a few boozy business types lounging around smoking and nursing their drinks, disinterestedly studying the strippers while the waitresses gossiped in the back. I toked up in the men's room, and when the mai tai went to work things started looking up.

The first stripper was a young willowy blond with vacant eyes, long legs and pendulous breasts, which she mechanically fondled as she haphazardly roamed the stage, shedding her costume to a slow '50s tune, *The Great Pretender*. I remembered dancing to it at the Youth Activities Center with Isabel Thompson, whose luscious breasts featured prominently in many young men's wet dreams, including my own. I wondered what the stripper, who resembled Isabel, saw in stripping. I wanted to talk with her even though we would have nothing in common. Still, I wanted to know her story; I was sick and tired of clever women.

The next dancer, a redhead, was about the same age but shorter and marginally cuter than the blond. Her routine was equally lame, a cowgirl act. She pranced around the stage like a high-stepping quarter horse letting out whoopees and yipee-yi-kiyays as she divested herself of chaps embroidered with penis-shaped sequined cacti, a fringed white leather vest and a ten-gallon hat. The grand finale involved clichéd intercourse with a six-gun.

By this time, well into my second mai tai, it was happy trails; the memories had stopped.

The third dancer was a humorous Filipina whose gymnastic act involved a number of extremely vulgar and erotic poses. Orientals don't seem to have the same sense of shame as Occidentals. At the end she front-loaded her vagina with a hard-boiled egg and sent it rocketing directly at me with a wild gyration of the pelvis.

The lights dimmed for the first act of the final set. Expecting either the horsey girl or the Filipina, I was blown away when a classy, statuesque woman in her thirties appeared, dressed like a belly dancer, wearing a white turban decorated with a huge diamond. Her elegantly designed costume conjured up images of gypsies, crystal balls and oriental harems. She was in a class by herself, regal and self-contained. Though the club was nearly deserted, she performed earnestly, as if her set was a sacred ritual feeding her soul. Her skin and features made me think she was a mulatto, but her race was hard to determine. I watched with complete attention; she seemed familiar. I wondered if I had seen her before but was too stoned to remember. The moment before she left the stage she turned and looked directly at me. It was the woman from the beach!

I hurried out, drove around the block and parked about fifty feet from the entrance, thinking she'd probably go out for a bite to eat before going home. I figured I would follow her and accidentally bump into her at the restaurant. I sat for half an hour, my heart racing, practicing my lines, but she didn't show. Suddenly I realized what a silly fantasy I had concocted. She would have thought I was a John anyway. In fact when I came down I wasn't even sure it was the same woman, so I turned the key and drove home; it was well past three and I had a meeting with the accountant at nine.

Magdalena was dragging her feet on the sale and I didn't want to trip in Waikiki, for obvious reasons, so I flew to Kauai for the weekend. LSD was a distinct improvement on alcohol because it revealed what alcohol concealed. To sort myself I had to touch that place where I dissolved and the self began. The Sandoz blotter I purchased from Bob, a charismatic acid *guru* and head honcho of a Berkeley commune, insured five or six hours of ecstatic tripping and produced none of alcohol's toxic side effects. Yes, I often felt tired the morning after, no more than after a night of love and a lot less than from a hangover, but with so much to process the downtime was welcome. I thought deeply about my experiences, gleaning insights about myself and the world.

On one trip I got a reasonably clear picture of where I was going. I checked in at the Coco Palms and walked up the beach, wondering what the trip had to offer. I came upon a deserted cove ringed with palms, sat on the warm sand, removed my shirt and opened my day pack, extracting a small jade box with an intricately-carved lotus on the top, a souvenir from Hong Kong. I unfolded a square packet of aluminum foil wrapped in yellow silk, revealing several small blue squares of blotter paper in the center of which were printed the Hindu symbol of Spirit, *Om*. Bob said it meant Truth.

I took a square from the packet, placed it in my palm, made a fist, put it in the center of my chest and bowed my head. An electric current began to flow, sending a chill wave of excitement through the body. I asked for guidance, carefully chewed the blotter and waited.

Time, radiating from the center of the mind, spread out in ever-expanding concentric rings and merged into the horizon. The thoughts of Magdalena and the business dribbled off the rim of my consciousness and dropped like ballast into the electric void opening up within. I felt myself lift off, a shuttle straining into space. A gull appeared high up, soaring on an invisible stream. I became the gull and then an eagle, alert and far-seeing, weaving and winding though the fine residue of thought and feeling hanging like mist, shrouding the mysterious center toward which I felt myself, a spirit body, traveling.

Suddenly the fog lifted, my vehicle dissolved, and I melted into a radiance greater than scores of suns, a place I would soon come to call "the crystal palace." Bodiless and deathless, I rested there, observing an endless display of exquisite kaleidoscopic, multi-colored *mandalas* forming and unforming against a background of cosmic sound, the *Om*, gauzy light refracting in every direction from a silent emptiness.

The thought "who am I?" filled my consciousness. In answer I saw myself sitting in full lotus, a fully awakened, infinitely blissful, supremely wise being with all virtues: purity, forbearance, fearlessness, compassion, wisdom, discrimination, straightforwardness, peace, patience and truth.

Hours later I returned to earth and walked slowly down the beach toward the hotel and my messy life, wondering how to close the chasm between who I really was and my present self. For a moment I dismissed the vision as a drug-induced hallucination, a perverse divine taunt, and lost heart. When the depression lifted I realized I had been blessed with an unshakable conviction of my divinity and knew, beyond a shadow of a doubt, I couldn't stop until I made it real.

What I didn't know, however, was that the sinner could not become the saint; the self I saw could not be created by wanting it or through any therapy. Had I been able to accept my disgusting, dishonest parts I would have saved a lot of time, but I believed I had to pay for all the suffering I'd inflicted on myself and others.

The following Monday there was still no word from Magdalena. I went to bed late and dreamed I was walking through the dark heart of Africa, stalked by heavily-armed black foes who leapt out from behind trees and rocks to do battle. I fought them off but lost energy with every encounter. When I was at my wit's end I took an inviting path leading into the mountains and arrived at a pristine lake. Looking into the water I saw the exotic dancer from the Forbidden City dressed in silky white with a marvelous headdress made of luxurious gems and feathers. With one hand she seemed to be offering a benediction and the long elegant fingers of the other clasped a large book whose cover bore several ancient hieroglyphic-like letters, fixed in a circle and glowing like emerald radium. I tried to decipher the meaning but the more I tried, the more indistinct the letters seemed. The dancer watched compassionately and held out the book so I could see it better.

I woke up late to Charlie's call.

"Got to hand it to you, James," he said enthusiastically. "She went for it. You're out of the business! Remember, a trip for two to Tahiti! She's going to sign at one on Friday."

Thursday evening, with less than twenty-four hours to go, I took a walk on the beach to calm my nerves. I was about to turn around near the rocks at the foot of Diamond Head when I came upon Madame Zora, the gypsy stripper from Forbidden City. Monday's dream flashed through my mind, and she invited me to sit. "Aren't you worried, sitting here alone at night?" I said.

"No."

"What about me?"

"You wouldn't hurt a fly. What do you want?"

"You were in my dream Monday night."

"In my business all the men have dreams."

"Not like that. Would you like to hear it?"

"Okay."

I described the dream and asked what she thought.

"Africa is your dark side and the black men are parts of you that are unhealthy, parts that you don't love and understand. You've been in conflict for a long time. It's making you weary. You want out. So a path opens up. It goes into the mountains. 'Mountains' means away from the world, looking into yourself. On this path you see a lake. This lake is your spirit, your soul. And when you look in you see a goddess figure holding a book. This book is the book of knowledge..."

"What knowledge are you talking about?" I interrupted.

"Knowledge of yourself."

I felt a thrill, wild excitement. "What self are you talking about?" I asked. I wanted to talk to her forever.

"It's a long story and it's time for my next set," she replied, getting up.

"You're leaving? We just got started. I want to know more about this business."

"Think about what I said," she replied as I followed her to the parking lot. "We'll meet again."

"How about phoning in sick? Get one of the girls to cover for you. I'll give you a hundred bucks if you'll talk to me."

"Take it easy, man," she said. "I want to go. I have my job. It's my duty. I'm not interested in your money."

"When will we meet? How about after your set?"

"After my set I go home and go to bed. I'm tired. It's been a long day."

"Thanks for talking with me. I needed that."

"Okay, bye," she replied unsentimentally. "See you around."

***

Magdalena and her lawyer were already seated when I arrived. I expected a raft of bad vibes, but she seemed composed, even peaceful. In fact she was absolutely beautiful. Her words, uttered in a moment of spite, "You'll always love me," came flooding back.

"Mrs. Taylor would like to ask you a question," Charlie said, pulling me out of my thoughts.

I nodded.

"What guarantee do I have you won't contact the IRS?"

"I'm sick and tired of the whole thing," I replied. "I just want to get on with my life. Very good things are happening for me and I don't want to think about the past. I'm sure you realize that if the Feds are involved they'll come after me too."

She nodded at the lawyer, who said, "Mrs. Taylor is satisfied. Let's sign the papers."

On the way out I saw her standing on the curb, waiting for a ride. "I'm sorry I had to do it that way," I said. "It really wasn't personal."

"It's okay, James," she said. "I'm glad it's over."

"Can I ask you a question?" I said.

"Why not?" she replied in her inscrutable way.

"Why did you believe me?"

"It sounded like the truth," she said as her Mercedes pulled up and she got in. "Good-bye, James."

I stood expressionless as she drove off, thinking of what might have been.

***

When I showed up at the club for the last set the horsey girl was down to her g-string, getting ready for a little fun with her six-gun. Madame Zora came on a few minutes later and went through her artistic routine. Her subtle, suggestive movements were tastefully erotic, not blatantly sexual like the others. I noticed a satirical slant to her last act, a subtle spoof of the whole sex business.

I went backstage and invited her for a drink.

"I just want to ask you about what you said last time," I said when she sat down.

"What did I say? I can't remember," she replied.

"You said I was searching for self-knowledge. I want to know what you mean by that. And the dream. How did you get in my dream? Something's going on. First I saw God in the post office, then I got turned on to acid, had this dream and met you. This is not how I had it figured. What's going on?"

"I told you. You're waking up."

"From what?"

"From your sleep."

"You're not making this easy," I said, "Please trust me. I just want to know. I'm not after you. I can get plenty of women, believe me."

"Okay, I'll meet you tomorrow."

"What's the matter with now? I'll take you out for breakfast."

"I told you I'm a working girl, not a rich playboy. I have my routine. I go home after my set and sleep. I don't go out with the customers after work. Here's my number, call me tomorrow about noon."

"By the way," I said, "I'm James. What's your name?"

"For now I'm Madame Zora," she said smiling. "If you're a good boy maybe I'll tell you tomorrow."

We met on the beach in front of the Royal Hawaiian at four.

"Sorry I'm such a pest," I said after we settled in under a large striped umbrella, "But I have the feeling you can help me."

"So what's wrong with you? You look okay to me," she said.

"Yeah, I'm okay moneywise, but my life's a mess otherwise. You want to hear about it?"

"Okay, but make it short. I can't handle much misery on days off."

I told her about the affair with Magdalena, the business, the epiphany in the post office and my first trip. She listened dispassionately, nodding here and there, asking the odd question.

"So what's the doubt? What do you want to know?" she said.

"I'd like to know what you make of it."

She sat quietly, looking out at the ocean, observing the sunburned tourists playing in the shallow surf. "Well, it bears out what I said the other night. You don't know who you are."

"You're the second woman who's told me this. I don't get it."

"I'm not trying to be difficult," she said. It's just that I can't tell you in so many words. It's not a verbal thing."

"So what kind of thing is it?"

"A spiritual thing."

"Are you saying I'm spiritual?"

"Not exactly. Spiritual's not an act, not something you do to make yourself feel good."

"So what is it?"

"It's what you are."

"What do you mean?"

"Remember how you felt on your first trip when you stepped out on the edge of the hills and the sun was setting, and you felt as if you were dissolving in light?"

"You bet! How could I forget?"

"And you said you felt like you didn't exist, as if you'd died but you didn't die?"

"Yes."

"Well, that light you dissolved into was you. The one who dissolved and died was James, your ego."

I still didn't get it, but it didn't matter. I could see what an unselfish and compassionate person she was. A great love for her arose. "When I hear you talk I have the feeling that you're saying something very important, but it's as if your words are filtering through cotton. I'm only understanding part of them."

"As time goes by you'll understand," she said. "Spirit unfolds in its own time. You can't force it."

"What about you? I've been pretty rude, talking only about myself."

"Me, I'm nobody, just a stripper at a second-rate Mafia joint," she replied.

We spent the rest of the afternoon together and met the following day. I went to her flat near the club to pick her up and asked her about a small black box-like object nestled in the center of a group of plants on an antique parlor table.

"An orgone energy accumulator," she said.

"A what?"

"Orgone energy accumulator."

"God, Linda, are you all right? What the hell is that?"

"It collects orgone energy."

"What's orgone energy?"

"The cosmic energy. It's spread evenly throughout the universe, but this box concentrates it here."

"The box concentrates it? How do you know?"

"I can feel it. It's like the pyramids, only more powerful."

"The pyramids? What do the pyramids have to do with energy? I thought they were tombs."

"They are, but they also play an occult role."

"Occult?"

"Hidden. Their builders had secret spiritual knowledge and made the pyramids according to certain occult principles that take into account the fact that the universe is a spiritual entity, not just a material one. That box acts on the same principle, focusing cosmic energy."

"How do you know this, Linda? All due respect, but it sounds pretty far-fetched to me."

"There's a lot you don't know, James," she replied. "I know it because I know it."

"But how, Linda? How?"

"I feel it."

"I don't get it. I don't feel anything coming from that box."

"You're just not sensitive, James. You think too much."

"Yeah, but Linda, are we talking about the same energy I experience when I take acid?"

"There's only one energy, James."

"Only one energy?"

"Yes."

"Tell me about it."

"What's to tell? Either you experience it or you don't."

"So we're talking cosmic energy here?"

"Right."

"Okay, then how does the acid release the cosmic energy? That whole trip is happening inside my mind, not out there in the universe."

"That's right, James, but the whole universe is inside you."

"Jesus, Linda, some of this stuff is pretty hard to swallow."

"Well, you don't have to swallow it. I'm not trying to convince you of anything, believe me. The way it works is I say certain things and you either get it or you don't. If you don't get it, it doesn't matter. It will make sense someday when you've had certain experiences."

"I'll take your word for it. Now back to the box. If it puts out the same energy I get when I take acid, why have the box?"

"Look, James, you can't take acid all your life, can you? You'll end up a space case. You've got to figure out how to get it naturally. This box brings it in naturally. It's better than dope because it's healing all the time."

"Healing what, Linda? You sick?"

"We're all sick. It's nothing physical. The soul's sick. It's suffering the disease of ignorance and needs healing."

"So how does a box heal the soul?"

"It's not the box, James. It's the energy. Energy heals."

"Who invented the box?"

"Wilhelm Reich."

"Who's that?

"A great man. A great man who was locked up by the government and died in a nuthouse because of his ideas. He said the universe is made up of orgone energy and sold these boxes to collect it. The government said he was a quack and persecuted him. He's a saint. Let's go to the beach. I can't handle too much of the spiritual stuff so early in the day."

The conversation continued a couple of days later.

"I had a chance to think about what you said last time," I said. "Remember we were talking about the orgone energy and how it healed the soul?"

"Yes."

"So what's this disease of ignorance you're talking about?"

"It's a long story. You sure you're up for it?"

"Sure, Linda, I don't work. I've got time on my hands."

"A long time ago," she began, "all souls were one with the energy. And everything was fine, each soul knew that it was pure energy. But then somehow they got cut off and forgot who they were. And the forgetting made them choose to live in physical bodies and suffer pleasure and pain. But there was a deep longing to go back to where they came from. And that's what we're doing, going back."

"You believe that, Linda?"

"Yes. More than that, James, I know it."

"How do you know it?"

"We've been through that with the pyramids. You know it when you know it. Something has to happen."

"Okay, so where does the disease of ignorance come in?"

"When the souls forget who they are, then they're ignorant. They want to know because that is the only thing that makes them happy."

"I hate to say this, Linda, but that sounds very simple-minded, like a fairy tale."

"It sounds like a fairy tale, James, because of your state of mind. If I told it to you the day the energy turned your life around or during your first acid trip you wouldn't have had a problem with it. As long as you're in the dream, the truth seems false. When you wake up it makes sense."

"But…"

"No buts, James. I don't argue. Either you get it or you don't. If you don't, it's okay with me."

Linda was right, I couldn't see the connection between the powerful experience of God, the inner energy and this balmy doctrine. At the same time her ideas touched something in me I couldn't explain. She had been sent to plant a seed.

***

I think I may have unconsciously seen dropping out of school, taking up with a married woman and doing business as a rebellion against my parents' conventional and decent ambitions for me. Yet even after I realized that rebellion is immature and futile, a deeper impulse pushed me down a dangerous path to freedom.

I would have preferred a painless, rosy-cheeked, born-again awakening, an enthusiastic acceptance of the hair shirt and the mind-numbing certainty of church doctrine, but the path laid out was more complex and subtle, a patient gleaning of the intention of the total as it unfolded through the events of my life.

The day Magdalena signed the papers, I ordered a dumpster and ruthlessly jettisoned everything associated with that life. I quit drinking and took up vegetarianism, shedding the excess weight. One day I met a sexy blond coed from Washington, DC, and left the island for good with no regrets. We flew to California, hitched to the Mexican border and partying hard caught the train El Ferocarrill del Pacífico for points south.

In Mazatlan I went for a morning stroll while Cindy had her hair done. Suddenly, on a back street, without provocation, a police car pulled up, two cops jumped out and unceremoniously shoved me inside. We drove a couple of blocks and passed through the gates of the local prison, where I was ushered into the clichéd third-world cell: a bare bulb illumining pocked, decaying walls, a filthy toilet, a rusted iron bed sporting a stained mattress, the obligatory horde of cockroaches and flocks of flies. The door slammed and I was left to cool my heels and contemplate my misdeeds.

In about an hour another cliché, a beady-eyed plain-clothes cop with greasy slicked-back hair entered and with cheerful sarcasm spoke the following obviously well-rehearsed lines. "Ah, señor, welcome to the Mazatlan Hilton. I hope you enjoy your stay."

I forced a smile at his witticism.

"Perhaps you are wondering why you are here, señor," he said nonchalantly, with a hint of menace.

"Yes, I am," I said with forced humility.

"Well, señor," he said eyeing my Omega, "You have committed a serious crime."

"Oh? What did I do?" I replied dispassionately, trying to keep my anxiety under control.

"You do not know, señor?"

"No, I was just taking a walk when you picked me up."

"Oh, señor, it is such a shame that you do not remember. You have violated the sacred laws of Mexico. Come with me, señor, I will help you remember."

He led me out of the cell and down a corridor into a room that had obviously witnessed its share of human depravity. He pushed a button next to an electric cord, whose bare ends were dangling near a metal bucket half-filled with water. A gargantuan man with rippling muscles, a protruding jaw and vacant stare lumbered into the room.

"Ah, señor, this is my assistant, Pedro. I hope I will not need his services."

Pedro moved a step closer.

"What work do you do in your country, señor?"

"I'm a businessman, sir, the executive vice-president of a retail corporation," I said, handing him my card.

"Ah, the señor is an important person," he said, turning to Pedro, who nodded like a robot.

"But I think the señor is not telling the truth," he said with menace. "He breaks our laws and tells lies. How can a man like you wear such long hair?" he said contemptuously. "Perhaps the señor is a rock star?"

"Just a businessman on vacation with my wife," I said.

"Oh, señor has a señora?" he replied, obviously unhappy I was not alone.

"Yes, she's the daughter of the ambassador to Uruguay and speaks Spanish," I replied, which happened to be the truth. "And when she discovers I'm not back for lunch she'll start looking for me."

I could see him thinking, so I decided to do business. "I think there is some way we can make things right, señor. Perhaps I was making a violation of your law, but I am just a foolish gringo, señor. I did not know what I was doing. I am sorry I made a mistake. Perhaps I can give you this nice Omega to pay my fine."

"Ah, I can see the señor is a reasonable man. It is important to confess your crimes. But the watch is not enough, señor. These are serious charges against you."

"Perhaps the watch and twenty dollars would be correct," I said.

"Now the señor understands the importance of the situation. But there is one more thing you must give me, señor."

"Yes, what's that?" I replied, amazed at his greed.

"Your hair, señor. Such hair is in violation of the laws of Mexico."

I was shown a seat in a nearby room, where a barber humorlessly removed every hair – except the mustache.

The detective appeared and laughed uproariously at what could only have been a well-worn joke, "Ah, señor, you look just like Pancho Villa!"

When I got back to the hotel Cindy burst into tears; she wanted a flower child, not a Pancho Villa lookalike.

That the police were not in the business of guaranteeing the safety of the citizenry was a tad unsettling, but the knowledge that the greased palm neutralized a host of crimes and misdemeanors made it possible to continue our hedonistic extravaganza. We hit all the mandatory tourist spots and ingested copious quantities of controlled substances too numerous to catalogue. Weeks later we crossed the border at Brownsville and hitched to DC, but at an aging twenty-seven I simply couldn't party hard enough to suit Cindy and fell by the wayside.

The Holy Man Jam

I flew to California and stayed with my brother in Redwood City, not far from Woodside where Ken Kesey and The Merry Pranksters, immortalized in Tom

Wolfe's *Electric Kool-Aid Acid Test*, made their home. Though the revolution had peaked, it was far from over, so I set out to make up for lost time, practicing both low- and high-church psychedelic: dancing all night at Winterland, the Fillmore West or the Family Dog, making free love with an assortment of hippie chicks, reading Watts and Huxley, and practicing *yoga* and photography.

I went wherever the flow carried me, marveling at the weirdness of the straight and psychedelic worlds. One day, walking down Market Street, I was blessed with the prismatic vision of a fly, seeing thousands of skyscrapers through each eye. And in the middle of each tiny image, I saw Giulia, a girlfriend from Amsterdam, and me walking arm in arm down Market Street!

Often I would be tripping and suddenly someone would enter my energy bubble or I theirs, and for however long, a few minutes or days, two lives would be welded together by the intimacy that comes from sharing a common vision. When it ended, it ended; each unemotionally wandered off into an unknown future.

I never knew where I would sleep or what I would do from one day to the next: head off into the Sierras with a sleeping bag and ten pounds of brown rice or spend a week romancing a beautiful woman in an elegant apartment on Telegraph Hill. Whatever it was, each experience was pervaded by a sense of richness and promise, a feeling of abundance and adventure.

But reality, which I preferred to think of as unreality, seemed to enjoy raining on my parade. One day, dressed in an expensive fringed leather jacket, striped pants and tie-dye T-shirt, I was sitting on the fender of my rig in a posh San Mateo neighborhood waiting for a girlfriend when the cops appeared and demanded my ID. Failure to register my vehicle on time had resulted in a citation a few months before, putting me in hock to the State for seventeen dollars. I offered to pay on the spot, but the police had other ideas.

"No way. You're under arrest, buddy. Spread 'em!" the officer said, gleefully spinning me around and pushing me toward their vehicle.

My mind entered a state of hyper-anxiety because a tiny bag of grass, two hits of mescaline, a tab of acid, a piece of hash, a pack of Zig Zag rolling papers and a stone hash pipe were hidden in the breast pocket of my jacket!

By the grace of God, however, the lining containing the pocket had worked loose from the seams by virtue of excessive use, so when I leaned against the car it hung in the space between my body and the jacket and the officer missed it when he patted me down.

The search complete, I was handcuffed by one officer while the other opened the back door.

"Watch your head," he said as he violently kicked me in the backside, sending me crashing headfirst into the steel screen separating the front from the back of the car.

I was meant to rant and rave and accuse them of a great injustice to provide them with an opportunity for further abuse, but I remained silent. I think my non-response caused them to become aware of their own guilt because they seemed almost subdued when we arrived at the station.

We entered the building and took the elevator up to the jail. A light blinked on above a steel door, a buzzer sounded and the door opened. On the right I noticed a glassed-in area, housing jail personnel. In a large holding cell on the left my cuffs were removed and I was left to cool my heels in the company of a couple of fellow miscreants as the cops sauntered off to start the paperwork.

As I was contemplating how to rid myself of the offending items, two burly deputies deposited a huge, wild-eyed, tattooed, jack-booted Hell's Angel, the type for whom jails are intended, in the holding cell. Judging by the vibes, he'd probably just murdered his girlfriend, shot a cop or robbed a bank.

He stood trancelike, staring into some private hell for a few minutes and then, without warning, ran into the glass separating the holding cell from the common area, beating it with his fists, screaming with rage at the top of his lungs.

All hell broke loose when the officers returned to subdue him. Secretly hoping he would bust a couple of heads, I swallowed the dope, quite a feat without water, ripped the bottom off one of the attorney/visitor phones, stashed the paraphernalia inside, and sat patiently in the corner hoping the booking would end before I came on to what promised to be, in the jargon of the times, a bummer.

Mercifully, twenty minutes later I was booked, searched, fingerprinted, allowed to pay my fine and released. When the drugs wore off the following afternoon I began to think seriously about cleaning up my act.

A couple of weeks later I met a fellow in a café in the Haight who turned me on to two hits of mescaline and told me about a rock concert at the Family Dog on the Great Highway across from Seal Rock, next to Playland. "Don't miss it," he said. "The Dead and Eric Clapton are on the bill."

The parking lot was jammed when I pulled up just after sunset. I walked across the highway, sat on the beach, snorted both capsules, one in each nostril, and waited for the explosion.

Expecting to be entertained by the Dead's weird, happy, psychedelic vibes when I opened the door, I was treated instead to the sight of Allen Ginsberg

French-kissing a young man in the entranceway. The main room was crawling with spiritual types: ochre-clad Hare Krishnas with drums and cymbals, chanting the *maha-mantra*, turbaned Sikhs and healthy granola-fed women wearing Birkenstocks, with sparkling eyes, dressed mostly in white. On one wall a movie showing Satya Sai Baba vomiting a huge stone Shiva *lingam* from his innards played, viewed by a crowd of otherworldly types.

I noticed Steve Gaskin – former San Francisco State professor turned hippie and an acid-age *guru* famous for his Monday Night Class, who eventually ran off to Tennessee with several hundred dedicated followers – standing in one corner, surrounded by members of his flock. A blissful Yogi Bhajan sat stage center, a beam of light emitting from what appeared to be a diamond between his eyebrows.

The vibes were a little strange, but good. Along the wall blond California *yogi* surfer types dressed like Indian *naga-babas* sat twisting their beautiful, lithe bodies like pretzels.

After I wandered around in a daze for a few minutes, an attractive young woman dressed in white came up bearing a tray with fruit juice and banana bread.

"Electric Kool-Aid?" I queried cleverly.

She looked at me with adoring eyes, missing the joke.

"Wow," she said, "Are you beautiful! Your energy is incredible. What meditation are you doing?"

"Two hits of mescaline," I said, her look of devotion changing to one of horror.

"You mean you're high?" she said in disbelief.

"Sure. They told me The Grateful Dead was playing. I snorted a couple of caps of mescaline and came to dance. But it's clear even to me that this isn't a rock concert."

"You're really high on drugs," she said. "Really?"

"Sure, why not?"

"You poor dear, don't you know?"

"Don't I know what?" I replied.

"Drugs aren't where it's at."

"Okay. So what's where's it at?"

"God. It's the highest high."

Something in me believed her. "Okay, God. That's fine," I said, "so where's God?"

"India," she said smiling.

"India?"

"Yes, my *guru* is in India. He's a perfect master. He's God."

"Come on, you don't believe that, do you?" I replied. "God's a kind of energy, a power, a force. It's not a person."

"It's a person too," she replied. "But we're not supposed to argue with people who don't believe."

"Who's 'we'?" I asked, my curiosity piqued.

"The devotees," she said enigmatically.

"What devotees?"

"The devotees of my *guru*."

"So who's your *guru*?"

"Guru Maharaji. Want to see his picture? It's full of *shakti*."

"What's *shakti*?"

"Boy, you don't know anything, do you?! *Shakti's* energy, divine energy. Here." She showed me a picture of a teenage boy dressed in silks, sitting on a throne.

"That's God?"

"You have to have *darshan* and get *shaktipat* before you can see it," she replied.

"What are these words you're talking? This isn't English."

"Sanskrit. The language of God."

"God has a special language?"

"That's right, Sanskrit. It comes from India. It's thousands of years old. The oldest language in the world."

Cynical as I was, some part of me was fascinated by this young woman and what she had to say.

"So what's this *dar... shat*?" I asked.

"*Darshan*," she said.

"Okay, *darshan*. What is it?"

"*Darshan's* when the *guru* gives you the experience of God."

"You're kidding. Nobody can do that. It just happens," I countered.

"I don't argue," she said. "You have to come and see for yourself."

"Here," she said giving me a card with an address and telephone number, "come and meditate with us. See for yourself."

A few minutes later I made the acquaintance of a tall, skinny fellow with a turban. "So what's your trip?" I asked.

"*Kundalini*, man. Breath of fire."

"Breath of fire?"

"Yeah, it's like this." He started what seemed like hyperventilating, his eyes glassing over, the veins in his forehead popping out.

"So what's that do?" I asked after he'd finished.

"Wakes up the *kundalini*," he replied sincerely.

"Okay, so what's the *kundalini*?"

"It's like a snake-energy in the spine. It gets woken up and blows your mind. That's enlightenment."

It was news to me. "So you're enlightened?" I said.

"No," he said sadly, "I'm not ready yet. I'm still too impure."

I wandered off wondering if the poor fellow hadn't done a bit too much acid.

The movie of Sai Baba, a meaty, weird-looking guy with orange clothes and an Afro, started replaying. He was walking in front of hundreds of people who were reaching out to touch him as if he were a rock star. He stopped in front of someone and waved his hand several times in a circular motion, and a little shower of sacred ash poured into the devotee's hand, seemingly out of thin air. A picture of one of the Hindu gods, Ram, was blessed by the *avatar* and continuously generated ash. He produced watches and jewelry from nowhere like a magician.

"That's pretty weird," I said to the fellow standing next to me, his hands folded in a prayerful attitude.

"It's not weird," he said, offended. "Not if you know who he is."

"So who is he?" I asked.

"He's an *avatar*," the man replied.

"So what's an *avatar*?"

"He's God."

"How can he be God?" I said, "I just met a woman who said that her *guru* was God."

"Oh, a lot of people think their *gurus* are God," he said with certainty, "but they're deluded. Sai Baba is the one true God. Who can do that?" he said as the part where God vomited up a huge phallic stone object started re-running.

"I don't know," I said, "probably God."

"There is no God," said a small, clean-shaven fellow with a bald head, wearing a purple caftan and carrying an odd oriental rosary when I asked him about Sai Baba. "There is no God and there is no self. There is nothing but *bodhi*, the Suchness. The Hindus are deluded."

"What's *bodhi*?"

"Enlightenment."

"Okay, what's enlightenment?"

"He who says doesn't know, and he who knows doesn't say," he replied inscrutably, his hands fairly zipping around the beads.

"There is one God and his name is Allah," said a scruffy, long-haired hippie who purported to be a Sufi.

"What's a Sufi?" I asked.

"A lover of God. God is the Beloved and we are his lovers."

"You mean sex? How can you have sex with God?"

"Everyone's God, so when you're having sex, it's with God," he said, employing an irrefutable logic.

"So what you into, man?" I said to an emaciated young man with sunken eyes who looked like he'd just been released from Auschwitz.

"Macrobiotics," he replied.

"Oh. What's that?"

"Balancing the *yin* and *yang* in your food."

"The *yin* and *yang*?" I replied.

"Do you eat meat?" he said, changing the subject.

"Some, why not?"

"If you don't know, you're beyond help," he replied walking off.

I must have talked to fifty people about God, *gurus, buddhas, avatars, kundalini, chakras, yin-yang,* acupuncture and meditation before the event wound down around midnight. Nobody was touting better living through chemistry. And, not surprisingly, nobody was witnessing for Jesus.

A Setback

I swore off drugs and decided to head for India. A few days later I met a woman, light years ahead of me spiritually, in Caffe Trieste, an Italian coffee shop in North Beach, to whom I showed a recently-purchased book on *hatha yoga.*

"Meatballs," she said unable to conceal her scorn. "Look at them. Beef on the hoof. This is not spiritual. This is gymnastics."

On a subsequent occasion she showed me a book with pictures of a different type of *yogi.* "Look at them," she said. "The grace, the poise. See how they aren't really here."

"Aren't here?" I said, bewildered.

"In meditation. They're looking inward at the light within. This is *yoga.* It has nothing to do with the body."

It was news to me.

A day later I came across a book entitled *The Yoga of Knowledge* by an Indian, Swami Vivekananda, who visited the States around the turn of the century. As I read, each consciousness-soaked word gave form to the vision I'd had on the beach in Kauai. And, like Linda, it spoke of the disease of ignorance. When I put it down I realized with renewed conviction I had to know who I was.

So I made up my mind to go to India and find God. I know it sounds eminently laughable, a real cliché, but that was my thinking. I won't chronicle the events that led up to my next near-disaster and will cut to the chase, but a few months later I found myself in New York City, the proud proprietor of a booming dope business. One afternoon my partner and I, a young Jewish woman from Brooklyn with nerves of steel and a good head for business, fixed over two hundred lids, stashed them in her granny's embroidered antique bag and caught a taxi for Randall's Island, where Jimi Hendrix and Jethro Tull were headlining.

I hunkered down in the row of dealers and started selling while Inez wandered around looking at the freaks. Within minutes I was surrounded by dozens of hands thrusting greenbacks in my direction. As the supply dwindled and my pockets filled with money, I noticed two young blacks worming their way to the front of the crowd. Suddenly one lunged at me, his knife slashing my jacket pocket, sending a flurry of greenbacks into the air. I swung the nearly empty bag at the second, whose blade cut it open, spilling the dope. As the crowd groped for the bonanza I took off at full speed, powered by adrenaline and a tab of acid. When I got to the corner of the grandstand I took the twenty-five-foot leap onto the freeway into the path of an oncoming taxi, which squealed to a stop inches away. I climbed in, thrust a twenty in the face of the driver and gave my assailants the finger as we sped off to the Village, where I changed, stashed the money and returned to the concert just as Jimi Hendrix was bashing a flaming guitar to bits on the stage.

We went to a party after the concert, and just as we were about to have sex the cops showed up. I was barely able to get dressed before being handcuffed and tossed in a paddy wagon with my fellow revelers. I pled guilty to disorderly conduct, paid the fine and when I walked out into the early morning air, I realized that I was on the wrong path. I'm obviously a slow learner.

I gave Inez ten thousand, kissed her goodbye and flew to Montana, where the family had a log cabin on the Big Blackfoot River. Early one morning a few days after I arrived, I dreamt I was in an exotic Oriental country standing on a series of stone steps, waiting for a boat on the banks of a large, calm blue-gray river in front of a group of ancient temples, majestic snow-capped peaks in the distance.

I woke up, grabbed my stash and walked down the river. Slowly, ceremoniously, I threw my dope into the river. As the last bit passed from view I saw a wriggling, snakelike, bluish light emerge from the depths, hover over the surface for what seemed an eternity and rise up glimmering and winking until it merged into the first glow of dawn suffusing the top of Sheep Mountain.

Within a week I walked into Icelandic Air's San Francisco office and bought a ticket for Europe, first stop on the way to India, Land of Light.

The Thrill Is Gone

Though treated to faint glimmerings, I didn't know that life was not about being different from who I was, but about understanding why I was as I was. So when I had the dream, threw away the dope and saw the mystic snake rise out of the river, I resolved to pursue a more pure style of life. If I had to do it all over, I wouldn't do it differently, because disillusionment and broken resolutions are as important as inspiration and kept ones if they teach the why.

An improved and subtler version of the alcoholic, the druggie – though a kinder, gentler fool – was doomed to extinction too. Yes, I went to a rock concert on the Isle of Wight, a wet, miserable, typically English affair, hit the clubs in Amsterdam, Paradiso's and the like, smoked a bit of hash – the European equivalent of pot – and had a couple of hot little episodes with the ladies. But the not-high days started to outnumber the high days, and I noticed a curious fact: the not-high days were sometimes higher than the high days, which made me suspect that something other than dope was making me feel good. Before long I would have to face the blasphemous prospect that dope was bringing me down.

I bought a bicycle in Paris and worked my way down the French coast to Spain, stopped off in Madrid where I initiated a bizarre bit of *karma* involving the President of the United States, of which more will be said later, and ended up in Malaga where I caught the ferry for Morocco, surrendering my hair at the border.

It Is Not Here on Earth that I Am Seeking

After another love affair in Tangiers, I shucked my hippie rags, bought a *jellabia* and caught the Marrakech Express. In Marrakech I discreetly smoked hash in the cafés, drank opium tea made from poppies, readily available in the *souks*, traded books with travelers, rode camels in the desert and socialized with consumer society's flotsam and jetsam, an assortment of crazy and incurable romantics in search of pleasure and adventure: a pair of lipstick lesbians from New York on vacation from the modeling trade, a diminutive bald dealer from California named Jason who walked through the streets wildly banging on a drum, a born-again Cherokee from Muskogee, Oklahoma, on the lam from a bank robbery in New York, who whiled away his days spouting scripture, a merchant seaman from San Francisco, who appeared later at critical points in my life, and a fellow whose presence in Morocco was probably a consequence of reading *Dune* on acid, a tall, rich, upper-middle-class WASP from Los Angeles who spoke Arabic, wore a blue burnoose and turban, and tried to encourage me to join a camel-riding band of revolutionary guerrillas who hung out in the desert to the south.

Exotic as it all was, the more I played, the less meaningful it was. As the libertine extravaganza slowly wound down I found myself turning down nights of love for the silence of the desert, where in sacred moments I became acutely aware of a wonderful seed sprouting in the depths, the spiritual force striving to articulate itself. Because it had saved me from myself so many times I started to think of It as a friend and guide. And one day, sitting alone on a rock in the desert at dawn, the Friend called me Ram, "the one who revels in the Heart."

This power, the exquisitely beautiful, "thumb-sized Person sitting in the Heart," as the *Upanishad* says, attracted me like nothing else and set in motion a way of thinking which would slowly transform me into an ascetic and a mystic. A power longing to be known, it created a restlessness no earthly experience could satisfy, an immense longing for liberation.

Bored with Marrakech, I took a bus to a small village of simple, domed, whitewashed houses tucked away in the Riff Mountains, checked into a tourist hotel and visited one of the local cafés where a skinny, frizzy blond astrologer from Philadelphia, who must have intuited my soft spot for eccentrics, made a bee-line for my table.

George, a walking, talking guide to the galaxies, had the whole planetary system and beyond wired. As we sipped our tea I was informed that Venus-conjunct-Mars-in-the-something-house had decreed our meeting. The stars also insisted we take a trip into the mountains to search for the remains of a lost civilization. Always one for a bit of a hike, I agreed to go and met her the next morning after breakfast.

As we climbed she revealed the startling cosmic information that we were fated to take acid and make love. There was a time, in the not terribly distant past, when such a prospect, even with a skinny girl like George, might have proved an interesting proposition, but I found myself remarkably disinterested.

George, and indeed the whole world, seemed a million miles away. I politely made my excuses, further endearing me to her. Perhaps she figured I was playing hard to get, a critical planet gone retrograde for a few minutes. Arriving at the crest of a peak with an awesome view of the mountains and the desert beyond, we sat down to take a break, and in a well-choreographed move, George broke out her stash.

"Okay, man," she said with complete authority, "at exactly 9:43 we're supposed to take this dope."

"George, I've got something to tell you."

"Okay, Jim, let it fly."

"With all due respect to the planets, I don't feel much like taking any more acid."

Her face dropped. "Suit yourself, Jim," she said coldly, "but you have to take responsibility."

"For what, George? Responsibility for what?"

"For messing up the *karma*, man. This is supposed to happen. You take the *karma*."

"What *karma*, George?"

"Look, Jim, can I level with you?" she said, the wheels spinning. She wasn't going to give up without a fight.

"Sure, George, let me have it."

"Everything in this whole cosmos is connected to everything else. Dig? And that means if one little thing doesn't do what it's supposed to do it causes all kinds of problems for everything else."

"What you're saying, George," I interrupted, "is that you'll be bummed out if I don't trip with you, right?"

"It's not just me, Jim, it's the whole cosmos that suffers in many ways. You can't fight the stars. You fight the stars and you come out a loser. That's the way it is. Now, we've got ten minutes until exactly 9:43, and I want you to think long and hard about your decision and I'll be back to get your reply after I take a pee." She got up and wandered off behind some boulders.

I didn't think very long or very hard, because it really didn't matter if I tripped or not. I was inclined against it because I objected to the way she tried to work the guilt angle.

"Well, you've got two minutes," she said, appearing from behind the rock. "Did you make up your mind?"

"No, George, I haven't. On one hand, I don't want to foul up the cosmos, and on the other, I don't feel that much like tripping. I've tripped enough for ten people in the last couple of years and I can't see it's going to change me that much."

"One minute, Jim, you've got one minute. Don't blow it."

I decided to let the deadline pass just to see what she would do next when The Voice said, "Take the dope, Jim."

So I said, "Okay," and George handed me a tab of acid with a big smile. I made her day. And I didn't know when I popped George's acid at exactly 9:43 a.m. that I was taking the trip that put the nail in the coffin of LSD.

I don't pretend to be an authority, but here is my theory on the psychology of drugs: in the beginning there is the you that wants to be different. Then you ingest the stuff that makes you different, "high" in drug vernacular. Finally, the drug wears off and the different you changes back to the original you. However, if you're not the boring you that you think you are in the first place, you won't mind if the boring you stays bored. Therefore you'll have no need for drugs.

As George's acid coursed through my veins I rediscovered what I actually knew all along but chose not to believe: I wasn't whoever or whatever was getting high. Within minutes the doors of perception opened on the rich inner world where the waving, pulsating life force strained against the thin film of matter struggling to contain it.

But I didn't change at all!

As the drug generated the standard hallucinations, I observed the mind expanding like a rapid-fill helium balloon, pervading subtler layers of existence, producing an indescribable lightness of being until it dissolved entirely, creating delicious ecstasy.

But it didn't affect me at all!

Suddenly I realized I was seated on an infinitely high inner mountain, one so high it was not high at all, indifferently watching an insignificant display of psychedelic pyrotechnics.

I was much more than the paltry body sitting on the earthy mountaintop or the expanding pleasure-filled mind.

I was the unblinking all-seeing eye of awareness, the unchanging center around which the mind and the world, like faraway planets, spin.

George had her day too. We didn't make love, but she stumbled on a monstrous fossilized vertebrae, perhaps a dinosaur part, which she lovingly lugged down the mountain, her interest in astrology vindicated. After all, hadn't the planets said we would uncover lost treasures from the past?

Apart from the pleasure I believed was inherent in them, I think I strove to possess and enjoy things simply to find out what they were. And I discovered a fact that should turn off anyone rushing around in the world looking for happiness: once an object or activity is understood for what it is, it loses its hold on you. It was like that with money and sex. And then drugs. Everything here is limited, but the human heart is unlimited; it will not rest until it has rediscovered itself.

To say I gave up those things is to miss the point. I lived through them, like a needle passing through many layers of fabric, emerging free on the other side. All resolutions are ultimately futile, although they may be helpful in the short run because will power is not enough. Vanity made me think I could overcome these things, but live it to the fullest and life will graciously take everything away in its own time.

It is not up to us.

Though I would take a few more trips, more or less out of habit, the experience on the mountain provided such a clear and powerful affirmation of who I really was that I could no longer take drugs seriously. So I decided to make life my drug and hitchhike alone to Cairo, vowing to rely for my highs only on that all-knowing being sitting on the peak of my consciousness, whose supreme dispassion put all my drug-induced hallucinations in perspective.

A week after the trip with George I was sitting cross-legged in the courtyard of an old Catholic church, warmed by the slanting rays of the autumnal sun, in a small town on the edge of the desert. The shadows deepened, the sky glowed electric blue and an orange aura appeared over the austere mountains as the sun dipped below the horizon. My consciousness emptied and an unearthly silence descended. Suddenly the mind began spinning like a top, picking up momentum, compacting itself into a tiny point of consciousness. Then, as if it knew exactly what it was doing, it left the body through the left eye and hovered in front of my face a few inches away!

Like a spaceship it took off at astronomical speed, propelled by an unknown force. Try as I might I cannot find words to describe what happened as it traveled through myriad worlds gathering experience. All I can say is that I discovered that our little planet is only one of many worlds evolving in a sea of transcendental consciousness.

After a while it returned and I saw it hovering in front of a bearded man sleeping in the back of a local café, as if it was trying to enter his body. My awareness caused it to reappear in front of my left eye, hover like a humming-bird, pierce the center of the eye, expand to the size of the body and come to rest, its strange mission completed.

Casablanca to Cairo

Tanned and fit, wearing a *jellabia* and sandals, looking every inch the latter-day mystic, I hiked to the edge of town and stuck out my thumb, a small French World War I army pack on my back, a large bamboo flute adorned with zodiacal signs slung over my shoulder. I would like to report adventure, intrigue and romance, but the Morocco I experienced from this point on was a different journey. I spent most of the long and uneventful days sitting by the roadside waiting for a ride, watching the mind run the gamut of emotion, trying to keep it anchored in the present. At the end of the day, more exhausted than if I had lugged the cross to Calvary, I walked into the desert, curled up in my *jellabia* and slept.

Different cultures view the same symbols differently. In the West, for example, a cloudy day symbolizes unhappiness, confusion and depression. But in India, an unbearably hot country, clouds are a symbol of hope, joy and abundance because they bring the rains. In the West the desert carries the projection of an inhospitable lifeless world, but throughout the Orient it has come to symbolize the vastness of Allah, the stark, pristine, immaterial energy of spirit. Christ's trip into the desert symbolizes an inward-turning, a movement in the direction of life itself, a journey into the hot heart of Allah.

The Saharan air burned away the heaviness and meatiness in the body, cleansed the breath and worked its way inward to gently purify toxins in the cells. I felt radiant and alive like never before. One day in a small town near the Algerian border I took my first *hammam*, Turkish bath. Sitting in the tub I noticed a greenish film collecting on the surface and called the attendant. "Monsieur, what is this?" I said in French.

"Monsieur is a smoker. That is the nicotine," he replied.

"I haven't smoked for two years," I replied.

"It doesn't matter," he replied, trundling out a well-worn story. "I have been the attendant in these baths for many years, monsieur. One day a man came in, and like you, saw the green film and he became very angry. He said the tubs are filthy, that we do not keep our bath clean. I said, 'You are a smoker, monsieur,' as I said to you. But he denied it. Then he remembered that he had smoked twenty years before. The nicotine was still in his body."

The desert's vast expanse and the endless horizon exert a magical effect on the mind. There are moments when outward and inward blend, the mind empties, sublime emotions come into play and an overwhelming sense of reality informs every perception.

The words *"In sha Allah,"* Lord willing, appear frequently in the speech of the locals. A statement is made and the Lord remembered. Life cannot proceed without the blessing. Disinclined to pray at regular intervals like my Muslim brothers, my soul prayed when it felt the urge — which was often.

One day a man driving a camel cart picked me up and called me *"sufi."* I nodded and smiled because I understood. I am here, I am a denizen of the inner desert. I am a mystic by default.

At the Algerian border the police smiled, said "LSD! LSD!" and gave a big thumbs-up. I continued on, day after day, making respectable progress, a persistent current of joy running through my being.

About three weeks into the trip, I caught a ride in eastern Algeria with a Libyan oil tanker, passing in the late afternoon through rolling hills covered with olive trees. Though I intended to ride all the way to Tripoli, I felt called to get down. The body seemed to have a mind of its own and led me into the landscape for a couple of miles until I came to the top of a small hill with a commanding view. I played the flute, watched the sunset and fell into a deep sleep, waking just before dawn to see dozens of pairs of eyes peering intently at me from the dark shadows ringing the edge of the clearing. As I lay in the half-light trying to make out what was going on, I became aware of an unearthly silence pressing down, as if I were lying on the bottom of a deep ocean. At the same time I felt light and high, as if I were floating in the upper reaches of the atmosphere in a body made of fine energy, a holy white radiance, an island of light in a sea of darkness.

It was then that I realized that my body, squeezed between these two forces, was hovering a full six inches off the ground! The mind raced, fracturing the spell, and the body dropped to earth and broke the silence, jiggling the ring of eyes, a herd of goats intently staring in my direction. Hoping to repeat the experience, I lay totally still for a long time, but nothing happened.

Like a visitor from another world, I walked for several days through the countryside until the mind gradually merged into physical reality. I made my way to Tunis, where I hung out for a few days and moved on, working my way across Libya to Benghazi where a young, blond Englishwoman, working in her father's oil firm, spied me walking through the market and invited me to tea. Love came easily and we spent two idyllic weeks together, our tearful departure one of the most tender and romantic moments of my life.

Chapter IV

Land *of the* Pharoahs

The Trick from California

PEOPLE IN ISLAMIC countries often find it difficult to get along with each other; their list of hatreds stretches back to the beginning of time. A British post-war politician, Clement Atlee, once perceptively and humorously remarked that politics – he might as well have included religion – was the "organization of hatred." Perhaps hatred keeps you on your toes so some enemy doesn't sneak up and snitch your camel or your wife. I found it peculiar that in a land where the name of Allah the Merciful is on every set of lips, hatred, cruelty and brutality have evolved to the level of fine arts.

My desire to continue overland to the Nile was unfulfilled because the Libyan-Egyptian border, a "sensitive area," was closed, and Aeroflot, the Russian national airline, was the only access to Cairo. I wondered how my first flesh-and-blood encounter with the Evil Empire would turn out. Although business and drugs had pretty much decimated my political views, I may have harbored unconscious sympathetic Communist resonances from my days as a beret-wearing, umbrella-toting, cappuccino-drinking coffee shop revolutionary, son of a "pinko" town judge, who earned radical credentials screwing his girlfriend on Joe McCarthy's grave. Were I to encounter a hostile, highly disciplined, steely-eyed cadre of uniformed anti-capitalist commies, I felt I could rely on my *karma* to pull me through.

Much to my surprise, at the entrance to the plane I was warmly greeted by a roly-poly *babushka* type with the calves of a front lineman, who might well have been recently recruited from a Ukrainian potato collective. Two disheveled pilots, sitting in the cockpit of their aging, inattentively-maintained Ilyushin jet, were laughing and joking with an attractive blond stewardess as the unmistakable smell of distilled spirits wafted from the cabin. We taxied down the runway, the plane straining mightily into Gaddafi's none-too-friendly skies, vibrating like an overloaded washing machine on spin cycle. Scarcely had the seat belt light been turned off than the vodka started flowing. Wishing to keep a clear head in the land of the pharaohs, I refrained.

My heart leapt to my throat as the Nile and the pyramids came into view during our descent, awakening ancient spiritual feelings – the perfect landing greeted by a spontaneous outburst of applause.

Emerging from the dingy terminal, contemplating the interface between the First and Third Worlds, the embarrassing moment when haves and have-nots cease to be ideas and actually touch, my state changed. Does a five-dollar taxi ride actually mean life or death to the children of this emaciated, hawk-eyed fellow pulling so frantically at my sleeve? I sympathize with the tourist's propensity to throw money at the problem, the insistence on being met inside the terminal by a well-dressed, well-spoken young man from the travel agency, the desire to be ceremoniously whisked from the airport in an air-conditioned limousine, deposited safely on the steps of a luxury hotel.

I could have ridden the limo, but it was the incorrect path, not out of mawkish liberal sympathy with the struggling and dispossessed, but because somewhere along the line, incrementally and imperceptibly, an island of aware-ness had opened in the mind, a point from which to dispassionately view the world. To nurture that awareness and redeem myself it was important not to insulate it against unpleasantness. It was mandatory that I rub the soul raw on life's realities – hands and knees over cobblestones to Lourdes.

I did not wade into that angry mass to lose myself in an Egypt that would test me to the limit because recent experiences had transformed me into a saint. My aware inner island was less a major land mass than a tiny atoll surrounded by an ocean of ignorance, hardly within easy reach.

I cautiously stepped off the curb and picked my way through the army of touts like a soldier gingerly crossing a minefield, anger and paranoia seeping in. Taxis are not the ticket when you are paranoid; one imagines every turn seemingly leading to a disreputable section of town where worst fears become realities.

So I caught the bus and sat in silence, looking out the window at the unes-thetic grayness of the slummy, polluted city, contemplating the sheer volume of unfortunate humanity. I had no need for further information after the scene at the terminal, but the bus allowed me a good read of the nation's psyche; what I saw was little cause for optimism – every eighth or ninth person a soldier, fully armed.

I got down near the Nile Hilton and began searching for a traveler's hotel, but drew a blank. Spying a park on the other side of the river, I set out to cross a bridge a quarter of a mile downstream. At the bridge approach, challenged by sullen soldiers sporting automatic weapons, I showed my visa and was allowed to pass. Shaken, I retreated to the deserted park and sat on a bench facing the river, lost in thought as traffic ground humorously along on the other side. Based on recent evidence, I faced the possibility that my romantic sojourn in the land of the Pharoahs was going to fail.

Coming out of my thoughts I found the sun setting and myself homeless. Cautiously exploring the park, I discovered a secluded and secure spot, stashed my valuables under a rock, spread the mat and slept without incident, awakening rested and refreshed shortly after dawn. With my wavy, blonding hair, beard, *jellabia* and bamboo flute, I must have seemed more an apparition than flesh and blood. Against a backdrop of military vehicles, soldiers, anti-aircraft-gun-adorned rooftops and sandbagged buildings, perhaps they viewed me as comic relief.

Sucking images from the air, a new musical style emerged – Saharan psychedelic. The crowd swelled and I wondered how it would end, not knowing I should have polished off the tune, bowed and beat a hasty retreat. Welded to the spot, my destiny drew near.

Suddenly, as if conjured by a malevolent *djin*, the vibes about-faced and from the back of the crowd I heard the strident voice of poverty, injustice and sexual frustration yelling, "Passaport! Passaport!"

"Passaport! Passaport!"

A shower of pebbles from the kids, like telltales, indicated a storm. I retreated into the music, fear ripping off my attention, the tune contorting. Released from its spell, minds wandered, amplifying the angry cries as bodies inched ominously closer, a nightmare about to happen.

The music stopped. Surrounded by a wild, excited crowd, two nasty young men were in my face, menacing, pulling my *jellabia* and shouting, "Passaport! Passaport!"

"No way, man, no way. Fuck you!" I thought, stepping back, my strength waning.

Then – hope! Four battered blue-black police vans raced into the courtyard and braked abruptly, vomiting bodies. Long leather straps flailing, the boys in khaki dispersed the crowd.

In sha Allah, someone called the cops!

As I bumped through the streets in the back of the van, the hostile stares of my fellow detainees indicted me for the sudden change in fortune. Deposited on station house steps, I was ushered into the cavernous interior and found myself at the end of the queue, blessed with ample time to contemplate an uncertain future.

A humorless, pen-wielding scribe stood at a tall desk at the head of the line, entering the accused's particulars in a large, dog-eared ledger. The paperwork completed, the hapless subject was ushered down a long hall and disappeared. The clank of steel sent shudders down my spine. The line shrank, images of Mazatlan flashing. When it was my turn the wheels of justice ground to a halt.

"English, English! Speaking English!" I said frantically.

He looked around uneasily, unsure of the next move.

"English, English!" I repeated.

Dead silence and time expanded into eternity. A door opened and a well-dressed officer filled the corridor with his presence. "What is the matter?" he said in excellent English, sauntering over.

"There has been a mistake, sir," I said, verging on obsequious. "I've been arrested for playing the flute in public."

He looked at me as if I were mad, said something to the scribe and ushered me into his office.

Contemplating his amused countenance, I relaxed.

The captain seemed supremely uninterested as I recounted the morning's events in self-serving detail.

"You see the people are very unhappy these days," he said. "They think every foreigner is a Jewish spy. You are German?"

"No, American. My grandfather was German. And what will happen to them?" I said, amazed at my concern.

"Nothing. We will leave them for a few hours and send them home. Public demonstrations are forbidden," he replied. "And where do you stay?"

"Nile Hilton," I said jokingly.

"Seriously," he said.

"I just got in and have been unable to find a hotel. I was looking for one when this business happened."

"Perhaps you are poor and can't afford a proper hotel."

"No, it's not that," I said showing him my money pouch. "I could stay at the Hilton. I'm looking for a small, clean hotel in a neighborhood where I can experience a bit of your culture. I hate tourist hotels."

He smiled. "You are in the wrong area," he replied helpfully, directing me to a group of local hotels on the other side of the river about half-an-hour's walk away.

"Thank you," I said. "I assume I'm free to go."

"Why not have a cup of tea?" he said. "I have always wanted to know about America. I went to school in England but did not get to see America. Of course

I should not be talking with you, because America supports the Jews, but to tell the truth, I am sick and tired of war."

So we spent the next half-hour talking sports, politics, religion and women.

Convinced someone up there loved me, but obviously shaken, I followed instructions that took me to a group of small hotels catering to locals, one of which sported a neon sign with a palm tree and the sentimentally appealing name Hotel Hawaii. Within minutes I was ensconced in a small, clean, reasonably priced room on the third floor with a verandah looking out over a *souk*, which provided ample local color. I deposited the pack, showered, grabbed the flute and hit the streets. Things were looking up.

Having come up with the short end of the stick in the Sinai the previous year, Egyptians were angry. I walked in the crowded downtown area for nearly an hour before I saw a smile, a little boy whose father treated him to a hot buttered sweet potato from a street vendor.

About noon I stumbled on a large café with a smattering of bored middle-aged men aimlessly puffing hookahs and staring mindlessly into the street. I ordered mint tea and accepted an invitation to smoke from one of the patrons, a fat businessman who deftly crumbled a generous chunk of blond Lebanese hash on the glowing coals. A few minutes later, properly stoned, I walked out into the afternoon, feeling ever so pleased, the morning's incident a faint memory. So this was Egypt, land of the pharaohs. Not bad.

After wandering aimlessly for about thirty minutes I ascended a small hill offering an excellent vista of the city, an easy trek up a gentle incline. In a few minutes, about two hundred feet from the top, I encountered a barbed wire fence hung with signs in Arabic placed at regular intervals, certain they said "Keep out!"

Though denied the all-around views the top provided, memory of the morning's folly suggesting discretion was the better part of valor, I pulled up twenty yards short of the fence, parked my bottom on a rock and took in a city stretching as far as the eye could see, melting mysteriously into the Sahara at the horizon. The maternal domes and phallic minarets of many mosques added an air of old-world inscrutability to the picture, inflaming my romantic soul, inspiring a haunting melody.

I played for a few minutes when suddenly the mind's eye saw my bullet-riddled body rolling down the hill! Trying to grasp the full significance of this disturbing image, I stopped playing and heard the metallic sound of a round of ammunition being injected into the chamber of a gun. Turning around, I found myself confronting a soldier with his rifle trained on me! With great deliberation I put the flute on the ground and raised my hands, signal for three or four heavily-armed soldiers to emerge from the brush along the fence. Two climbed over, covered by their companions, one picking up the flute, the other herding me up the hill, the tip of his rifle jabbing the small of my back.

Experiencing a fairly serious case of anxiety, unable to figure out our destination, because there was no sign of life as we approached the summit, and suffering the reason-distorting effects of a powerful surge of adrenaline, for a moment I foolishly thought of bolting, but wisely reined in the overtaxed mind.

About fifty feet short of the summit we approached an artfully camouflaged entrance near a couple of large boulders in a clump of brush, which, activated by an electronic device, opened automatically.

Ushered into the bowels of the earth, I was confronted with a reasonably large room filled with communications equipment, manned by half a dozen soldiers. After a rough strip search and examination of my documents, I was shown a wooden chair under a bare bulb. It was like a scene out of a bad movie, and I half expected to hear the hackneyed line, "Where were you on the night of...?"

Had I been wearing a button-down shirt, polyester slacks, baseball cap and been carrying a snappie, my story might have carried a little more weight — tourist wanders off the beaten track. But minus the flute, to the untrained eye I could have passed as a rank-and-file camel jock.

Discounting their justifiable paranoia, my story, at least on the surface, did not make sense, because I was not real — camel jock just the latest in a long line of honestly-come-by inauthenticities. People don't change identities like a chameleon unless there is something to hide. I wasn't hiding the obvious, an identity as a Jewish spy, but I was hiding nonetheless. From myself.

Somehow I garnered the impression that the niceties of our legal system, Miranda, habeas corpus and a free call to an attorney of one's choice, sensible as they are, were not excessively popular in Egyptian legal circles. This was war and they had just snagged a scumbag Jew.

Though family stock on both sides for several generations is pure WASP, I had occasionally been told by close friends that my features, particularly in the nasal area, could pass for Semitic. This, coupled with tanned skin, *jellabia* and insensitive choice of location for an afternoon stroll, lent justifiable credence to their suspicions. Tourists sit in air-conditioned bars, take group tours to the pyramids, squander their hard-earned capital in the *souks*, dine in fancy restaurants and wallow in the brothels.

An officer who spoke good English interrogated me. I told him that I was a businessman on holiday, omitting the story of the morning brush with the law, but including the stop in the café for a smoke, figuring the truth might play well: stoned hippie stumbles on sensitive military installation.

"What are you doing here?" he asked.

"I was taking a walk, saw this little hill, thought I'd get a view of the city."

"But did you not know that this was a military base?"

"No. I didn't. I saw the signs on the fence and figured they said 'keep out,' so I didn't cross. If your man hadn't showed himself I wouldn't have known anything. I rested a few minutes, played the flute and was about to leave."

In the background an examination of the flute was in progress.

Then out of the blue he said, "So what do you think of President Nixon?"

Dumbfounded, I replied, "I don't have any politics, sir."

"Everyone has politics," he said menacingly.

I was too frightened to see what he was getting at: America had supported the Jews, and Nixon to an Egyptian was the Great Satan. "Really, sir, I don't know much about the President."

He nodded to a soldier standing behind me and I felt a searing pain as the butt of a rifle crashed into the back of my neck. When I regained my seat and my composure, he said, "Everyone has an opinion about Nixon."

It seemed reasonable to develop an opinion. "Well," I said picking my way cautiously, "I don't think he's an honest man."

He seemed interested.

"People say, 'Would you buy a used car from this man?'" He missed the joke, so I tried again. "People ask, 'Would you by an old camel from this man?'"

The hint of a smile crossed his face.

"Honestly, I don't know that much. I live in Hawaii and make business with the tourists. I saved my money to make a trip around the world. I don't know what's happening in politics. I find it interesting to learn about different people. I came to see the pyramids and the Nile. I don't read the papers."

"So what do you think about Israel?"

"I don't know anything about Israel."

Suddenly I found myself sitting on the floor, the chair kicked out from under me.

"I do not believe you," he said, his voice quivering with anger as he loomed menacingly over me. It suddenly dawned on me what was going on in his head.

I started to get up, but he viciously kicked me down.

"Are you a Jew?"

"No way."

"You look like a Jew."

"I am not a Jew. I was born in Montana. There are no Jews in Montana. It is impossible."

"So what do you think of Jews?"

At this point he gestured to another soldier who came over, received instructions and left the room with a companion and my passport, giving me time to think about my reply. The energy changed and it seemed I'd been through the worst.

"So what do you think of Jews?"

"Not much," I said meaning I didn't have an opinion – which I didn't.

"You mean you don't like Jews?"

"You see, sir, I don't know any Jews. Where I come from there are no Jews. But people in America think Jews are only after money."

He seemed familiar with this view. "They are pigs," he said with complete contempt, violently hitting the table with a baton. "Pigs!"

Nearby, several clearly baffled men speaking in low tones clustered around the flute, tapping it on a table, carefully examining the inside, holding it up to the light, poking it with a knife, looking for my transmitter, secret codes and cyanide capsules.

"And what about that?" said my interrogator, indicating the flute.

"It's only a flute. Shall I show you how it works?"

He nodded and gestured toward the men, one of whom brought the flute.

The sweet, full tones of *Row, Row, Row Your Boat* oozed from the big bamboo flute and the bunker went silent. "It's an old folk song from my country. Would you like to hear the words?"

To my surprise, he nodded.

When I said, "Life is but a dream," I distinctly noticed a softening around his eyes and the corners of his mouth.

The interrogation abruptly stopped and I sat alone in the center of the room as the men went about their business. For the next two hours I was treated to a practical demonstration in the relativity of time, seconds stretching to eons as battalions of angry and fearful thoughts goose-stepped across my consciousness.

Eventually the two men returned, said a few words to the captain and went to their stations.

The captain approached. "It is as you say. We have checked with the CIA and you are not a spy. I am sorry for the inconvenience, but war is war. Perhaps you should not smoke the hashish. My driver will take you to your hotel. Do not mention this place to anyone, do you understand?" he said, handing back my passport.

I nodded.

I followed the driver down the hill to a jeep parked on a nearby side street. Twenty minutes later we pulled up in front of the hotel. Oddly, it seemed to carry a sleazy, almost sinister, vibe. I was glad to see it nonetheless, chalked the perception up to lingering paranoia from the day's events and dragged my exhausted and aching body up the stairs to the quiet sanctuary of my room.

I sat on the verandah as the sun set, watching the activity in the bazaar, listening to a bad recording of call to prayers crackling from a faulty loudspeaker wired to the minaret of the local mosque, musing on the old days when the *muezzin* sang in his own voice. A crow landed on the railing of an adjacent verandah, mindlessly cawing. Unconscious and hectic as it all was, I took great solace in the noise of the city winding down. At last the day was over!

Exhausted, I stumbled into the room and fell into a deep sleep, only to be awakened a few minutes later by insistent pounding on the door. Thinking the army had changed its mind, I jumped up, grabbed my pack and headed for the verandah and a quick exit over the rooftops when The Voice, on vacation all day, said, "Open the door, Jim."

I dropped the pack and opened the door.

An obese man with beady eyes, three days' stubble on his slack jowls and a food-stained *jellabia*, the kind of person only a mother could love, lumbered carelessly into the room, stopped in front of me, reached into the hood of his *jellabia*, extracted a small wad of money and offered it to me. As I inched back to put myself out of range of his decaying breath, he grabbed me in a bear hug and planted a sloppy kiss on my lips.

The cops, okay, the military, maybe, but this? Full of rage, I wiggled free, stepped back and threw a blow that connected solidly, sending him careening out the door and across the hall where he collapsed in a heap against the wall. Letting fly a stream of invective, I slammed the door, locked it and lay on the bed shaking.

No sooner had I regained my composure than another barrage of knocking shook the door. Thinking it might be the lover boy with the cops, I again contemplated the alternative exit, but The Voice repeated, "Open the door, Jim."

I reluctantly followed the advice and was confronted with a second man, not quite as disgusting as the first, but with similar intentions. Before he could make any moves I slammed the door hard in his face.

It seems I am a slow learner. After the third episode, bells started ringing. The Hotel Hawaii, so innocent and peaceful during the day, transformed itself into a male whorehouse when the sun set. And in a realization that put me in such a state I didn't know whether to laugh or cry, I was the trick from California!

Judging the situation non-life-threatening and too weary to dig up alternative accommodations, I jammed the couch and a chest of drawers between the door and a wall, reducing the possibility of forcible entry to manageable odds and fell into a deep sleep, awaking early to a real-life nightmare, one that had me longing for the relative pleasures of a military interrogation or life in the slammer. The body, barely moveable, was on fire, as if sand was coursing through the veins! I dragged myself up and looked in the mirror to discover I was covered from head to toe with ugly red welts.

The bedbug is a pernicious insect, the bite not particularly serious unless he is diseased – a distinct possibility in rat-infested Cairo. But a handful of bites can almost drive you crazy. And a body-full is dangerous.

Once in India I met a nice young man, a French junkie, who was bitten on the legs while sleeping in a sleazy ten-rupee hotel. In his torpid state he scratched the bites with none-too-clean fingernails, bringing on an infection which, left untreated, turned into a serious case of gangrene.

As one would imagine, life is cheap in India. Humans go for under a hundred dollars, a hit man will bump off an enemy for thirty, so what is the fuss about an arm or a leg? They charged him eight dollars and sawed it off just below the knee. When we met he was hobbling around Connaught Circus on a hand-made wooden crutch, begging for a ticket home, an idea that suddenly sprang to mind as I stood in utter agony looking at myself in the mirror.

My luck seemed to be running out; perhaps it was time to bag it. But The Voice, which had been working overtime recently, said, "Hang in there, Jim."

"Okay," I thought, "It can't get any worse."

But I was so wrong.

While my straight clothes, reserved for visas and special events, were getting a proper pressing at a little tailor shop around the corner, I ran down the local dealer, purchased enough opium to kill a horse and had my hair trimmed. Returning to the hotel, I showered and changed – Bedouin to businessman in the blink of an eye.

When I stopped at the desk to drop off the key, the clerk exhibited signs of what could only be called awe. Whether it was my makeover, the story of the night's events or a combination of both, I will never know.

I checked into a posh, colonial-style hotel with hardwood floors, immaculate tiled baths, high ceilings with brass-fitted fans and dark mahogany blades, tall, generous windows with louvered shutters, huge four-poster beds, a snooty staff and spendy prices.

Like a scientist obtaining chemicals for an experiment or a doctor supplying a prescription, not a low-life junkie, it was knowledge, not depravity, that sent me to the street to score. So when I undressed and lay on the cool, clean, white sheets under the ceiling fan, the soft light and sounds of the city filtering in through thick wooden shutters, and ingested the opium, I was not blindly groping for *nirvana*. I knew exactly where it was and how to get there. With the help of the poppy my consciousness lifted out of the body to the point where the bites were too distant to scratch. Within minutes I rediscovered that inner space where pleasure bubbles up in endless self-generating waves, wiping away even the memory of pain.

A couple of days later, I re-entered the body. The bites, still ugly as sin, had lost most of their sting, and the wad of opium had been reduced to the size of a raisin. I was eager to get on with my life, such as it was, but was not feeling well. I had not eaten for two days and was experiencing a hard pain in my bowels. On examination, my stool, ordinarily inert waste, proved to be host to hundreds of wiggling, maggot-like white worms!

As one might suspect, the Third World takes a reasonably casual approach to public health. In Rajasthan, India's western desert, the dentist squats by the side of the road on a small mat, surrounded by the tools of his trade: a hand-painted sign showing red lips and white teeth, a couple of pairs of dusty dentures, which he will graciously consent to wipe clean with his soiled shirt tail should you wish to fit them, a few metal picks and several pairs of pliers. For a pittance, upwards of a dollar, you can relieve yourself of an offending molar or an unpleasant incisor. You squat, mouth open; he peers in, identifies the culprit, grabs the pliers and yanks.

In those days Egypt's street-level health care system was probably on a par with India's; to my knowledge no Food and Drug Administration intent on protecting the health of the population existed. At least it would be fair to say that people with whom I came in contact in my search of a remedy did not have access to the latest pharmaceuticals. Long-standing formulas available in the bazaar had to suffice. The strange brown fluid I purchased, probably a close kin to carbolic acid, had obviously not been excessively scrutinized, analyzed and rigorously tested by teams of steely-eyed, white-smocked government scientists before grudgingly receiving the imprimatur of officialdom. The man who sold it knew one small fact: it was toxic enough to kill the little white worms cavorting in my gut, but not quite toxic enough to kill me.

As I suffered the cure and parasites by the score met an untimely demise, I contemplated my options: plan A had me on the next available flight to New York, a cop-out. Plan B saw me booking the next available flight to Bombay, an eminently reasonable idea, and plan C would take me up the Nile into the Sudan, down to Uganda, over to Kenya and across the Indian Ocean to Bombay – total folly. And my heart's desire.

Though I have since changed my philosophy and learned to cut my losses, I could not see myself heading back to the States, tail between my legs. The flights to Bombay were booked a month out, scotching that option. So without even visiting the pyramids, I caught the first train south, figuring, based on information I had picked up on the street, I could procure a Sudanese visa at Aswan, and hoping that with a bit of luck Egypt would soon be history.

In my rush to get out I took the milk run, a boxcar without window panes featuring tightly packed rows of straight-backed wooden benches. As the train inched out of the station I wondered if it was truly more sensible to put my life in jeopardy in the land of the pharaohs than to subject it to the vacuous world of TV, Kleenex and Lycra spandex. Had my hatred of plastic, which mocks a psyche weaned on millions of years of organic life, been the ultimate cause of my present torture: rubbing elbows with the most humorless, sullen, God-forsaken human beings I had ever encountered? After about twenty seconds I definitely wished I were back in Mom's Formica kitchen drinking a Coke.

For two hours nobody spoke. Hostility, so thick you could cut it with a knife, gave lie to the liberal notion of a stalwart, simple, fun-loving peasantry; I had obviously read too much Marxist propaganda in college. These people were as hard as the benches on which they sat, as unfeeling as the desert wind sending its stinging sand raining into our faces. Yet, in spite of it all, I was happy to be leaving a city that seemed to have only ill will for a good-hearted but naive traveler.

Traveling is a strange game. You find your destiny rolling out like a ribbon in front and the past receding into the distance behind. The trick is to find the still point, the here-and-now moment when everything is in perfect balance. Get ahead of yourself or fall back into the past and you suffer. Like the pole a tightrope walker uses to maintain balance, you carefully adjust the past and the future to keep the mind awake and centered. If you are skillful, at some point your vision shifts, things are known as they are and the simple profundity of existence is fully appreciated.

For a few hours I achieved that state in spite of the ache in my guts and the torturous conditions. The memory of the ugly city receded into the past, balanced by the vision of ancient Egypt: Thebes, Luxor and Abu Simbel. Perhaps I had made the right move. At one point, several hours down the line, the journey seemed almost festive as the train stopped in the middle of a sugar cane field, permitting the passengers to evacuate and harvest as much sweet cane as they could carry.

Things seemed to be picking up when I found a seat in a second-class compartment next to a window with a pane, but my bliss was short-lived. After about an hour I noticed everyone in the compartment staring suspiciously at me, awakening much-too-recent memories. I tried to ignore them, but to no avail. When the tension reached a certain pitch, as if under orders, a soldier, clutching a rifle, sitting near the door on the opposite side of the compartment came over and demanded to see the pack wedged between my feet. Had I been driven by a hidden force to purchase this World War I French army pack several months ago in a Paris flea market just to incite the suspicions of a paranoid Egyptian soldier?

I undid the straps and gently snapped my blanket like a carpet merchant, all eyes tracking my movements. Next, I removed the velvet cover from my *I Ching*, scrolled through the pages and lifted it heavenward, saying, "Allah," to indicate that it was a holy book.

The moment I spoke the Lord's name a well-dressed man passing in the aisle stopped to observe.

I modeled the dress shirt and tie. No smiles, but the energy was not getting worse. Finally, I dry-brushed my teeth with a yellow toothbrush. Just as I ran out of possessions and ideas the man in the aisle said, "Well, done! Bravo! An excellent performance!" in perfect English.

He stepped through the door, filling the compartment with his presence, speaking Arabic and chiding, perhaps scolding, the passengers, rendering them docile as lambs. I breathed a sigh of relief and joined him for tea in the dining car.

"What did you tell them?" I asked, once we were sitting comfortably in the diner.

"I told them they should behave as if you were a guest. It is our tradition that strangers are to be treated as guests."

"I'm very pleased you happened along," I said. "I don't know how to thank you. It seems everywhere I turn I find myself in a tight situation. The people are very angry."

"It is the war. They cannot forget the humiliation. One cannot blame them."

"But how do you feel? Are you Egyptian?"

"Well, yes and no," he said enigmatically.

"How do you mean?"

"Here we have two Egypts – Arab Egypt and the real Egypt. What you saw in that compartment is Arab Egypt."

"And the real Egypt?"

"The reason I intervened was for the real Egypt."

"You mean the pharaohs, the pyramids, the Nile?"

"Yes."

Something in me stirred and my head spun as if I were coming on to a psychedelic. For a moment it seemed as if the train were stationary and the desert moving.

"Spiritual Egypt?"

"Yes," he said, and my cells tingled with bliss.

Some part of me had been waiting for this conversation for a long time.

I heard his voice, speaking out of a blaze of radiance, say, "I intervened because I owe you a favor."

"A favor? But I don't know you," I replied, realizing it was not true as soon as I said it.

"As far as this life is concerned," he replied.

"This life?"

"A long time ago, not far from here," he said motioned upstream, "we were best of friends. You helped me. Today it was my turn to repay my debt."

"But how do you know this?"

"It is hard to say. Something in me told me to get up and walk through the train. When I saw you standing there entertaining those fools I remembered something. I do not know what it was exactly. I recognized you. I knew you."

"You knew me?"

"Yes, not your body, but you, the real you, your soul. I knew you and I knew why you had returned."

I told him about the first few days in Egypt and suggested that I had come to suffer. He laughed.

"No, that's not what I mean," he said. "You will suffer, no doubt, but that is not the reason you are here."

When he said "here" I had the feeling he meant "on earth" or "in this life."

"You are looking for something, and a piece of the puzzle is here."

In a flash of illumination I saw that nothing in my life had worked like I thought it should because God had Its own ideas about what was good for me. I was not running away or rebelling for the reasons I thought. The granola girl's words, "God is where it's at," flashed in my mind. I was searching for Him – all of this a necessary part of that.

I heard the voice of God speaking through him.

"You have forgotten who you are. That is all," he said with compassion. "Before long you will remember."

"Just who am I then?"

"That's for you to discover," he said smiling, his eyes pools of light.

The Second Time Around

Because they were footing the bill for the dam, Russians called the shots in Aswan. Proffering my passport at several of the better hotels proved futile, so I had to settle for an Arab joint. Predictably, morning found me covered with bites. To add insult to injury the embassy informed me that Sudanese visas were only available in Cairo! Chastened, I caught the train back. Though I was through with Egypt, she was obviously not through with me.

I booked through to Cairo but felt inspired to get down as the train pulled into Thebes. Near what had once been a small bathing pool I encountered a tall, slim black man with an Afro sitting in meditation in the sun next to an orange pup tent, naked except for a G-string. I sat down and waited until he opened his eyes. "What's happening, man?"

"Not much, just hanging out," he replied.

"I take it you're not working on your tan," I said.

He smiled.

"So, what's going on?

"Meditation. Meditation."

"Okay, but what's it all about? What you meditating on?"

"It's a long story."

"Tell me, I've got time. I'll buy you a beer."

He perked up. "It's a long walk to the nearest beer. Let's have a smoke."

"Okay."

So we hunkered down in the shade of a ruined temple, toked up and he began. "I was working in a savings and loan in LA. It was nothing much, just a job to pay the rent. One day during lunch break I went to the library and was thumbing through a big art book on Egypt. As I turned the pages I felt a strange energy come over me, as if I knew all about this stuff. In the middle of the book was a full-page bust of Nefertiti that completely captivated me. As I looked at her the image came alive. My eyes were drawn to a spot on her neck just below her ear and when I concentrated on it I suddenly zoomed into her and woke up in ancient Egypt. And I realized I was not who I thought I was.

"From that point on I couldn't stand my job. Something told me it was time to bag it, but I didn't have anything to fall back on. I was living hand to mouth, like a slave, even though I wore a coat and tie. I couldn't get the picture of the goddess out of my mind. It was like an obsession. There were times when I would work myself into such a state that I'd journey back and relive past lives. It was all very real, but I couldn't tell anyone. The crowd I ran with would have laughed me off the block.

"Then one day at the beach I bumped into a white chick, the hippie type, who took a liking to me, so I took a chance and told her what was happening. She said I was having a spiritual awakening and if I wanted help I should say this *mantra*. She was a member of a Japanese Buddhist sect and gave me a little altar, called a *gahanzan,* and a set of beads, and taught me this chant, *Nam Yoho Renge Kyo.* She said if you chanted it you would get your heart's desire."

"What's it mean?" I said.

"All hail to the *Diamond Sutra.*"

"The *Diamond Sutra?*"

"Enlightenment."

He continued. "It seemed crazy, so I put the beads on a bookshelf and forgot about them. But they didn't forget me. One night I woke up about two. As I lay there staring at the ceiling I was aware of a light coming from the direction of the bookshelf. I thought I was dreaming, my mind playing tricks. I got up and went over. It blew my mind! There was an unearthly light surrounding the beads. I picked them up and the *mantra* started coming spontaneously, my fingers moving the beads automatically. I never felt so much power.

"So I started saying the *mantra* every day and discovered that I got much peace. My life, which had been a little stale until then, started to take off. About a month later I got a call from a brother who had been a good friend years before. We'd had a falling out because he didn't repay a debt. It turned out he was cleaning up his life and while he didn't have the money, wanted to give me a Mercedes left him in a will. I sold the Mercedes, which was worth a lot more than he owed, quit my job and bought a ticket for Cairo."

Danny was planning to travel up the Nile to Uganda and the Congo, so we joined forces. After recent experiences I was happy to have a companion.

Though not an asset in Egypt, black skin might have advantages in the Sudan and points south. It seemed things were finally looking up.

We hung around Thebes for a couple of days soaking up the atmosphere, exchanging ideas, and caught the train for Cairo on Friday. Monday was a holiday and it took three days to get the visa, so we had a week to kill. Because Danny had seen the pyramids, I set off on my own.

I took the profound feeling that arose when I saw them from the plane as confirmation of my belief that the ancients had known God. True, the culture that created these powerful and egoless symbols of the Divine was gone, but I had a strong conviction that the real Egyptians were wandering the earth today, directing inquiring minds to God, the sacred inner pyramid.

What else would explain the man on the train? And Danny. These were not ordinary people, caught in the reality of the visible. Though too cynical to think of myself as religious, in my heart of hearts I caught the bus to Giza to go to church.

When the pyramids came into view this time I felt a subtle movement deep inside and noticed that the world was suddenly bathed in a rain of unearthly light! When I got down, the people clustered at the base seemed more like cartoon characters beamed from an alien world and superimposed on the timeless screen of reality than camel drivers, trinket vendors and foreign tourists. Experiencing fits of ecstasy, I climbed the face of Cheop's pyramid to a small entrance that led up a long, gently inclined flight of stairs to the tomb.

At the top I came upon a small room, the King's Chamber, containing the sarcophagus of the pharaoh, a deep, lidless, rectangular stone box, not much to look at. In lieu of alternatives, I sat on one corner and began to play my flute. As music, whose source I could only guess at, welled up from within and currents of joy played through my body, images of the distant past, like reclaimed memories, floated through my consciousness. Like Danny, I had been in Egypt before.

My reverie was broken by the backlit form of an elegant black woman standing in the entrance to the tomb, frozen to stillness by the music.

The haunting strains stopped and I found myself back in the twentieth century confronting an interesting destiny.

Obviously moved by the music, she said, "Who are you?"

"I'm not sure," I replied. "The way things have been going, I'm pretty sure I'm not me."

She laughed. "That music. Where did you learn it?"

"I don't know how to say this. You'll think I'm crazy."

"Don't worry," she said. "I'm open to anything."

"I didn't learn it. It just happened. All I know is that it came from a long time ago."

"That's for sure," she replied. "It was so familiar. For a minute it seemed as if I weren't here at all. I started to remember something... I don't know... as if I had been here before... as if I had come home... very strange."

"That's what I felt too. It was as if I were entering a time warp."

I hopped down from the sarcophagus. We were nearly touching in the small room.

"I should be on my way," I said, a little embarrassed. "I imagine you'd like to be here on your own."

"Not at all," she replied. "There's not much to see, is there? Let's talk, if you don't mind." She reached out and took my hand, awakening a not-so-mystical energy.

We slowly made our way down, making nervous bits of conversation to diffuse the sexual tension. In the narrow, unventilated passageway the fragrance of her body was overpowering. The ancient tranquility gave way to the excitement of the moment.

When we stepped out in the open I was stunned by her beauty: refined and carefully-sculpted features framed by a full Afro, a tall, perfectly-proportioned body and slim, elegant hands and arms, like those of the goddess Nut holding up the cosmic sky.

"I'd like to see them from a distance, from the desert," she said.

"Let's rent a couple of those horses," I replied.

When we reached the bottom I sat in the sun on the edge of the pyramid thinking about the vicissitudes of fate while she went to notify the tour guide. Less than a month before love had blessed me in Benghazi, and here it was again, staring me in the face.

Uncharacteristically, I felt a pang of conscience, followed by the startling realization that what I was thinking about was not love. The feelings were as tawdry as the human scene playing itself out below – the silly tourists, the touts, the trinket vendors. Amazed at the clarity and dispassion with which I observed these thoughts, it struck me that somewhere along the line a part of me had split off and become a disinterested witness.

"Let's go for a ride!" she said enthusiastically, grabbing my hand, jerking me out of my reverie.

We galloped into the desert.

"This is fantastic," she said as we turned to look at the pyramids. "How do you think they did it?"

"I don't buy the materialist idea that they were monuments to the colossal egos of the pharoahs. I think they had a spiritual view of life, a whole philosophy of reincarnation and transcendence. The pyramids were an expression of a deep religious feeling."

"I never thought of it like that," she said. "But it makes sense."

We rode for a while, caught the bus back to town, wandered the streets in the afternoon, had dinner and strolled along the Nile arm in arm on the way to the Hilton.

A man who had been following for a couple of blocks came up and offered hash. "Very cheap price. Five dollars."

"I want to smoke," Amanda said. "Would you join me?"

"I've been trying to quit, but sure, why not?"

I dug the tobacco out of a cigarette with a toothpick, mixed it with the hash and repacked it as we sat together on a luxurious couch overlooking the Nile. She leaned over to examine the hash, her breast brushing lightly against me.

"Would you like a drink?" she asked.

"Do you think they can manage a margarita?"

She phoned room service and the boy brought the drinks.

"Here's to a lovely day," she said raising her glass. "You've been so nice. You've given me a lot."

"You're great company," I answered. "It was my pleasure."

"And I'd like to give you something special too," she replied, planting a luscious kiss on my cheek.

I fired up the joint and passed it to her.

In a few minutes she got up and left the room. Too high to pay much attention, I thought about the big diamond on her ring finger and contemplated ruining the evening by asking the obvious, but before I could make up my mind, she said, "Would you like to come in here?" in a voice that could not be refused.

I looked in the direction of the bedroom. She was standing in the doorway, stark naked.

"I would," I replied. And I did.

***

"So where you been?" said Danny.

"Taking in the sights, wandering around, nothing much."

"You look pretty happy for a sightseer," he replied.

"Having a bit of luck with the ladies, if the truth must be known."

"A lady of the night, perhaps?"

"Not my style, Danny. A tourist from New York on a trip around the world. Met her at the pyramids."

Sensing a hint of envy, I changed the subject. I particularly did not want to mention her color. Later, when we were a bit tighter, I might tell him the whole story.

The visas came through and we made it to Aswan without incident. I booked a classy cabin on the upper deck of the boat that plied the backwater of the dam, but Danny had to settle for a cramped spot on a barge affixed to the front of the steamer, carrying goats, chickens, longhorn cattle and a colorful sea of poverty-stricken humanity.

We sat in stillness while the evening embraced the desert, our toes trailing in the crystal-clear water as the barge chugged slowly toward the heart of Africa. Overwhelmed by the immensity of the Sahara, the intense blue of a night sky in which a crescent moon was rising in the east, the placid dignity of the cattle, whose elegant horns and majestic heads were silhouetted against the sky, the mantric drone of the engine and the smells of evening meals cooking on little charcoal fires, I found myself traveling inward toward the still point, the limitless center from which the world is projected.

Glowing like a saint, I left the barge and joined the first class passengers for dinner, where I was seated next to a young couple from California, ex-flower children, who, as a result of a series of miraculous events, had been drawn into the orbit of The Mother, a Frenchwoman and consort of one of twentieth-century India's spiritual giants, Sri Aurobindo. Aurobindo was an upper-caste Tamil who, after completing his education at Oxford, returned to join the struggle for India's independence. For his trouble he landed in jail, where he experienced enlightenment and exchanged the political world for the spiritual world. He eventually settled in Pondicherry, a French enclave on the Indian Ocean, where an *ashram*, catering to thousands of Indian intelligentsia and European intellectuals, grew up. When he died, The Mother, a visionary type, founded a spiritual "city" named Auroville, where select aspirants could prepare themselves for the next great evolutionary leap in human consciousness. Barbara and Mark felt "called" and were on their way to join the grand experiment, an idea that did not appeal to me.

As the evening progressed I told them of recent experiences: the astral travel in Morocco, the levitation in Tunisia and the reincarnation experience in the Great Pyramid. Mark went to his cabin and returned with a book entitled *Sri Aurobindo, or the Adventure of Consciousness*.

"It will put your experiences in perspective," he said.

"You mean you don't think I'm going crazy?" I said, voicing a doubt common to anyone awakening to their true nature.

"Not a bit. In fact I envy you. I'd give my eye teeth to have things like that happen to me."

What were the odds that an American from Montana would find answers to his existential questions in a book by a French devotee of an Indian *guru*, given to him by a pair of Californians on a paddle-wheel steamer chugging up the Nile on a journey into the heart of Africa? "In mysterious ways His wonders to perform."

Their support and the book, which indicated that my experiences were relatively commonplace on the spiritual path, went a long way to assuage doubts about my sanity and generated a sense of purpose and self-confidence that came in handy in the coming weeks. The realization that I was about to experience a culture that venerated mysticism made my lonely pilgrimage much more bearable.

The following morning we docked at Abu Simbel, a sight that predictably set up strong seismic vibrations in my soul, convincing me once again that I had been an Egyptian a long time ago.

Khartoum

We were delayed at Wadi Halfa by an altercation between a group of seven Bedouins, rumored to be packing a quarter of a million dollars worth of gold on their way to the Khartoum camel market, and Sudanese officialdom. The officials decreed that all barge passengers would be deloused before gaining entry, a blatant act of discrimination. The traders were powerful, steely-eyed men, armed to the teeth. Just by looking at them you could see that they were as uncompromising as their desert environment and as tough and amoral as the beasts they tended. The argument ended when the traders drew their guns and officialdom backed down, much to the relief of everyone.

In those days Wadi Halfa was a ramshackle, dusty outpost on the Sudanese-Egyptian border, a place to catch the train to Khartoum. We boarded enthusiastically, elbowing and shoving like the locals to claim seats on rows of backless benches bolted to the floor. However, lack of windowpanes, a must in the desert, permitted sand, smoke and cinders to blow into the coach. When we pulled into Khartoum my short-lived love affair with desert trains had come to an end.

Mark and Barb, whom I bumped into in Delhi months later, opted for the flight to Nairobi, but Danny, who wanted to go to Uganda and the Congo to explore his "roots," told me about a weekly boat up the Nile through the Sud to a town called Juba, not far from the Ugandan border, that piqued my curiosity. The bad news was that a particularly brutal civil war was in progress, one still going on today, and Juba was a besieged outpost in the heart of rebel territory. It was a classic case of ethnic cleansing. The Islamic Sudanese, who controlled the northern part of the country, were trying to eradicate the southern animists. The overland route out of Juba to the south was impassable, the only option was a once-a-week flight to Entebbe.

The war was a risk we were willing to take to pass through one of the most mysterious and isolated environments on the planet, a risk that nearly resulted in the forfeiture of our lives. Travel was off limits without permission from the government. Permission meant bribes.

We put up in a laid-back hotel, a backwater eddy that had amassed a peculiar collection of human flotsam from the river of life: a shifty pair of Afghans who claimed to be political refugees but were obviously involved in the drug trade; a cross-eyed, uptight English nurse on a humanitarian mission; a moon-faced South African mulatto transvestite who disappeared about dusk; a bearded, pipe-smoking, Swiss intellectual on a grant to study Sudanese irrigation needs; an ageing Italian junkie and his child bride, a nubile young lass of thirteen with the IQ of a monitor lizard; a barrel-chested Argentinean merchant seaman in search of adventure; a couple of Indian traders, and others. Our arrival added a black and a white American hippie, and two devotees of The Mother. A devout Indian couple ran the hotel, whose walls were covered with pictures of many-armed gods and goddesses. A votive candle burned eternally in the office, and the air was thick with incense.

We showed up at the government office first thing in the morning.

"You want to go to Juba?" the bureaucrat said with undisguised contempt, looking us up and down as we stood meekly in front of his cluttered desk.

"Yes, sir."

"It is impossible. It is forbidden. Why do you want to go there?"

"Just to see the Sud. We have come all the way from America to see the Sud."

"But there is war. It is not possible. I cannot guarantee your safety."

"I understand you are winning the war," said Danny, concealing his contempt for the Islamic government. "They were saying on the radio last night that only small pockets of resistance remained."

"This is true," said the bureaucrat, flattered that we had an interest in what was going on in his country.

Danny pressed on. "You see, we only want to ride the boat. We will not be stopping. When we get to Juba we will catch the plane to Entebbe. The boat is secure and Juba is secure, so it should be no problem. Besides, what would the rebels want with us? I am sure there must be a way we can get permission to ride on that boat," he said, discreetly tucking a twenty-dollar bill under some papers on the desk.

"Well, you see, sir," the bureaucrat continued, "it is possible for certain people, but not for tourists. Perhaps if you come back tomorrow I can see if it is possible."

The next day the conversation continued.

"I have been instructed to let you make an application," he said. "This does not mean you will automatically be granted permission. This is a sensitive area and we must clear all applications with the department of defense, so it will take time and there is much paperwork."

"This is very good news. I understand that we may not be granted permission, but let me just give you a little something to grease the wheels," he said diplomatically, putting another twenty on the desk.

The bureaucrat nodded, stood up and shook our hands, glancing furtively at the twenty. "Well, gentlemen, come back on Friday and I will tell you about the progress of your application."

On Friday the application was still in process and we left depressed.

Danny dealt with the frustration by smoking *bango*, a particularly psychedelic strain of African weed worthy of its name, but I amused myself by wandering the city, hanging out by the Nile thinking about God, practicing *yoga* and reading the *Bhagavad Gita*, the Bible of the Hindus, a gift from the hotel owner, Mr. Patel, whose friendship I cultivated.

You see," he said, "this book is most auspicious. It is something everyone should read. It reveals the Brahma Vidya."

"Excuse me, Mr. Patel, but what is the Brahma Vidya?"

"Good question, young man. I am glad you asked. Brahma Vidya is the science of God-realization."

"Science?" I replied skeptically. "What do science and God have to do with each other?"

"Just you read," he said with great love, lighting another incense stick. "Just you read and you will see."

***

"You're no fun anymore," said Danny when he came into my room to smoke a joint and found me standing on my head. "You going religious on me? Better watch out or you'll end up like Mark and Barb."

At the end of the second week the application was still mired in the bureaucratic swamp, sending us into a deeper funk.

By five on Friday of the third week it seemed we had been suckered. I woke up depressed on Saturday about nine and stayed in bed, the clock ticking off the final hours. At eleven-thirty the depression lifted and I got up to go out and book a flight for Nairobi. As I entered the lobby where Danny was sprawled out on a couch reading the book on *hatha yoga* given to me by Mr. Patel, killing time until his bus left for Addis Ababa, a car screeched to a halt in front of the hotel and our official came running through the door. "They're here! The papers have come! Come with me. I'll drive you to the boat. There's no time to lose."

We arrived at the dock five minutes before noon.

The Sud

The Sud is an area in southern Uganda through which the Nile flows on its long journey out of sub-Saharan Africa to the Mediterranean. It is not so much a river as a gigantic swamp with large floating islands of vegetation, home to untold species: crocodiles, hippos, snakes, huge fish and a riotous aviary with birds of every shape, size and color. The boat, another paddle-wheel steamer, the only link between the tribes living in the south and Khartoum, picked up and dropped off people – mainly soldiers and traders – and goods on its ten-day journey.

On a physical level we saw no evidence of war, but the faces, body language and a spring-tight atmosphere left little doubt that fear and hatred were the dominant emotions playing in the swamp.

On the second day, within earshot of a village, the captain blew the horn signaling our arrival. Like a picture from *National Geographic*, a crowd of illiterate tribal people, who practice a way of life thousands of years old, gathered at the dock.

From the local's point of view, in addition to the commerce, the boat provided an opportunity to get news of the outside world and stare at the well-dressed, well-fed, civilian and military personnel who gathered on deck at every stop. Even before we had properly docked, naked and emaciated children

114

commenced begging from the shore. In response to their entreaties, passengers threw chunks of stale bread into the muddy waters just out of reach, forcing the children to brave the treacherous currents. Famine, one of the government's most effective weapons, made the game work.

As inevitably happens, competition for the bread caused the kids to kick, hit and scratch each other, much to the delight of the passengers. Before long the adults, unable to stand injustices visited on their children by other children, were drawn into the fray and a full-fledged melee ensued, which further encouraged the laughing passengers who fiendishly cast more bread from the boat.

When it was clear that somebody was about to get seriously hurt, a huge man, close to seven feet tall, rippling with muscles and armed with a bullwhip, appeared from the village and positioned himself on the bank above the fighting crowd. The tip of the whip darted out like the tongue of a snake, landing squarely on the back of a young boy who screamed in pain. Sensing the end of the fun, the passengers threw more bread into the water.

Obviously enjoying his work, the enforcer ruthlessly attacked all and sundry. Occasionally, the distance to a body was so carefully calculated and the force of the whip so powerful, a geyser of blood would spurt from the victim to a cheer of approval from the passengers. The ritual repeated itself three or four times during the ten-day trip.

One day the boat pulled up, the gangplank was lowered and I stepped onto the main street of a village with about fifty or sixty mud-and-wattle, grass-capped huts.

My appearance invariably provided locals, most of whom had never seen a Westerner, with much amusement. By this time I was sensitive to the nature of the conflict and found my sympathies on the side of the tribals, so I discarded my *jellabia*, which was too hot anyway, in favor of a pair of multi-colored, striped pants and a lime green T-shirt, which I had found in a market in Khartoum. However, my costume could hardly compete with that of an aristocratic young man approaching from the opposite end of the village, perhaps the only member of Sudanese counterculture in the history of the country. Well over six feet, he carried a spear and a long, thin drum, probably made from a hollowed root. Into his closely-cropped hair had been woven two springy spiral wires, to each of which were affixed half a dozen brightly-colored feathers that shook, dipped and quivered as he walked. The top half of his body was covered by a pink nylon see-through negligee, obviously made to order by the village tailor, and the lower half by underwear resembling a jock strap. He was also wearing gold-rimmed, glassless John Lennon spectacles and carrying a beat-up short wave radio, with a wire antennae tuned to a Nairobi station from which Credence Clearwater Revival was wailing its signature song, *Proud Mary*. A look of recognition crossed his face as we passed. A brother.

From dawn till dusk we whiled away our time sitting in easy chairs on the roof of the boat, a large screened area that effectively separated us from a fierce assortment of swamp insects. Even from that vantage point it was often impossible to determine the boundaries of the river whose powerful currents seemed to mirror the currents of subtle energy and light playing within. As I watched hippos munching water hyacinths and crocodiles sunning on the banks I realized that inner senses, even more acute than the outer, were developing, turning toward a mysterious and exotic spiritual land. And I felt deeply grateful when I understood that God was blessing me with a bird's-eye view of my little life as it, like the boat, meandered its way upstream on a timeless journey to the Source.

The euphoria ended and fear became a more or less permanent feature of the inner landscape when, on the tenth day a few miles upstream from Juba, I spotted a funnel of vultures circling above a half-submerged human corpse on which several smaller scavengers, mainly crows, were heartily feasting.

Juba is one of the most remote spots on earth, a green Timbuktu. There probably was a road south to Uganda, but we were explicitly told in Khartoum that, owing to the war, the only exit was a weekly flight to Entebbe. Outwardly, what appeared to be a fairly rundown provincial outpost seemed normal.

We checked into a hotel and were unpacking when a police car pulled up and disgorged a uniformed officer, who strode briskly through the lobby and up the stairs, and knocked loudly on the door.

"You have an appointment with the chief of police at nine-thirty tomorrow morning," he said humorlessly the minute I opened the door. "Be there." We had no doubt he meant business.

We drank beer and chatted until dark. At one point I woke from a fitful sleep to the sound of small-arms fire in the distance, which, coupled with the memory of the bloated corpse in the river, did not conduce to a blissful night. And it was no secret that a few hundred miles south, Idi Amin, one of the most bloodthirsty dictators of the modern era, was living it up in Kampala, the destination of our flight. When he was finally forced to flee, the conquering troops found a freezer full of human body parts in his residence.

In the morning we took breakfast at the hotel, showed up on time and presented our documents. The chief, like his emissary, was a man of few words with a war on his hands.

"You are in a war zone," he said. "Your lives are in danger. I have no time to look after you. I will tell you how to survive until Thursday, when your plane leaves for Entebbe."

"You will be approached by many people. You can talk all you want but no matter what, you are forbidden to give money or to buy food and medical supplies for anyone. The rebels need help and will contact you. We will be watching. If you do not follow these instructions you will be killed."

A smile crossed his face and he nodded toward the door. As I got up he handed me a slip of paper with his name and number. Assuring him we would comply to the letter, we left somewhat shaken.

"Real friendly chap," I said to Danny as we walked out.

"At least we know where we stand," he replied. "Actually, I liked him for some reason. Don't lose that number. It may come in handy. Does kind of rearrange a few brain cells, doesn't it, but I'm not going to hole up in that dive for a week. We'll have to play it cool, that's all. You don't seem too rattled. What gives?"

"The Voice, Danny."

He turned his head.

"It just said, 'Take it easy, Jim, everything's fine.' And then something about a goat."

"If this stuff didn't happen to me too, I'd think you were nuts," he said.

We discovered a small café on the main street and sipped tea for an hour. Danny felt like hanging out and I felt like napping, so I paid the bill, but when I stepped out on the street, I found myself confronted by a huge goat blocking my way. When I stepped the other way, it countered. Reality was trying to tell me something.

Then, clear as a bell, The Voice said, "It is not a goat, Jim." I looked into its eyes and was immediately possessed of the conviction that a non-animal conscious being was living in a goat's body!

Suddenly it struck me that if there were any place on earth where animals could be vehicles for higher powers, a common sub-Saharan belief known as animism, it would be Juba. Even if it was not what I thought, the idea of a pet was emotionally appealing, considering the stress. Studies have shown that prisoners attain acceptable levels of adjustment to prison life when permitted to care for pets.

Within minutes we were friends for life. I bought him bananas and we walked around town for about an hour taking in the sights until we bumped into Danny.

"So what you think, bro?" he said referring to the town.

"Not much, Danny. It's a real cow town. Can't imagine why they're fighting over it."

"I hate Muslims," he said. "They never get it right. I feel like joining the rebels. What's with the beast?"

I told him what I thought.

"Too much dope," he replied. "All those Purple Owsleys shorted your circuits. It's just a goat, man. You gave it bananas. It loves you. Don't worry, we'll make it through till Thursday."

"Humor me, Danny."

We returned to the café. In a few minutes a shifty-eyed fellow sitting in the corner came over and asked in broken English if he could join us. He claimed to be a student, and I could feel Danny, who was a real sucker for a sob story, softening. When he offered the man a seat the goat walked in, took my sleeve in his teeth and nearly pulled me off the chair. The patrons from a nearby table laughed, but I took it as the goat's way of saying the guy was trouble and suggested that we split, but Danny was not interested.

"Catch you later," he said, turning back to the man.

So I left, following the goat.

While the goat lay in the shade outside, I hung around the hotel for a couple of hours reading the *Bhagavad Gita*, thinking about a timely verse that said God was in everyone and everything, nervously wondering how Danny was getting on. At one point I got up to see if the goat was still there and saw Danny in a highly agitated state enter the courtyard in the company of a strange man. When he appeared at the door I could see a huge welt on the side of his head.

"Jesus! What happened to you!"

"It's a long story," he replied. "Will you get me a beer?"

"Sure. Who was that?"

"A cop. One of the chief's spies. He saved my life. At least he saved my passport and money. The beer, please," he said irritably.

I went down and sent the clerk out for beer. Danny was standing in front of the mirror examining his bump when I returned. I sat down and watched him for a few minutes.

"So what happened?"

"I'm coming to that," he snapped. "The guy told me about his miserable life, his sick mother, his brother who disappeared under mysterious circumstances, his sister who had to quit school to support the family, his dead father. The whole sad bit. I swallowed it all. He said he didn't want anything, just someone to practice his English on. He was very nice, very convincing. After a while he invited me home to have dinner with his family. I said okay, thinking that it was a great opportunity to get to see a little village life. Well, he led me into a very slummy area and when we turned a corner a big fellow hit me with a stick on the side of the head. It nearly knocked me out, but I was able to stay conscious and fight them off for a couple of minutes. Just when they were getting the upper hand a man showed up and fired a couple of shots. They ran for it. He wounded the one from the café, but the big one got away. We carried the wounded guy to the jail and the cop escorted me here. He was watching us all day," he continued. "I never saw him. They're using us as bait. This is one fucked-up city!" He took another long pull on his beer and said, "You sure split when that guy showed up."

"I didn't like his vibes. And the goat, Danny. It didn't want us there."

"Are you nuts, man! You and that fucking goat!"

The next morning the goat was waiting in front of the hotel when we went out.

"Oh, shit," said Danny, making menacing gestures as the goat watched with supreme indifference, "I can't stand that fucking creature."

We went to the café for breakfast and hung out for a couple of hours, the goat resting regally near the front door. Several men came over and tried to engage us in conversation, but the language barrier prevented any real communication. Just as we were about to leave, a very scary man with snake-like eyes came in, sat down and started eyeing us.

"I don't like the look of this guy," said Danny. "He's one scary fuck."

"Absolutely," I said. "Let's truck."

Suddenly I felt a tug on my sleeve.

Danny's resistance to the goat dissolved. For the next four days we let it take charge and nothing happened, which was exactly what we wanted.

Two days before the flight the goat did not appear. We took breakfast in the café and hung around most of the morning drinking tea. Mid-afternoon, Danny suggested a trip to the river. Things were peaceful, so we wandered upstream and sat down not far from a cluster of mud-and-grass huts where four village women were bathing.

Incredibly, they waved us over and turned us on to some very potent *bango*, which led to much laughter as we tried to communicate in sign language. Suddenly I realized the sun was setting.

"Hey, man," I said to Danny, "we've got to split. It will be dark before long; it's a bit of a walk to town and you know what goes on out here after dark."

"You crazy, man?" he replied. "Things are just heating up. Hang in there. We're sure to get laid."

"Are you nuts?!" I replied. "I'm not messing around with these women, believe me. We had a good time. Let's quit while we're ahead."

But he wasn't having any. I hung around a few more minutes and made an issue of it.

"Fuck, man! You go. I'm staying," he said decisively.

"Have it your way, Danny," I replied. "I'm outta here."

I turned and high-tailed it downriver. In a couple of minutes I heard him coming up behind.

"Christ, you're one uptight honky," he said as he caught up.

"I don't think with my dick, Danny. I don't intend to get mixed up with the locals on any level. This place is bad news. I'm going to be on that flight tomorrow. I can't stand the anxiety. Something happens, we get detained and it won't be fun. Is this the path?"

Because of the descending darkness, the dope and our mutual irritation, we became disoriented.

"Let's stick to the river," I said. "The town's on the river and eventually we'll hit it."

"Hey," said Danny, "this is where we turn. I remember it. We're almost there."

We turned and walked about a hundred yards when my worst fear materialized. A man shouted a command that could only mean, "Stop or I'll shoot!"

We froze in our tracks. A powerful light went on and I could make out several uniformed men with assault rifles coming toward us. There was nothing to do but raise our hands and wait until we were surrounded. They marched us about a hundred yards to an army outpost where we surrendered our passports and were shown seats on a wooden bench next to a bare wall. In a few minutes a tall officer with a cruel face, who spoke rudimentary English, came in.

We told him the facts, which he either did not understand or did not believe. He glanced at one of the soldiers who hit me on the side of the head with his gun butt, knocking me to the floor. I think the shock was so great I left my body because I didn't feel anything. As I was struggling to get up they attacked

Danny, hitting him several times. I felt great admiration for him because he took it so stoically. I was almost on my feet when one of the soldiers kicked me viciously in the side, sending me crashing against the wall.

Then, clear as a bell, The Voice said, "Show them the paper, Jim."

I reached into my pocket and produced the paper with the chief's name and number. The officer took it and left the room, accompanied by his henchmen.

"You okay?" I asked.

"Not bad," replied Danny, "how about you?"

"A hell of a headache, but I'll survive," I replied. "What do you think will happen?"

"I think the chief will bail us out."

An hour later the chief appeared, a big smile on his face. "I told you we meant business," he said. "What happened?"

We told him the story and he laughed.

"Come on," he said affectionately, "I'll take you back. Perhaps you shouldn't smoke so much hashish."

The next morning, our last, Danny suggested we stop by and thank the chief before our flight. "He may be on the wrong side, but he's a stand-up guy."

"Not a bad idea," I said.

The chief was happy to see us, impressed we'd stopped by, and offered a ride to the airport.

Uganda

If the Sudan was dangerous, Uganda, under the vicious rule of Idi Amin, was a Kafka-esque nightmare. Kampala, the capital, once a smart colonial city, was a mess: boarded-up shops, mountains of refuse rotting in the streets, bands of armed men and non-existent public services. People walked quickly with their heads down and eyes averted.

We found a cheap hotel and went out for a beer. I invited Danny to come to India.

"Sorry, man. India's not my thing. I want to head down to Zaire. You were right about Uganda. It's straight from hell. It'll take me a couple of days to get things set up. Hang around till I leave, will you? Two are better than one."

I agreed to stay. As we were walking along a narrow street on our way to the bus station to check the schedule, a late-model Mercedes came careening around the corner at the end of the block and screeched to a halt in front of a shop not forty yards away. Two soldiers leapt out, their guns drawn, and entered the shop.

We about-faced like mechanical dolls, walked hastily up the block, turned the corner and breathed a sigh of relief. Unable to resist, we peered around the corner to see a man leaving the shop at gunpoint. As he neared the car, he bolted and the teenage soldiers opened fire. Long after he was dead they continued to pump bullets into his body.

We hid in an alley until it seemed safe.

"Jesus!" said Danny. "This is bad news. Let's go down to the river where we can think."

"Did you notice they didn't care if anybody saw them?" I said. "They didn't even look around or try to be discreet. There's no law here."

"Put it this way," said Danny, "that was the law."

After about thirty minutes we came to the riverbank and found a secluded spot not far from what appeared to be a water-pumping station. Still shaken, we sat in silence for a few minutes.

"What's that?" said Danny referring to a cylindrical cement tube not far from shore.

"It looks like a pumping station, shall we check it out?"

Traversing a walkway onto the station we came to the pump room door, which was ajar. With the smell of decaying flesh filling the air, we looked down and saw two decomposing bodies caught in the intake grill.

A Taxi Ride

As I stood in the bus station the following morning watching Danny's bus recede into the distance, a line from Mr. Patel's *Bhagavad Gita* came to mind: "The Self is not killed when the body is killed," accompanied by a great wave of peace. In the stillness I heard The Voice say, "What does it matter? They know not what they do."

Instead of leaving immediately, I visited the famous Kampala bat caves, which proved to be highly overrated, a dark, malodorous experience. On the way back I stopped off for a beer before hitting the road. When I came out, a tall, hefty young woman came up and took my arm.

"Hey, you like me?" she said cheerfully. Before I could reply, she said, "You wanna fuck me?"

"I don't think so," I said, as politely as possible as I increased my pace.

She tightened her grip and kept up. "You fuck me, okay? Very cheap."

"Sorry, no money," I replied.

"Okay," she said surprisingly, "I fuck you free," rubbing her hand on my backside.

"Thank you very much. That's very nice of you, but not today. Maybe tomorrow," I replied, trying to extricate myself from her vice-like grip.

"I no like tomorrow."

The more I struggled to get away, the more she hung on.

Convinced the money was the issue, she repeated, "I fuck you, no money."

"That's very nice," I said without enthusiasm. "Why you want no money?"

"You white man. I like fuck white man. I like your hair," she said running her fingers through it.

Realizing words weren't doing the trick, I turned down an alley where I could force the issue without being seen. I had my work cut out because she was large and very muscular. Just as I was about to attack her she threw me down and groped the genital region, discovering my money belt. I feigned arousal, and she eased up a bit as she pulled my shirt out of my trousers. Then I kneed her with all my force in the stomach, throwing her against a wall. I scrambled to my feet and ran down the street, her curses ringing in my ears.

Shaken, I returned to the hotel, grabbed my pack, walked to the edge of town and stuck out my thumb. In about twenty minutes an English teacher on the way to his native village, about twenty miles from the Kenyan border, picked me up. He had the sensitivity not to ask what I thought of his country, and I had the manners not to discuss what I had seen.

When we arrived at his home his mother prepared a chicken dinner and we spent the evening in conversation. My stories of life in America gave him great pleasure. In the morning he offered to take me to the border, but I declined, to spare him the inconvenience.

I had not been waiting ten minutes when a beat-up taxi, with two large trunks on top and three male passengers, stopped and offered to take me to Nairobi for ten dollars.

The border was a small building with a rundown police car parked in front. To control traffic, a long, weighted, black and white pole haphazardly affixed to the top of a cement-filled fifty-gallon drum confronted us. We pulled up and I showed my passport, which the smiling officer stamped immediately. The driver seemed to be known, but the passengers' documents were non-existent. No worries. Such situations are tailor-made for *baksheesh*, the lifeblood of officialdom.

The officers pointed to the trunks, and a lively discussion ensued. The men were obviously concealing something, so the driver was instructed to park and we were ordered out. Once the trunks were untied the men became agitated, and when I noticed one stealthily feel inside his jacket I realized he was armed.

The trunks contained animal skins, ivory and two elephant feet. Realizing they were onto something, the officials inspected the luggage in the trunk and searched the taxi. In a few minutes a great pile of contraband lay on the ground in front of us.

An argument ensued and I gathered that the officials were threatening to confiscate the lot, meaning they wanted a bribe. Evidently the demand was excessive and the poachers refused. Voices were raised and body language became confrontational. Since I was legal, I felt disinclined to witness the proceedings and began to discreetly back away.

I would not swear to it, but I think my presence was keeping a lid on things because the moment I was out of the energy bubble the poachers went for their guns, catching the officials off-guard. I made it to the corner of the building when a shot rang out. Everyone dove for cover as I ducked behind the building and ran up the road in the direction of Nairobi, pack in hand. I heard several shots followed by a long silence.

Hitching would obviously not be promising until the dispute was resolved, so I ambled leisurely down the road enjoying the landscape, happy to have escaped unscathed.

About an hour later the taxi came chugging along, minus a significant fraction of the luggage. The poachers were a bit glum, particularly the one with a flesh wound in the upper arm, which was wrapped in a bundle of dirty rags. The driver wanted another ten, a rather cheeky idea, but I agreed, a decision that seemed to cheer them up a bit. Why they didn't rob me, I'll never know. *In sha Allah.*

I was overjoyed to see Nairobi, a large modern city where white skin was no longer an object of interest, but I quickly grew bored. So I hitched to Mombasa, a laid-back seaside playground on the Indian Ocean, where I whiled away the time eating seafood and tropical fruit, reading nineteenth-century English novels from the booksellers in Nairobi, fending off the whores and chatting with the locals and a motley assortment of travelers waiting for the bimonthly boat to the Seychelles, Karachi and Bombay.

Nothing happened outwardly or inwardly, much to my relief. Life's small details unfolded perfectly, as if a loving host had planned every minute of my visit. The tropical environment purified my mind until each perception was bathed in a fine, gauzy halo of light. The boat was old and slow, but the ten-day journey could have lasted forever as far as I was concerned. I recall sitting up at night in perfect peace, listening to the drone of the engines and watching the night sky, only to fall asleep an hour or two before dawn and awake excited and energetic as the sun burst over the horizon, lighting up the silver bodies of the flying fish that landed on the deck during the night.

Everyone experiences life in this awareful, immediate way one time or another. I know now that it is the experience of God, our natural state. How ironic I should be experiencing it and not know what it was. And of course it was doubly ironic that I was going to India to look for God.

Chapter V

The Inner Journey

"Once you go There, you never return."
~ Bhagavad Gita

MY ENERGY RETURNED after about three weeks with Kahlil, the Pakistani man who rescued me from death in Punjab. Early one morning I dreamt I was sitting in an audience in San Francisco listening to a lecture on Vedanta given by a bearded Hindu holy man dressed in orange silk. I awoke to see Kahlil coming up the stairs bearing a small bag.

He sat on the edge of the bed and said, "By the will of Allah you will go to Kabul today. Here is some money and food for the journey. And take this," he said, handing me a gold ring. "It will be of use. I will go now. The driver will take you to the bus. All the best." We shook hands and he left quickly so I would not see his feelings.

As the bus bumped along it seemed the path I had been given was as harsh and inhospitable as the rocky, mountainous land through which we were passing. And yet it had its beauty, like the Khyber Pass where we stopped, allowing the passengers to disembark, turn toward Mecca, roll out their rugs and pray. As I watched with interest I realized that my knowledge of God was very different from theirs. As their bodies turned westward and their heads repeatedly touched the ground, I marveled at such deep faith in a God they could not see because to me Allah was shining forth in every rock and mountain. I could feel Him in the air, hear Him in the wind and see Him in the hard and leathery faces of the Afghans.

Arriving in Kabul exhausted from the long journey, I found a small hotel and fell into a fitful sleep. In the middle of the night I was awakened by my own screams. A light went on next door and I heard a knock on my door. It was Jack, my friend from Morocco and Manali!

"I heard your screams and recognized your voice," he said. "What happened? You look like death warmed over."

We hung around Kabul for about three weeks, taking long walks through the city and far out into the countryside. I spent most of my time sleeping and reading. Jack read and smoked hash.

One day, sitting on one of the hills surrounding the city after a long climb, he offered dope, which I declined.

"What's the matter, man?" he said. "You used to be the biggest tripper on the block. You going religious on me?"

I recalled a similar conversation with Danny. "I don't think it's good for me right now," I said. "The body's still pretty weak."

"I don't know, man, the way you climbed up here makes me think you're in pretty good shape."

"You're right," I replied. "It's not the body. I love the smell and often feel like smoking, but it messes up the mind."

"That's just the point," he said, missing the point. "It makes the mind feel so good."

"Only in the short run, Jack. After a while it gets so dull you can't think properly. I wouldn't be in the mess I'm in today if I hadn't smoked that dope in Kulu. It cuts off my vision of God."

He looked at me incredulously. Even though he was a good friend I had not mentioned my religious experiences, because I knew he would not understand. "Your vision of God!" he said sarcastically.

"I didn't tell you before, because I know how you feel about religion and God."

He didn't reply and stared quizzically at me.

"It's not religion, Jack. Believe me," I continued. "I share your feelings about it. But God is different. I've seen Him. I see Him often. He's in my mind. If it's clear, I see Him. If it's dull, I feel lost."

"Lost?" he replied.

"Lost. Unhappy. Lonely."

"You're unbelievable," he replied. "The hepatitis must have done something to your mind."

"I don't think so, Jack," I replied. "The happiness you think is coming from the dope really comes from God."

He laughed. "Now I know you're nuts," he replied. But it was only his ego trying to keep things under control. His heart was listening.

"People always think I'm crazy," I said. "But I see something else. It's a very private thing."

There was a long pause during which I could see him thinking. "So what's this God business?" he finally asked.

"I don't know if I can explain it very clearly. It's all so new. Something is happening to my consciousness. I'm not the same person I was."

"Not the same person? You seem pretty much the same to me."

"That's true," I replied. "But only on the surface. Deep down my soul is changing. When the tectonic plates shift you have an earthquake. Well, I'm having earthquakes in my consciousness, things I can't control. And all my ideas and beliefs are changing as a result. In a few years you won't know me."

He was unconvinced. No matter what I put him through, his brotherly energy was what the doctor ordered to prepare me for the next leg of the journey. When the time came to move on he gave me the money to get to Istanbul.

The trip was uneventful. After a few days in Teheran the money ran low, so I hitchhiked through Turkey, picking up a ride with a fast lorry at the border. The sight of Mount Ararat, which predictably set off seismic vibrations in my soul, was the only event of interest. I rested for a week in Istanbul, sold the gold ring, bought a kilo of hash, sewed it into a vest and took a first-class sleeper ticket on the Orient Express to Amsterdam, where I sold the hash and bought a ticket to California.

A Hole in the Head

I did not really appreciate America until I returned from my travels. When I stepped off the plane, I felt like kissing the earth. What a pleasure to sleep in my own bug-free bed, take hot showers, eat Mom's bland meals, talk on the phone, zip around in one of Dad's big cars and visit the family doctor.

After several weeks I left Idaho for San Francisco. One day I wandered south of Market, an area thoughtfully set aside for the dregs of society. Sitting in a greasy-spoon café thinking about my next move, I observed all types of low-lifers acting out. I marveled at the irony of the attitude to which I had recently been treated by many middle-class Americans, that economic misfortune somehow disqualified India as a civilized country. Yet anyone with eyes could see that very few countries did human misery like America. With the exception of sub-Saharan Africa, the violence, anger, alienation and despair I observed here were infinitely worse. In fact the way India handled her poverty was head and shoulders above the way we handled our prosperity.

Walking through the Greyhound bus terminal, I passed an obese, odoriferous man clad in a tiny, soiled T-shirt and a pair of Hawaiian shorts, pounding meaninglessly on the doors of a bank of luggage lockers. Nearby, a lean, stubble-faced, hollow-eyed young man, probably a junkie, shaking like a leaf in the breeze, sat in a row of plastic TV chairs next to two sleeping blacks, sizing up the patrons, looking for a mark. Next to the ticket counter two chain-smoking, pudgy, bleach-blond whores in tank tops, tight jeans and stiletto heels argued with the clerk about a refund. Stepping out on the littered street, I was accosted by a drooling drunk demanding change.

But somewhere along the line I had forfeited my reactivity – at least to things outside myself. I was not cold and hard; I could feel the world's pain. But somehow my journey had turned inward and I was relating to my own unexamined and unhealed stuff, the poverty-stricken, larcenous, addictive and whorish parts of my mind.

My brother, always a great friend, let me have a charming little room in the back of his house in Redwood City where I could think about what to do at my leisure. Even had I been interested, the psychedelic party was winding down and grass was going mainstream, losing its allure. Cocaine, a high hardly worth mention, was just coming on the scene. The troops were gearing up for the sexual revolution, but thankfully my "wild oats," as Mother quaintly put it, had been sown.

For a moment, in a fit of madness I actually considered finishing my education, such as it was, and taking my place in society. But what that might be, I could not imagine. It was not a real consideration, because the travels, inner and outer, had awakened me to such a degree that I could never fall asleep long enough to take the American dream seriously. But where to turn? Christianity's simple-minded option was not a possibility. I wondered if the intensity of life on the road was not responsible for the epiphanies, but I was not about to set out again to test the theory. Months passed and nothing happened. I got a girlfriend and discovered that my brother's address got its ten seconds of national fame on my account.

A year before I had mailed him a gift parcel containing several items, including a hash-filled candle from Madrid. In the meantime the President decided to help customs obtain increased appropriations from Congress to strike terror in the hearts of drug kingpins everywhere. The press was invited to view a nationally televised demonstration on the White House lawn of the uncanny ability of dogs to ferret out dope – the government's latest heavy weapon in the war on drugs. Five or six parcels had been selected at random from the mails and mixed with the planted parcel. Released by his handlers, the dog made a bee-line for the marked package, the officials smiled and Nixon seemed pleased. But the dog, a true professional, moved down the line and sniffed out another, which of course was my parcel! The officials were embarrassed and Nixon furious. A couple of weeks later the FBI showed up, inquiring about my whereabouts.

"Somewhere between Casablanca and Katmandu," my brother said, offering them a beer. Nothing came of it.

One day I got tired of killing time and decided – against my better judgment – to write off my frustrating longing for God and drop back into the world.

"It's about time. You've got to grow up sometime, James," Mother said, when I called her to tell her the news. The next day I got up, went into the bathroom, hung a little mirror on the shower wall so I could trim my beard when it was soft, turned on the shower and thought about my day; after lunch I would head over to the campus and pick up an application for admission.

In the middle of this very ordinary stream of consciousness my mind suddenly went blank and I experienced powerful and strange vibrations coming from the solar plexus. An unearthly silence, thick as a morning fog, descended on the room and I heard the *mantra* "*om namah shivaya*" rising spontaneously out of the depths, bringing deep peace, inundating my soul with sweetness. I looked in the mirror and saw a face transfixed, bathed in an otherworldly radiance. In the space between and above my eyebrows a tiny jet-black dot appeared. The *mantra* continued, churning as the spot expanded to about the size of a dime, opened up and became a hole! The flesh on the forehead liquefied and cascaded into the hole at an incredible velocity. My whole face, including the eyes, became a shimmering, vibrant river of energy and dissolved into nothingness!

As I observed my body disappear I found myself in my soul body, speeding purposefully into the unknown. In nanoseconds my small bundle of consciousness burst its skin and dissolved.

Not that I was without self. I was no longer a limited bundle of consciousness but had become what I always was, a limitless eye seeing in all dimensions in a realm of endless spiritual light! Simultaneously, a gossamer strand of consciousness miraculously connected me to a body toweling off in a shower on a tiny planet in an insignificant solar system somewhere in one of myriad galaxies stretching endlessly before me.

Enthroned in my hidden, light-filled kingdom, powerful and glorious, I observed the body I once thought belonged to me exit the shower, dress and walk out to the road. A car pulled up and the driver, a complete stranger, whom I recognized as myself, offered a ride.

"I'll drop you off at the Bayshore," he said as the little me nodded in agreement. His mind was immediately overcome with peace, and we sat comfortably all the way down the hill, intimately connected but silent like an old married couple. No sooner did I step out at the San Francisco on-ramp than another car pulled up and the driver cheerfully offered to take me to the city. He dropped me off downtown and I aimlessly wandered the streets, guided by an unseen hand.

Blessed with universal vision, I saw lives, both mine and others, stretching back in history to the time when the soul leapt like a spark from the eternal fire. Preceded by a wave of peace, emitting energy like an over-amped transformer, my presence indiscriminately raised the vibrations of all those around me. People woke from their waking sleep, looked around quizzically, experiencing a fresh new world and proceeded on with renewed purpose. Rays of the light that I am refracted from the perfect mirror of my mind, conveying messages and planting seeds that would serve in their long journeys home. The real "I" did more good in the space of minutes than the little "I" had done in its lifetime. And all the while I was completely hidden, a thief in the night, inconceivably minute, yet expansive beyond limit.

As evening fell I found myself walking up Market Street, totally in the moment, a great joy welling in the heart. An out-of-service bus pulled up. The door opened and the long-haired driver said, "Get in, I'm off duty. I'll give you a ride. Don't tell me where you're going. I will know."

We had driven through the streets for about ten minutes when the bus stopped in the avenues east of the Park.

"Here we are," he said. "Right?"

I had no clue, but thanked him and nodded. Any place was just fine. He drove off smiling. Stripped of will, the body walked down the block and up the steps to a small house and into a life from which I would never return.

I opened the door and noticed a crowd of about thirty sitting quietly, facing a raised platform. When I entered, heads turned as if I had been expected. I took a seat in the second row, the silence deepening to such a point that a few shuffled and coughed nervously.

I tuned into an orange-clad Indian *yogi* sitting directly in front of me and realized we were in the same state! Radiant light streaming from every cell of his body, he got up to speak and the dream on the seventeenth day of my rooftop recuperation in Lahore flooded my consciousness.

It had become reality.

I had met my teacher.

I was terribly impressed by his dignity and presence. Every idea seemed personally relevant. He said that this wonderful state of God-consciousness, just beyond our waking, dream and sleep states, was the nature of every human being. Just as eyes and ears were necessary to know forms and sounds, Vedanta, or *brahma vidya,* the science of self-knowledge, could give the knowledge and experience of God, liberating the soul from suffering and limitation. The words of Mr. Patel from the hotel in Khartoum flashed into my mind. As the *yogi* supplied the overarching idea welding my epiphanies together, I could see how every event in my life had been pointing to this moment.

The exhilaration of our meeting gave way to a delicate clarity as his carefully-chosen words concentrated the rays of my mind into a beautiful *mandala.* Like a small child lifted by a loving parent to see out a window, he showed me a landscape stretching infinitely in all directions, offering endless possibilities, empowering me with boundless self-confidence. At the same time I experienced deep humility and realized that, except for this and other moments in the presence of God, my short thirty years had been a terrible waste. Behind every lofty idea, eloquent word and graceful gesture the knowledge of God gushed through this extraordinary channel. Seeing in him the perfect expression of my innermost desire, I vowed to attain the knowledge of who I was and make my state permanent.

When I stepped into the still, warm night every object seemed hollow and empty, physical reality a one-dimensional image reflected on the screen of Infinite Consciousness. I immediately understood scripture's idea that only the omnipresent radiance suffusing the world, not the world itself, was real. A man and his dog out for a stroll seemed more like a movie, a walking idea, than flesh-and-blood beings. Seeing the thought animating them like puppets caused me to burst out laughing.

Within minutes the silence swallowed the thoughts generated by the talk, chewed them carefully and refined them into purposeful energy. I knew what had to be done, laughing at the irony of the idea of going back to university. By the grace of God I had been enrolled in quite a different school.

On my way to the bus I came upon a bloody and bruised young woman wretchedly whining and crying as she pursued a drunken, leather-clad man down the block. Scratching and kicking, she attacked him and grabbed him by the arm, trying to pull him back. He cursed her violently, broke loose, hit her savagely and struck off with renewed vigor. The scene played over and over as they moved down the street. For a moment I thought of intervening, but realized that everything was perfect between them, that they had unconsciously evolved this tawdry game for reasons known only to them. Or not. Within an hour they would be passionately clinging to each other in "love." Contemplating their sordid drama, which seemed like a life metaphor, I understood that the only way out was to see what I was seeing. Their cartoon-like figures receded down an alley, and I continued on my way, lost in the glory of God.

A Great Man

Swami Chinmaya was a very famous and highly-respected Indian holy man. A college-educated, upper-caste Hindu from Kerala, he had abandoned a fledgling career in journalism to study spirituality with Swami Shivananda, one of India's most loved saints of the last century, in front of whose *ashram* on the Ganges I had entered the stream. Eventually he journeyed further up the Ganges to Uttarkashi, where he met his *guru*, Swami Tapovan, a Himalayan sage of great wisdom and purity. Sometime during his seven-year stay he attained enlightenment.

When it was time for him to move on, the *guru* suggested he stay in the Himalayas and live a simple life. He said, "Why run around on the plains chasing devotees? Stay here and those meant to get something from you will come."

Exceptionally dynamic and charismatic, a genius by any standard, the Swami was unable to keep his light under a bushel, so he ignored the *guru's* advice and descended to the plains. The first talk drew five, but before long he was waking them up in the thousands, not unusual for an exceptional orator with immense energy in a country where spirituality is a great draw. Not since Vivekananda founded the Ramakrishna Mission had Indians taken to the path of knowledge with such enthusiasm. Inspired by an intense love of Vedic culture, he could not have burst on the scene at a better time. The educated elite and emerging middle class, for whom British secular culture was tantamount to a strong religious identity, had spiritually disenfranchised themselves in a land whose only claim to fame was God. Longing to get back to their roots, they took to his English presentation of their heritage like ducks to water.

The teaching was called a *jnana yagna*, a Sanskrit term meaning "sacrifice of knowledge." Because it is consistent with a duty-based idea of life, the backbone of Indian society, and invokes the power, mystery and spirituality of the Vedic Age, the idea of sacrifice resonates powerfully with the Indian mind. The "knowledge sacrifice" involved his talks on the *Bhagavad Gita* and the *Upanishads,* the source of the Vedanta. During my stay with him I met many enlightened disciples. Once they had realized the self, most stayed in the Chinmaya Mission carrying on the tradition under the direction of their *guru*, who quickly became a national figure.

By the time the sixties rolled around he was ready to spread the message abroad and took his first trip to the West in 1965. The fatal night at the Shivananda Center was the first stop on his second trip to the West. How ironic that I should undertake a long pilgrimage to India in search of a *guru* only to meet him a mile from the Family Dog where I had been informed two years before that God, not dope, was "where it's at."

As fate would have it, I did not have attachments and I did have money in the bank, so when the Swami moved on, I followed.

Overpowering and intense, the experience of God continued. Completely inspired, vibrating with energy, I was happy as a clam. It did not take long to realize that my situation was unique.

One afternoon I asked the Swami, "Are there degrees of God-experience? Some people seem to get only a glimpse while others are completely absorbed. Why is that?"

"Strictly speaking," he replied, "there are no degrees. Either you experience it or you do not. But you're right too. The mind is the instrument through which the self is experienced. Imagine looking at the sun. If the sky is clear, you see it in all its brightness. If there is a thin layer of clouds, you see it, but not clearly. If the clouds are heavy you do not see it at all. Similarly, if the mind is pure you will experience the self intensely, and so on. That is why I'm talking so much about spiritual practice. It purifies the mind so the experience of God is clear. If you experience the self directly you can know It as yourself."

"I haven't done much spiritual practice, yet my experience is so powerful I think at times I can't stand it. And I've met devotees who have been practicing a long time who admittedly don't have much of an experience at all. How do you explain that?"

"Well," he said, "sometimes people live in such a way that they purify the mind unconsciously and when the awakening comes, it is intense. Others practice in the wrong spirit, so nothing happens."

"But, sir," I replied, "my experience is intense and I have not lived a pure life at all."

To my surprise he didn't answer the question. "You see," he said, "it is not a good idea to call attention to your experience. It doesn't really matter what you experience. Vedanta is not about experience. It is about what you know. You experience the self all day long because this is a non-dual reality made of consciousness, but without the knowledge that you are the self, it does not do you much good. You have probably had many transcendent experiences, but they came to an end."

I nodded.

"This is because the self was not known for what it is. When the self is known as oneself the experience of it continues forever because it is you. When do you ever not exist? Spiritual experience is fine as long as the ego does not try to co-opt it. It will think it is special because it is experiencing God."

He looked knowingly at me and continued. "In reality, the self is everything and everything is the self. There is no duality, no 'experience of the self' as separate from worldly experience. Whatever you are experiencing, call it spiritual or not, is the self. You seek self-experience because you think this world and all your mundane experiences are not also the self. So what you are trying to solve by getting another experience can only be solved by understanding that everything is non-dual consciousness."

So that was it! I had been hankering after a particular kind of experience. To stay in this state I needed knowledge. But what exactly was that knowledge?

"It's not a knowledge like we think of knowledge," he replied the following day in *satsang*, showering me with smiles. "There are two kinds of knowledge – relative and absolute. Relative knowledge is knowledge that arises when a subject contacts an object. The ego experiences the world and knowledge arises. This knowledge is imperfect, subject to error because the subject and objects are conditioned by time. Absolute knowledge, on the other hand, is non-dual, out of time, because its object, awareness, is eternal. It removes the misconception that you are the body-mind complex and reveals the self. Once you have this kind of knowledge you never forget who you are."

After ten days in San Francisco we moved to an idyllic setting in the Napa hills for a retreat, sharing the venue with another spiritual group. Isolated by business, dope and my lonely pilgrimage, I did not realize the scope of the spiritual ferment that was taking place in California. Many Indian *swamis*, most notably the Maharishi and Swami Satchidananda, judged America ripe for teaching and built up large followings overnight. The Buddhists were hard at work. Within thirty years the Dalai Lama would become a world famous media celebrity and young girls in tank tops would sashay through suburban shopping malls with *Om* tattooed on their backsides. Occult and esoteric groups of all ilk sprang up like mushrooms after a rain. Tens, perhaps hundreds, of thousands of psychedelic pioneers like myself, whose experience had opened them up to higher ideas, were fertile ground for the pre-Biblical teachings that would later be called "New Age."

I believe the conviction arising from legitimate spiritual experiences induced by drugs – that there is something beyond the realm of the senses and the mind's mad craving for pleasure and security – not drugs themselves, is the most enduring and important legacy of the sixties and forms the basis of a spiritual revolution that continues today.

In any case, a week before we arrived a psychologist, vowing not to move until he attained enlightenment, locked himself in a cabin and began meditating. A few days later, alerted by his screams, the authorities broke in and hauled him off to the state insane asylum a few miles down the road.

"It is dangerous to take this sort of an attitude," said the Swami of the incident. "Enlightenment does not come simply because you want it. You have to be prepared. This is why in our country we have the *guru*-disciple lineage. The disciple must cultivate the requisite ethical and moral standards, a keen sense of discrimination, dispassion and a calm mind. And he should have a teacher, someone who has already successfully walked the path. This is typical of the independent and egocentric approach to life in America."

The retreat felt like a family gathering. Witnessing more happy faces in ten days than I had seen in the last ten years, I spent all day in his presence, listening to the science of self-knowledge.

"Why is it a science?" I asked one afternoon during the informal discussion period, hoping for more than Mr. Patel had offered. "It seems more like a religion."

"It is a science in this sense," he replied. "In science you have certain theories that have to be proven by experiment before they can be accepted as knowledge. Vedanta presents the theory that there is a God, which we call the self, and it provides methods for verifying the truth of that theory. If they are used properly, the practices and techniques will deliver the experience and knowledge of God.

"Religion asks that you merely believe in the existence of something you cannot practically verify," he continued. "You are promised release later on in heaven, but the idea of actually knowing God intimately and directly as your own self is considered blasphemy. Our idea is that God must be of practical use. Faith alone is not enough. We want to experience God, to live in God as God. Only then can we accept the theory of God's existence, which at that time is no longer a theory but knowledge.

"Of course God can never die, but God has died here because faith has killed Him. If you believe God can be known only through faith, you rob yourself of the here-and-now experience of God.

"The West has the idea that the physical universe is reality and that it is made up of matter only. And consciousness supposedly comes out of matter. To us this is a ridiculous idea because matter is insentient. How can sentience, consciousness, come out of matter? Vedanta says that the universe is consciousness from the very beginning. In fact before the beginning. It does not evolve once the material universe gets to a certain stage. Even if it did, how would the universe evolve without consciousness? Evolution, any kind of change, implies consciousness or energy.

"So you think that the only reality is the material world and you explore that. The way you explore it is called science. And you have been very successful in exploring and explaining it using the scientific method. We do not quarrel with you on this point. In practical ways your use of science has exceeded ours. This is why your standard of living is much better than ours. But long before there was a Western civilization our sages were exploring the inner world, the world of mind or consciousness with a scientific mentality. So over thousands of years we have developed a proven subjective science. It is not just theories. It is not the opinion or system of some brilliant man, like Nietzsche or Sartre or Freud, or religious dogma, but the accumulated knowledge and experience of tens of thousands of subjective scientists.

"Our science goes beyond yours. We accept the knowledge that comes from the scientific method and the senses. Today, psychology is trying to establish itself on a scientific footing. Eventually the general public will accept the existence of the subjective as a fact, a reality equal to the reality of matter, because of science. We already fully accept the existence of the mind. We have very carefully documented its reality, how it works, how it interacts with matter. But we have also gone beyond mind. Our science has three divisions: the material universe, the psychological universe and consciousness, the self."

This information was terribly important because it meant there was a method for integrating my experience of God into my life. With the help of this extraordinary sage, the riddle was about to be solved.

"Please don't think I am arguing with you, sir," I said, "but you said that the goal of spiritual life was to live in God as God. But this is surely not possible, because I am certainly not the creator of the universe."

"Very good thinking, Ram. It does seem that there is a contradiction. By 'God' I did not mean the creator of the universe, although that is the conventional meaning of the word. I meant that because of which it was possible for a creation to happen, pure consciousness. Our idea of creation is quite radical compared to religion's view of an external God and an external creation. I have no time to go into it now, as it is a very subtle topic that involves a lot of background information, but if you continue with your study of Vedanta it will become clear."

***

Suddenly I had a life. Every day I attended every talk, meditation and *satsang*. In my spare time I prayed, meditated and studied scripture. My experience of the self was exhilarating and almost constant. When I was tuned in, the Swami was always "there," unlike the Rishikesh *yogi*. I wondered how he could maintain an impeccable human façade and a clear mind while such tremendous happenings were going on within him. I would often get so caught up in my amazing inner unfolding that I could not properly think or speak. Yet he nonchalantly dished up brilliant and detailed lectures on every aspect of the science of self-realization without compromising his meditation. Later I would discover that for him, in keeping with the teaching that this was a non-dual reality, there was no separation between "inner" and "outer" and that there was no meditation to keep up. Nothing was taking place in him at all. He was the empty but full consciousness of which he spoke, not a person experiencing it.

His teaching was a fine work of art. The ideas had been so cleverly arranged and skillfully expressed that simply by paying attention, a point would inevitably come when nearly every mind in the room would transcend itself and the vision of the self would ensue. But it would never last. When they came down they would cluster at his feet again looking for another trip to the beyond.

"Any fool can sit down with a rosary on the Ganges' banks and realize God in no time," said the Swami with characteristic hyperbole. "The problem is staying there. The unconscious is very powerful. It will generate a strong extroverted pressure and force the mind to come back and accept its limited view of reality. The idea is to learn to live in that state. Great work is required before the mind can divest itself of its identification with and attachment to the ego and its thought system. We call this work *sadhana*, the means of accomplishment."

The picture was complete. When the last obstacle was out of the way, the experience would be constant. Though I would eventually realize this was a rather crude formulation of a much subtler truth, it was perfect for me at the time because it channeled my prodigious energy into an endeavor that completely appealed to my heart. I had found my calling.

When I learned that the Swami was headed for Hawaii, I sold my car, broke off with my girlfriend and called my parents. Dad did not seem to mind. I think he had written me off a long time ago, but Mother, as usual, was disappointed. To have given birth to a son who at the tender age of twenty-nine was traipsing off to India with a long-haired, brown-skinned *swami* dressed in flaming orange was about all she could bear. How was this going to play to Mildred and Mona over tea?

I may have been intoxicated, but I was not a fool. To this day I am suspicious of big personalities. Everything about the Swami was glorious, verging on extravagant, and conflicted with my minimalist view of enlightened souls. I had read a little too much Zen literature, I believe. Although his flyers presented him as a scriptural master and made no grandiose spiritual claims, everything about him seemed to be shouting, "I am God," to the rooftops. On several occasions in intimate settings he used the pronoun "I" to refer to himself as God. Was the ego claiming divinity or was God actually speaking?

I too felt godlike during my mystic experiences, but what did it mean to say you are God? Even if you are non-separate from God, which we all are in our innermost selves, how could the claim be objectively verified? And if it could not, then what would be the point of claiming it – unless you were using it to make your ego look big?

Many devotees, whose level-headed spirituality I admired, claimed they saw him as God. And when I saw the vast crowds that came for his *darshan* in India it was hard to discount this view. Additionally, I had developed the conviction without a shred of evidence – except intuition – that he had "called" me with the *mantra* in the shower and generated the miraculous events that led me to him. It was unlikely that a human being could do such things. Nor, to my knowledge, did human beings serve the world so selflessly.

For example, one chilly morning we showed up at six for meditation at a local school and found the doors locked. While the organizer ran off to dig up the janitor, the Swami, who always started on time, sat down on the cold concrete next to a trash can in a thin silk *dhoti* and shawl and began his talk, totally oblivious of the surroundings. A grandiose ego would probably never sit next to a trash can – unless it was showing off to make a point – but God might.

All things considered, however, I still had my doubts. Although I could not know it at the time, my knowledge of God, not the Swami, needed a bit of work.

An Honest Man

A group of smiling, well-dressed, prosperous devotees garlanded him as he emerged from the terminal in Honolulu and whisked him off in a late-model automobile to a suite on the top floor of one of Hawaii's best beach hotels. He lectured to an attentive crowd in a packed auditorium at the University of Hawaii. To keep the fire burning when he left town, study groups were formed and there was the usual talk of setting up a "center." At the end of the ten-day event the donation envelopes filled two large boxes. The take probably amounted to tens of thousands of dollars, a lot of money in those days.

Just when everything was sunny and warm, a dark cloud appeared. It is the habit of devotees to hang around the premises of a *mahatma* to catch a glimpse when he or she transits from one place to another, like fans of rock stars and famous people everywhere. But instead of asking for an autograph, they bask in the radiance and perhaps – if they have the courage – ask for a small personal blessing.

One day I was standing with a group of devotees when the Swami emerged from lunch at the home of the *yagna's* sponsor in a state of exceptional radiance and waited at the end of the driveway for his ride to his next function. We clustered around him like iron filings drawn to a magnet. When the car pulled up I opened the door, stepped back and did *namaskar*, a prayerful salute. Suddenly he became deadly serious, looked at me with terrifying fierceness and nearly shouted, "Do not do *namaskar!*" Then he got in, nodded to the driver, and the car pulled quickly out of the drive.

What had I done wrong? One moment he gives great love and the next he yells at me, embarrassing me in front of the devotees. What was he trying to say? The thought of heading back to California entered my mind. Had this *guru* business been just another of my wretched excesses?

I walked over to Waikiki Beach and sat on the sand at almost the same spot where I met Madame Zora two years before, and cleared my mind. Then The Voice spoke the following remarkable words, "He wants a disciple, not a devotee, Ram."

As often happened when I had a question, it was answered before I could ask it. The next day in an afternoon *satsang*, I was surprised when someone asked about the difference between a devotee and a disciple!

"A devotee enters into an emotional relationship with God," he said. "It is the most common path because the average person is situated at the emotional level, responding to situations and people with their feelings. Such people often subordinate reason to their feelings, lose their discrimination and find themselves unable to control their own lives. But if they can learn to love unselfishly and surrender to Him their lives will work well and they will eventually attain union with God.

"A disciple, on the other hand, keeps reason in the driver's seat. He must have a clear mind so he can separate the real from the unreal, the one sure way to self-realization. Such a person does not want to be dependent on anyone outside himself, including, except for a short time perhaps, the *guru*. The danger on this path is that the heart can shrivel and the ego grow."

So that was it! My devotion was a display of personal love rather than devotion for the principle he represented. The heart is a slow learner, wanting what it wants no matter what. A year later, it seems I still did not get it. We were in Haridwar, an ancient city where the Ganges leaves the Himalayas and begins its long journey across the hot dusty plains. After an especially good day, I showed excessive familiarity in front of dinner guests, prompting him to set the record straight in a statement that still comes regularly to mind.

"I think you have the wrong idea, Ram," he said icily. "I am not a person. I am an institution."

One day, near the end of his stay in Honolulu, I attended an afternoon *satsang* at his hotel. The Swami came out tired and cranky, and asked for questions. As I listened I found myself becoming irritated at his replies. He seemed to be using the questions to talk about what he wanted to talk about, not to resolve the person's doubt. I watched each questioner's face for the light-bulb effect, but nothing was happening. The answer to the next question, a pat explanation of the three states of consciousness, seemed to miss the point entirely.

When he took up the third question I quit paying attention and studied him dispassionately, like a lizard watching a bug or a cat observing a grasshopper. He seemed cut off, locked in his own private world. The words sounded hollow and I wondered if his whole thing was not a big bluff. True, he did not seem to be squirreling away millions in a Swiss bank or messing with the many obviously smitten women who were always clustered around, but perhaps he was just a huge egomaniac, in it for the power and glory. Did my god have feet of clay?

He finished an answer, which seemed only slightly more relevant than the last, took a pinch of snuff and called for another question. A red light went on. How did the snuff habit fit into the spiritual path? When he felt the urge, which was frequently, he would take a pinch from a beautiful, hand-chased gold box and suck it up his gargantuan nose with relish, handling the preparations with flair. First, he would remove an immaculate, neatly folded, orange handkerchief from his pocket and indifferently clean the snotty, black residue without scrambling the stream of ideas or disturbing a single word in the highly polished flow. Then he would flip open the lid, nonchalantly take a pinch and shake it to get rid of the excess grains, and when he had a second between ideas, inhale it with great relish. How did he justify this obviously unspiritual, downright unhealthy habit?

I began to suspect that an exotic oriental psychedelic concoction was the source of his inspiration. Having held friends spellbound for hours when I was high on acid, I knew what dope could do.

Fortunately, I had enough sense to realize that maybe I was just cooking something up, so I sat on my suspicions, hoping they would disappear. But it was too late. The Swami, irrespective of his state of mind, seemed to know exactly what anyone was thinking at any time and he also seemed to enjoy making issues.

He finished handling a question, looked me right in the eye and, holding up the gold box, said, "You have a doubt about this, Ram?"

My first impulse was to deny it, but I heard myself say, "As a matter of fact I do."

Every head in the room turned. I had broken a cardinal rule of devotee-dom: never challenge the *guru*. If his talks created a meditative state, it was nothing compared to the silence brought on by my reply. I decided to see it through.

"I'd like to know what's in the box," I said calmly.

"Snuff," he said with a twinkle in his eye. "Would you like to try some?"

"As a matter of fact I would," I said.

The crowd fidgeted.

He gestured for me to come forward and I picked my way carefully through the mash of bodies.

"You know how to take it, I suppose," he said, handing me the box. Having made no bones about my drug history, I knew he was having me on.

"I believe I do," I said, expertly laying a line out on the back of my hand and inhaling it efficiently. When the snuff hit my palate it took every ounce of self-control not to sneeze on the Swami's neatly pressed silk *dhoti*. "Seems to be like you said," I said, wiping tears from my eyes.

He smiled blandly and called for another question. While the woman formulated her question he looked directly into me as only a *mahatma* can do, eyes brimming with compassion. Then he drove the stake in the heart of my ego: "Trust me, Ram. I'm an honest man."

***

The incident cleared much subconscious resistance, raising my vibration, kicking me into tighter orbit around the center of my being. At the time I noticed a constant halo around my body, which had become particularly limber and graceful since I met him and capable of sitting for long periods without moving.

My skin glowed with the freshness of youth and my senses became remarkably acute.

And significantly, the power to non-verbally resolve doubt arose, bringing to mind a science fiction movie I had seen years before, featuring a slimy, brain-like creature with one huge eye, Hollywood's idea of the cosmic intelligence, floating in ambrosial fluid in the center of an otherworldly room in the middle of a distant galaxy. The race of mutants serving the brain simply thought their problems into it and, presto chango, out came the answer! My answer was not always a word or idea but an experience, a knowing, that would clear the mind.

Many strange things took place. One night, for no apparent reason, I awoke in the dead of night and suddenly became aware that the Swami was in the room, not physically, but as a presence! Was he actually there or had he become so deeply established in my consciousness that he seemed to be there? Or was he simply my personal symbol for the presence that illumined all the activities of my inner world? Within a week, five thousand miles away the experience would repeat itself with an unusual twist.

Chapter VI

The Turning Point

Miracles and Such

WONDERING HOW THE Swami would react, I unilaterally decided to attend the next *yagna*. When I entered the first-class cabin on the flight to Hong Kong the Swami's face lit up and he said, "Ram, Ram, Hong Kong too?"

"Hong Kong too, Swamiji," I replied. "This Vedanta is good stuff."

As I turned toward my seat a stream of energy passed from his brow *chakra* to mine and catapulted me out of the body into deep meditation. I staggered to my seat, delicious waves of bliss bubbling up from the depths.

Flying while flying, I spent the next five hours lost in ecstasy, pondering the mysteries of the inner sky and observing the lustrous beauty all around: the wonderful construction of the wing and its rows of perfectly spaced rivets, the marvel of the tray table, the rich weave of the seat fabric, the luminosity hidden in the hearts of the passengers, the is-ness of everything.

I did not ask for permission to come, because I did not want him to see me as a needy devotee. I saw him roll his eyes when they moused into his room with personal problems. "Should I sell my house, Swamiji? Should I quit my job?" Charming displays of innocent devotion perhaps, but ultimately futile because the purpose of the spiritual path, as taught by His Holiness, was to develop discrimination and set oneself free from dependence on objects, including the *guru*. Besides, it was hardly an adventure; I had been to Hong Kong dozens of times.

It was a decision a mature person would take and it was in harmony with my conditioning. I was the only child to appear at school on the first day without my mother. When asked where she was I replied, "She is busy; I can answer your questions." I was completely amazed when they insisted that I fetch my mom. "Everyone has a mother on the first day," they said.

An incident in San Francisco a couple of days after I met the Swami sheds light on my psychology. When the Swami was chanting several repetitions of a *mantra* during an evening meditation, I experienced a super-charge of power and intense pressure inside the body, as if the top of my head were about to be blown open. The discomfort forced me to make my way out of the room, disturbing the gathering. Once outside, the energy dissolved into the star-filled firmament, and I felt better.

A few minutes later I was back, drawn like a moth to the flame, upsetting the meditators, trying to get comfortable, but the claustrophobia returned in spades, and unable to help myself, I left again.

When I appeared in the doorway a second time, I heard the Swami's angry voice, "What is the idea?"

I left, full of shame.

I think it was just my ego's reaction to my strong feelings for him. The ego, which had never loved a man in this pure way except as a child, could not bear it and forced me out. When it calmed down the heart regained control and allowed me to return, only to have the ego assert itself and eject me once again. What a peculiar tug-of-war! For the ego, love meant fear of control by the love object, hence its valuing independence. After thinking about it for some time, I concluded that this tendency was actually a blessing, although there was no reason for it in this case, because he would never take advantage of his relationship with someone; he was too noble. I read a *sutra* once that reinforced my belief. It said, "The desire to love and be loved is the cause of all suffering."

A few weeks before, when he was innocently asked how many devotees he had, he looked at the questioner as if she were mad, and in a voice verging on contempt said, "None! You cannot be devoted to me. I am nothing. If you are a devotee, you are a devotee of Truth. Truth is the *guru*." I liked that idea because surrendering to a principle is a lot less messy than surrendering to a human being with all his or her peculiarities, preferences and foibles. But then, in the highest sense God and the word of "God" are one, so consulting him about my future would have been tantamount to consulting truth. Still, God is God; if It panders to every neurotic fear and desire of human beings, the whole creation would quickly cease to function.

Maybe the doubt about who was in charge of my life stemmed from the wealth of conflicting feelings occasioned by our extraordinary relationship. At times I felt that he was my spiritual father. At other times, my mother. Sometimes I saw him as my son, an inappropriate and difficult feeling considering the situation. Not long after we met I realized that a womanly part of me loved him with passion, a shocking discovery! Tender, almost matronly feelings I had never known in the presence of a man began to surface, enriching my experience immeasurably.

As that aspect of our relationship unfolded, even my appearance became more feminine. At first I chalked it up to unisex, the idea of gender-blending that was all the rage at the time, but when I read the biography of Ramakrishna Paramahamsa, which chronicled a phase of the great *mahatma's* life during which his identification with the Divine had him dressing and behaving like a woman, I realized that the feeling was nothing to worry about.

Feminine energies come to the fore as the path approaches the source because the mind is surrendering to God. Christianity projects a male divinity, and devotees, regardless of gender, often conceive of themselves as brides of Christ. Similarly, in India, holy men wear shawls in the manner of women to symbolize marriage and submission to God.

Had I wanted to step off the deep end, I could have joined a Vaishnavite Hindu sect called the Shakti-Bhavas, "those who have a deep and passionate feeling for the Divine Mother." Devotees engage in worship of Radha, the consort of Krishna, one of the many popular symbols of divine love. I found the following passage in a book entitled *Krishna, The Divine Lover*, describing their peculiar style of worship:

"This sect is in favor with those with an effeminate turn of mind. The faith of members of this order focuses on Radha, consort of Sri Krishna. They declare themselves to be her female companions with the idea of paying homage to and establishing identity with her, even taking on the manner of speech, gait, gestures and dress of women. At monthly intervals, in the manner of menstruating women, they put on red-colored clothes as if affected by menstruation and pass three days in this state. After the period of 'menstruation' is over, they take a ceremonial bath. In the manner of married women anxious to be physically united with their husbands as enjoined in the scriptures, they take to themselves on the fourth night a painting of Sri Krishna and stretch themselves into an erotic pose. Raising both legs, they utter 'ahs' and 'oohs,' adopt coy manners and cry aloud, 'Ah, Krishna, I die! Krishna, I die!' Through practices like these they believe that they earn great merit and please the Lord by engaging themselves the whole night."

Fear I would run off and join the Shakti-Bhavas must have caused the Swami to reprimand me in public when I was sitting on the women's side in a meditation one day. "Never forget that you're a man!" he shouted as I moved to the men's section.

Seriously, the most common feeling that surfaced was brotherly, in the manner of Krishna and Arjuna, two of India's most revered spiritual giants and lifelong friends, one a realized soul, the other a seeker of truth. Krishna imparted enlightenment to Arjuna during a great civil war.

It would be disingenuous to say I would not have liked a personal relationship with the Swami, but personal relationships are virtually impossible with this type of *mahatma*, because they do not think of themselves as people. Or if they do, the person is a subordinate identity, not the essential identity. In his case it would probably be fair to say that, considering the thousands of people he came in contact with every month, it would be impossible to cultivate anything more than a very shallow relationship with a tiny fraction of them. I think he loved humans in general. As he surprisingly admitted in a rare moment, "I don't do well, one on one." I cannot complain, because he was there for me whenever I needed him, right up until the end.

In any case, our relationship, like perhaps most relationships, often seemed little more than a communication between me and my spiritual projections. Eventually the whole relationship idea turned out to be a wash because in the end there was simply no difference between us.

Finally, troubling myself about the decision to go to Hong Kong was pointless because Swami or not, I had permission from the Lord within, struggling to free itself from the burden of ignorance. It knew more, surely, than I that liberation depended on this animate *swami*. That I had not quite realized I was the Lord was the problem, although the following experience seemed to suggest I was.

One day, just before we left for Hawaii, I was sitting on my bed in the afternoon, totally absorbed in the deep and perfect peace of the inner self, suffused in light, full of energy, every cell pregnant with bliss, when the body disappeared! Not a problem during sleep, but definitely peculiar in the waking state. I was bodiless for a few moments and suddenly – I was no longer there!

Absurd of course, for how did I know I was not there unless I was there? But it was absolutely true, the person I thought I was had been automatically supplanted by a bodiless, mindless "I," and this "I" was living without taking a single breath! Because I did not have senses or a mind, I could not see or hear anything specific, but I could "see" myself as endless light and "hear" myself as silence without limit.

How long this non-experience, which was to become increasingly frequent as my practice progressed, lasted, I cannot say. Perhaps a few seconds, maybe minutes, but when the familiar "I" reappeared I thought it must be enlightenment. The fruit was the knowledge that "I" was beyond everything: me, my *guru* and the teachings. Although I was not quite there yet, I understood that nothing in the world, not even dismissal by my teacher, who was the only love object in my life, could change me.

The experience generated an indescribable feeling of otherness. When I got to Hong Kong and took a visa picture in a sit-down, four-for-a-dollar booth on the docks near the Star Ferry, I was startled – the unearthly eyes were seeing – but seeing nothing! There was nobody home!

I showed it to a devotee, who became visibly agitated.

"What's the matter?" I said.

"This is scary, Ram. This is scary. Who are you?" She clammed up and avoided me from then on, as if she had just viewed a "ten most wanted" flyer in the post office. From that I learned not to share my inner stuff. No matter how spiritual or close they are, those who have not experienced the great void never understand.

We deplaned at Guam and sat in the departure lounge with the Swami during refueling. Though we had been together every day for a month, he had never asked a personal question. Surprisingly, he inquired about my profession.

"Business, Swamiji," I said, a little ashamed.

"Nothing wrong with business, Ram," he said. "It is a noble occupation. Someone has to create wealth for the society. If it were not for businessmen there would be no Mission. Besides, it got you here. It is all a matter of how you think. If you are in it only for the money, then it is not good. But if you do it as a service, for your spiritual growth, it is as good as any spiritual practice. Do not look down on it."

"As spiritual practice, Swamiji?"

"Yes, definitely. Spirituality is not about what you do. We have great saints who were butchers, weavers, kings, even prostitutes. It is not what you do, but the state of mind in which you do it. You cannot always help your *karma*, but you can change your attitude. If you dedicate your work to the self and work dispassionately it will purify you as surely as meditation or any other practice."

During a break in the conversation a cockroach the size of a small mouse came ambling across the floor and stopped in front of the Swami, his antennae waving.

"He wants his *darshan*," I said.

The Swami laughed.

Shanti, who had been silent throughout, asked what attitude she should take toward sex.

"You cannot stop it all at once," he said. "The tendencies are too strong. It will disturb the mind if you try to control it completely. At this stage you need to sin intelligently, use your discrimination and keep practicing your spirituality. Eventually you will find that you start to feel good inside and the craving for sex will dry up. If you rely on it for pleasure you will not taste the great bliss of the self. At some point it will fall away naturally. That is the goal."

As we reboarded I marveled at the concept of intelligent sin. It would certainly not fly in Christian circles, but it made perfect sense. Why stress yourself repressing natural urges? And why go hog wild indulging them? Pick and choose your moments. What a perfectly wonderful idea.

A wealthy Indian stockbroker, the *yagna* sponsor, and a handful of smiling devotees met us in the terminal, garlanded the Swami and whisked us off to Hong Kong Island in a black Mercedes limousine. I was determined to take care of Shanti since it was her first time out of the country and asked to be let down on the street so I could dig up a hotel. But the Swami had a word with the organizers. After they installed him in a high-rise flat on the island we were taken to a Sikh temple a few miles away and given rooms there. The hotel in which the talks took place was the same hotel where a scant three years before I had spent many boozy, romantic weekends with my Filipino girlfriend.

By this time my meditation had stabilized and I no longer passed in and out of the God state, but with the Swami's help dove ever deeper. I eagerly attended every function, sat up front, stayed tuned in and watched the unfolding of each and every petal of the divine lotus with rapt attention.

One morning during *Upanishad* class I smelled a fragrance so subtle I nearly swooned. At first I thought one of the Indian women in the class was wearing a potent and exotic perfume, but the aroma continued as I walked back to the temple along a busy, smoggy roadway. The next day I heard celestial music welling up from within, as wave upon wave of tingly, blissful energy washed over the body. During the question session I told the Swami what had happened.

"It is a good sign, Ram. The mind is becoming subtle. Our *yoga* literature extensively documents these experiences. In themselves miraculous experiences are just temporary psychic phenomena, but this shows that you are on the right track. You must go beyond to the source."

That the mind, which is opposed to self-knowledge on principle because it effectively cancels its desires, was starting to think spiritually was the real miracle, not the petty *yogic* experiences. One day I noticed that I was starting to love Shanti in less than a platonic way. The feelings would not go no matter how hard I tried to ignore them, so I decided to get into them and see what they were really all about. And within minutes, at the end of a particularly juicy sequence of emotion-inspired thinking, the mind, with great confidence, said, "It is nothing, you are not the body. It is the self in her that you love." The lust dried up immediately.

When I mentioned this to the Swami he gave me a little speech. "Good," he said with characteristic enthusiasm, "the mind is coming around. You must continue to meditate on the teachings so that they become your own. The experience of the self is natural, but the power to bring it into the thick of life is rare. These teachings retrain the mind and wean it from its unholy alliance with the ego by teaching it to think from the self's point of view.

"Our work is showing the mind how to solve its problems. The spiritual science is based on reality, not the false reality the mind is caught up in. Problems are there because the mind is thinking unrealistically. It wants things to be as it wants them to be, not as they are. So it is always angry, frustrated, disappointed and dejected. But if it learns to think from a different premise, from the self's point of view, it will eventually come to know the self, and its problems will diminish and disappear. This is not brainwashing, because the self is the truth. It is reality.

"Most people do a little scripture study, listen to a few lectures, chant some *mantras* and when they do not get immediate results they move on to another teaching, another *guru*. The secret is to stick to one path, going into it deeply, hearing the same ideas over and over from different perspectives at different times, comparing them to your experience. It is boring, but it is the only way. I spent seven years with my *guru*. After six months I knew all the ideas, but this was not enough. The mind had to be retrained and the knowledge assimilated through contemplation, so I stayed on for seven years."

This subtle non-event, a small but important victory, meant the retraining had begun. Eventually, like the Ouroboros, the mind would consume itself as quickly as it grew. In the meantime the miracles continued.

Hong Kong was a watershed for Shanti who was having serious doubts about following the Swami. One night we talked about her concerns. I encouraged her to soldier on and offered to loan her the money to get to India. The next day, after morning class, the sponsor informed us we had been invited by the Swami to the afternoon *satsang* at his apartment.

No experience in this world, including the joy of sex, can compare to the *darshan* of a *mahatma* in transcendental ecstasy. When we entered the atmosphere was electric and the Swami was sitting ramrod straight on a sofa next to a picture window with a spectacular view of Hong Kong Harbour. He was surrounded by a blinding white aura, his eyes glowing coals, and his powerful voice cut the silence like a scythe, every word forceful, precise, eloquent and soaked in love. "The self alone is real," he was saying as we entered. "This world is only apparently real."

I had the sense that we were participating in an event of great significance. He motioned us up to the high-energy zone, and the devotees made room. When he had completed the teaching someone asked a question. He thought for a minute and said, "Suppose Ram here and Shanti were having a conversation last night and he said to her..." At this point he repeated enough of the conversation verbatim to let us know that he had obviously been there, even though in terms of physical reality he was five miles away when the conversation took place! Then without batting an eye he went on to weave the conversation into the answer. The ego did not enjoy contemplating the consequences of this event, because it meant there was nowhere to hide. Were all its wicked little thoughts and greedy emotions as accessible to this amazing God-man?

Feeling that he would scold me for mentioning it, since miracle talk was completely discouraged, I did not ask him about it, not that such things can be adequately explained anyway. Perhaps these powers had been so much a part of his life for so long he did not think them extraordinary.

The Oxygen Bottle

The Swami suffered a heart attack several years before we met and some years later he would undergo triple bypass surgery in Houston after a second attack. For years doctors advised him to take it easy, an option not in the cards for a man with a world to enlighten. And true to form, he would eventually die with his boots on, croaking out the teachings.

Little wonder his health was poor. By the time we met he had been teaching non-stop for over twenty-five years, a dawn-till-midnight schedule, three hundred sixty-five days a year, with no breaks except the day or two for travel between venues. He personally answered all mail, devoting the hours between three and five in the morning to the task. I have no idea how big the Mission was, but in spite of its relatively loose organization there was much to-do on a mundane level and the Swami, like a hands-on CEO, kept it all together. His schedule of international travel, fixed a year-and-a-half in advance, involved hopping from city to city, country to country, every ten days. Though he was taking steps to correct it when I met him, his diet consisted of spicy food and milky sweet tea. He suffered diabetes, snorted large quantities of snuff, religiously avoided exercise and talked eight or ten hours a day. With relish he often described the body as "a stinking bucket of feces and urine, food for worms." That he nearly lived eighty years was a tribute to the grace of God and the wonders of medical science.

A couple of days before the flight to Bombay he called me into his room. I touched his feet, and was offered a chair. Though I had not discussed my plans, he said, "You'll be going on to India, Ram?"

"Yes, Swamiji, if that's all right with you," I replied.

"Well, you've come this far. It would be a shame to quit now."

"It's been very good, Swamiji, much more than I ever expected. I think I've got the idea, but I need more practice. I was in India before and had many interesting experiences, but I really didn't know what was going on. It was hit and miss. I needed a comprehensive system like the Vedanta to bring it all together."

"Yes," he said and fell silent.

I felt something momentous about to happen.

"You know I have a heart condition, Ram?"

"Yes, Swamiji, the devotees speak of it often."

He picked up a small green oxygen bottle and looked at it bemusedly. "Sometimes I don't get enough oxygen and swoon. So the doctors have given me this bottle. Needless to say, I can't be carrying it all the time, so I need someone to carry it. When it looks like I'm going to pass out, give it to me. If I'm already unconscious put this piece of plastic in my mouth and open the valve. You probably won't have to use it, but it's a precaution. Do you understand?"

"How much do I give you?" I said.

"I don't know," he replied. "Use your own judgment."

I didn't like the idea of taking responsibility for him, but didn't say anything.

"Is it too much responsibility for you, Ram?" he said with a touch of sarcasm. "Are you worried I might die on you?"

"I think I can manage, Swamiji," I said. "After all, it's only the body."

He laughed.

My newfound "little duty," as they say in India, was the spiritual equivalent of winning the lottery. I had been granted virtually constant access to a great *mahatma*, the effect of which was that I became privy to every thought and feeling, every fluctuation in his energy, an invaluable development because the more closely I was attuned to his "equipment," as he liked to call it, the faster I evolved.

My new job also highlighted the fact that he might drop dead at any moment and leave my longing for freedom unfulfilled. And it made me realize that my uncontrollable and misdirected passion for experience was really an unbounded desire to know who I was. As a consequence I became even more of a fanatic for enlightenment. Fully owning this desire fixed me firmly on the path, an arrow flying to the mark.

About a year later, just before the end of my discipleship, I was hovering around the Swami, burning with such intensity that he turned around, although he was otherwise engaged.

"What is it, Ram?" he said irritably.

"What's what, Swamiji?" I said, unaware of my desire.

He seemed perplexed, realized what was going on and with a look of genuine amazement, said, "I've never seen anyone with such desire." Perhaps it reminded him of himself at that age.

His Holiness

It would be impossible to describe the feeling of excitement and promise as the jet touched down on the tarmac at Bombay International. The last time around, standing on the deck of the geriatric ship from Mombasa as it limped into the harbor, I was just a romantic hippie in search of adventure, inspired by the fateful words of the granola girl from the Holy Man Jam. This time I was blessed with the company of a *mahatma* and a clear idea of what I was seeking.

We entered the terminus, the Swami in front, Shanti and I behind, the oxygen bottle at the ready. Across the room behind the glass, a large crowd of devotees, garlands in hand, waited eagerly for the Swami to clear customs.

I noticed two officials coming straight towards the Swami, certain they were about to nab a rich export *guru* trying to sneak through with a cornucopia of watches, cameras, gold and transistors. In fact he was only packing silks and scripture. As they approached he turned his head and I distinctly saw a beam of energy, like a ray of light, pass from his mind into theirs! They went blank, stopped, looked around, could not remember what they were about to do, turned and walked leisurely back into the office. The Swami, indifferent as ever, passed through the doors into the embrace of the devotees who saluted and garlanded him as they sang traditional Sanskrit verses in praise of the *guru*.

On our way to the *ashram* we passed through one of the worst tin-and-burlap slums in India and I was amazed that our entourage of late-model automobiles with prosperous people chanting the name of God did not attract more attention. In the West, one might expect a poverty-stricken malcontent to hurl a rock through a windshield in such a situation, but nothing happened. At one point during a traffic jam a beggar put his hand though an open window but ambled off indifferently when his desire was unfulfilled. Some seemed to enjoy the chant. At an intersection a young boy danced to the music and a turbaned man with a monkey on his shoulder smiled.

Situated in a park-like atmosphere near a small lake amid rolling hills, the *ashram* nestles among tall trees behind a small hill near a man-made lake. It is endowed with generous walkways and well-tended gardens, and is capable of housing perhaps one hundred fifty students. In addition to two three-storey dorms, there is a dining hall, a lecture hall, the Swami's small three-room "hut," a bookstore and a couple of other buildings. On top of a hill commanding excellent views sits a stunning white marble Shiva temple.

Except for a skeleton crew, the *ashram* was deserted. Evidently a number of rich devotees, not expecting him to live, withdrew their support when he suffered his first heart attack, canceling all programs. But he surprised them, rising like the phoenix full of messianic zeal, jetting off around the world in search of greener pastures. Within a year the *ashram* would be fully functioning, hosting a two-year residential program of Vedic studies taught by his number one disciple.

I was given a room shaded by a huge mango tree in one of the dormitories along the perimeter. It sported barred windows and was furnished with a none-too-comfortable bed, table, chair and mosquito net. Mercifully, it included the most indispensable fixture in Asia, a ceiling fan. I soon discovered that keeping small articles on the window sill was pointless because groups of monkeys periodically swept through the *ashram*, lifting everything in sight. One of the boys told me the monkey was called *hari*, the thief. It is also one of the most common names of God, the inner monkey whose transcendent love steals the heart.

Life in the Swami's entourage rolled along as if on greased wheels. A second morning class and devotional items, temple worship, chanting and other small rituals were added to the program. For example, we all ate in silence after chanting the fifteenth chapter of the *Bhagavad Gita*, the Hindu "Bible," a moving ritual.

The Swami had obviously been holding back on tour, accepting the West's reluctance to venerate holy men by presenting himself as a scholarly lecturer on Indian philosophy. He had even cut his long hair. He was actually a duck out of water, experimenting with the strange and threatening idea that you are fine as you are. There is nothing to obtain here on earth. Occasionally he met with hostility and disrespect. But India does God like the Japanese do cars and the French do food. The first time around I had my glimpses, but this time I witnessed the world's spiritual superpower in all its glory.

Too high to sleep much, I awoke at dawn to a misty, ancient Indian morning. I bathed, put on my *dhoti* and *tilak*, grabbed my shawl and walked up the path to the Swami's hut, an unpretentious three-room bungalow with terrazzo floors and grilled windows, where a single light emanating from his bedroom spread an unearthly calm. I stood in the garden, enchanted by the fragrance of the plumerias, telling the beads, waiting for him to emerge.

In twenty minutes he appeared in the doorway in freshly pressed silks, *mala* in hand, obviously absorbed in his inner state, wavy crystalline lines of light emanating from his body. The handful of devotees who were hanging around came forward, offered flowers, touched his feet and withdrew without speaking a word. We fell in line behind him, joined by other sleepy devotees converging on the temple as he walked slowly through the gardens, occasionally muttering the Lord's name.

Mounting the long, steep stairway, the Swami stopped frequently to catch his breath and look out over the tops of the palms at the lake in the distance where the first rays of morning light were reflecting. I could see he was visibly moved by Mother India and the prospect of meditation in his own temple, after a long visit to the land of the heathens. He sighed deeply and held out his hand to the morning as if greeting an old friend, the Lord's name on his lips, "Narayana, Narayana."

The smell of jasmine saturated the air and oil lamps flickered in the sanctuary, a Brahmin priest, naked from the waist up and wearing the sacred thread, chanted in Sanskrit from the *Shiva Purana*, an ancient devotional work. The Swami walked slowly to the altar and gracefully prostrated before the gleaming white marble form of a smiling Shiva in meditation pose. "It is not the statue to which we bow," he often said, "but to That which it symbolizes."

We circumambulated the altar and sat on the immaculate marble floor, the Swami taking his seat on a platform at the side of the temple where the sun's rays would shortly come to warm him. Waiting until everyone settled in, he said a few words about meditation and led us into the cave of the Heart. A deep peace enveloped the room as forty bodies sat motionless, the silence broken only by the cawing of crows and an occasional horn from a faraway road.

Tears of devotion trickled down my face when I realized that I had discovered a non-dogmatic religion with a sense of true reverence. Coming from a country where churches are easily confused with dental clinics and devotional song is accompanied by electric guitars, I was overjoyed to discover true sanctity. It was now perfectly clear why the Swami was called His Holiness.

After meditation we silently walked down the hill to the kitchen to take tea before the *Upanishad* class. No one spoke. Each was absorbed in his or her inner world.

The Pope of India

India is a time warp. Invariably the modern filter dissolves and you are transported back to a different time. If you come upon a twelve-hundred-year-old temple and witness the ancient rituals, you quickly understand that nothing, including dress and hairstyles, has changed in hundreds, probably thousands, of years. In contrast to ours, which indiscriminately discards everything good and bad after a short honeymoon, then sets out to reinvent it, Indian culture has preserved humanity's most important legacy – love of Truth.

Vedic culture is based on the idea that all names and forms in this world are nothing but consciousness, which, not to put too fine a point on it, is roughly equivalent to God. God is not an extraterrestrial deity sitting in a faraway heaven, according to the science of self-knowledge. God created the world out of its own consciousness in the way that a spider creates a web out of its body. God is both the substance of the creation and the intelligence that shapes it. The purpose of life here is to extricate ourselves from the web of life's sticky threads by investigating the nature of reality. Those who are successful live free and fulfilled lives.

Several thousand years before the Christian era, this and a handful of ancillary revelations experienced by a group of forest-dwelling ascetics, called *rishis,* were enshrined in the *Vedas,* the oldest extant texts on the science of God-knowledge. A *rishi* is someone who "sees," or knows, God directly. The *rishis* established forest academies where the spiritually-inclined came to realize Truth. Since the knowledge of God is the ultimate knowledge and the means of realizing it has proved to be effective for thousands of years, it remains intact to this day. All lineages of enlightened souls ultimately stretch back to the Vedic Age and beyond.

By God's grace I had stumbled onto a bona fide *rishi* and his forest academy. One might think that because it was situated in suburban Bombay and the *rishi* flew in jets and wore an Omega watch things had changed. But Truth is Truth and it comes down like it always did. Merely to walk into the classroom, decorated with pictures of great *mahatmas,* including, in the place of honor, the Swami's *guru,* my spiritual grandfather, and hear the text in Sanskrit, a spiritual language unchanged in thousands of years, was to be transported back to the source.

Attractive as they were to me in the West, the teachings became immensely richer in India. As I slowly grasped the Idea animating the world of the visible, I came to understand that one could scratch the surface of any Indian cultural ritual and find the *mandala* of God hidden beneath, a realization that wiped out what little pessimism I had concerning the future of the human race. The Truth would be kept alive forever because it delivers fulfillment.

By the second day a steady stream of humanity beat a path to his door. I was allowed to stand in a corner behind his desk when he received devotees, guests, visitors and mission workers. What a privilege to witness the deep respect and love for the institution and observe the subtle way his words lifted them up, dissolving their cares and woes, giving new meaning to their quests.

It was easy to see how he had attracted such a large following. One day we were alone for a few minutes and I remarked that he had a pretty cushy deal, that all he had to do was sit back and let the Lord do it all.

He put down his pen, removed his glasses, rubbed his eyes and said wearily, "It's not like that, Ram. It looks that way to you because of your high state. But you do not know what is behind it. I started out with nothing. Five people attended my first talk. I've been hard at it for twenty-five years, building it up brick by brick. It is not a miracle at all, simply a lot of hard work. Why do you think this body is such a wreck?"

A few days later I realized what he meant. I was so empowered by my mystic experiences I rarely slept. Ever the bad boy, one afternoon, when everyone was napping, I decided to slip out of the *ashram* and have a cup of tea in a nearby park. When I approached the *ashram* gate I heard the Swami's raised voice. I ducked behind a tree to see what was happening and peeked out. He was standing in the middle of the path in the scorching afternoon sun, looking every inch the Old Testament prophet, sweat running down his face as he argued passionately with a young Brahmin boy, a temple priest who wanted to leave the *ashram* and return home. The boy was not interested in what the Swami had to say and met the angry words with sullen and resentful stares. Eventually, however, under the pressure of the Swami's logic and the force of his personality he reluctantly agreed to soldier on. Big man or not, to the boy he was just another Indian.

It also showed that Indians tend to take spirituality with a grain of salt because it is such an obvious part of their culture. A few days later I was talking with a devotee, a businessman from Bombay, about the urgency of attaining enlightenment.

"What's the hurry?" he asked humorously. "There is much time. You should enjoy yourself first, have a family and do something worthwhile for the society. If you do not get it this time, you can get it in your next birth. Why rush? Anyhow, what good does it do? We've had *mahatmas* for a long time and look at this country. It's a downright shame. We cannot even look after ourselves properly. We were better off under the British. These *yogis* should come out of their caves and get some honest work. The best and brightest minds in the society are sitting in *ashrams* going for *moksa*."

"Yes, but you're a devotee. You must be working for your enlightenment. The Swami talks day and night about *moksa*."

"Well, *moksa* is not something you get," he said. "It is something that comes from God. Only rich people can afford the leisure of chasing *moksa*."

"So why do you follow the Swami?" I said, intrigued.

"He is a great man, you see. He is teaching us to think for ourselves, not to get hoodwinked by religion."

"Hoodwinked by religion?"

"Yes, religion is the bane of Indian society. It stands for everything that is backward, superstitious. Religion is the most powerful and corrupt force in the land. Not one government has had the backbone to stand up to religion. The priests are in total control of the people's lives."

"But this is religion," I argued, referring to the Chinmaya Mission.

"Yes, but this is how religion was in the time of the *rishis*. It is religion for the thinking man and it puts something back into the society. The Swami is a great man. He is giving us back our heritage."

I did not make it to the tea stall for fear of incurring the Swami's wrath. In fact although I had occasionally tasted the lash I tended to forget that there was a fierce spiritual warrior behind the peaceful façade. I am reminded of an article in an Australian paper that called him the Pope of India and said he was "no peace-love pussy cat, but a real tiger."

Apart from confirming his contention that teaching was hard work, I realized that "holy" does not mean pious and nice, but whole and complete. This is not to say that he was not also unbelievably gentle, kind and very lovable. And although the Swami portrayed the goal of spiritual work as a desireless mind, I was secretly pleased to know he had strong desires – for the right thing – because desire was language I understood well. But it did seem a contradiction. If he was the ever-blissful, ever-peaceful self, then what was all the fuss over such a small thing, a homesick boy wanting to abandon his duty? I did not realize at the time that for someone with non-dual vision there is no big and small. Everything is equally important, if it is important at all.

The doubts created by the incident were resolved a few days later when a devotee asked, "What is the right attitude to take toward the *guru*, Swamiji?"

"The *guru*," he said forcefully, "is only a temporary psychological aid. He is supposed to wield the teachings that reveal the self. If he gives advice, it will be generic advice: seek the self and practice discrimination. When the self is known the self becomes the *guru*. You cannot rely on the outer *guru* to solve your problems. What does a *guru* know about the details of your life, especially *gurus* who have many devotees? Vedanta presupposes that you are a mature person, that you know how to negotiate the currents of existence. You should be very suspicious of *gurus* who are eager to take on your problems. If you maintain dispassion and discrimination and let Truth be the *guru*, you will move quickly toward the goal. Do not swallow everything the *guru* says or does."

He looked directly at me. Then, with a twinkle in his eye, dramatically stroking his long beard, he said, "When dealing with *gurus*, here is a good rule of thumb: the longer their beard, the greater your doubt about who they are should be!"

Everyone has an ego, the enlightened and the unenlightened, contrary to conventional wisdom, which claims that a *guru* by definition is egoless. Manifestations of gurugic ego are meant to be blithely dismissed as projections by others, as if egolessness, which undoubtedly has its points, were the ultimate spiritual goal. If egolessness were the ultimate goal, how to account for the many egoless people, like saints, who do not know who they are?

Like so many apparently important and easily misunderstood issues, however, worrying about the *guru's* ego turned out to be a waste of time because I had been given an ironclad inner assurance I would find fulfillment through him. So I took the warts-and-all approach – love somebody, love their stuff. When I got over wanting a saint, I found a very interesting and complicated man, outwardly joyful and fun-loving but pure steel inwardly. Sometimes I saw him as a huge raptor perched on a lofty crag waiting for a small rodent to appear. Often enough my ego was the rat. But he never toyed with me or seemed to enjoy the attacks, like a cat, but tore into me impersonally and mechanically with impeccable logic, a spider indifferently bundling up a moth fluttering in its web. Whether they came from his ego or not, the infrequent attacks were useful to me; I took what I thought valuable and left the rest.

Ninety/Ten

After serving the Bombay devotees we toured other cities and towns, repeating the ten-day routine with mantric regularity. Because I was young and inspired I had the energy to keep up with the schedule, but the Swami was not in good health and was forced to draw on meager reserves. One day the doctors put their collective feet down and insisted that he take a break. I received permission to accompany him, but he disappeared without giving me the details, so I found myself cooling my heels in the *ashram* while he flew to Hyderabad. The devotees had either been kept in the dark or been instructed not to give out the address, so I decided to track him down on my own.

The moment I stepped through the *ashram* gates a taxi stopped and took me to Andheri where the Bombay train was just pulling into the station. We reached the city an hour before the Hyderabad train departed. Though I held a third-class ticket, the conductor graciously offered me a berth in first class. I arrived rested and alert the following morning.

The Mission's number was out of service, a big blow to my plans. Though the Indian grapevine is second to none and the Swami was very famous, my inquiries proved useless. I sat down, depressed, ordered a cup of tea in a small café and eventually decided to get a hotel and think about my options. I paid my bill and turned down a narrow side street where I noticed a small shrine dedicated to the elephant god, Ganesh, remover of obstacles, one of the oldest and most popular gods in the Hindu pantheon. Having been recently worshipped with flowers and incense, a few coins lay in an ornate brass dish at his chubby feet. He seemed alive, a beatific smile on his elegant, elephantine face. Laying a rupee in the dish, I asked that the obstacles to my search be removed. The depression lifted and my mind entered a meditative state.

Suddenly the whole thing seemed ridiculous, a metaphor for the quest. How could I search for something I already had? He was my connection with the Lord, no doubt – but the Lord was right there in my heart.

My desire drained and I felt a miraculous infusion of energy. The body that seemed heavy and meaty before now seemed light and insubstantial. Then, without any help from me, it got up and headed down the street! It walked with mindless certainty for about ten minutes, automatically turning here and there until it stopped in front of the gate of a large Raj-era mansion.

The Voice said, "Ring the bell, Ram."

A servant came to the door, and The Voice said, "I'm a devotee of Swami Chinmaya," and I was ushered in. I walked into the front room just as Swamiji was entering from a hallway on the left, a look of genuine surprise on his normally inscrutable face.

"How did you find me?" he said. "I'd given instructions that no one was to come."

"You said I could come," I replied.

"Who told you?" he said suspiciously.

"No one, Swamiji. You forgot to leave instructions, so I decided to find you myself. I caught the train yesterday and wandered the streets today but had no luck. When I asked Ganesh to find you, the body knew exactly where to go, like a homing pigeon."

He paused for a second taking it all in, shook his head, said, "*Hare Ram!*" which more or less translates as "Holy cow!," and told one of the servants hovering around to give me a room.

Every morning I got up a few minutes before four, showered and peered down the hall to see if light was coming from under the Swami's door. I hovered in the hall until I was sure he had completed his toilet, then wormed my way in on the pretext of bringing him a cup of tea. Once inside, I stood like an usher in a corner, basking in his energy, meditating on the self.

The way God had taken me to him, virtually moving the body through the streets without my participation, convinced me that I could rely completely on the inner Swami, so attachment to the outer Swami's physical presence began to dissolve at this time and I entered a stage where just the thought of him kept me in meditation. It is easy to think continually about someone you love. The more I loved him, the more he became part of me. At some point we began to physically resemble each other. Fortunately, I did not suffer the anxiety of love, however, because I understood that the whole process was part of my *sadhana*, the will of God.

As recently as a month before I had secretly spent several nights sleeping in the garden outside his window like a faithful dog because I was afraid to lose contact. I knew I would not be discovered; first, because nobody would be so crazy, and second, because it was God's will. By the time we headed back to the West he had become completely internalized, as much a part of me as my own mind, allowing me to leave his physical presence for a short time, take care of some small family *karma* and return without breaking the transmission.

As I meditated on him over the months a pure form emerged in my mind, one corresponding with my own spiritual qualities because at the level behind the personality we are all the same divine person. Fixing my attention on that image as it played in the mind invariably led me to the self, the light enlivening it.

The Swami was my *guru* because his inner energy ignited mine. The subtle flow of divine energy between one soul and another is the only relationship pleasing to God, and a true teacher. Lesser *gurus* are quite happy to count bodies, bask in the adoration of devotees, tell people what to do and take satisfaction in the idea of *guru*-hood, but not the Swami, who eagerly held up his side of the equation once the *shakti* was activated. As our relationship progressed I realized that he was as devoted to my enlightenment as I was.

Usually, when I came to a new level he would acknowledge it in some way. After we had been in Hyderabad about a week we were sitting alone in the parlor waiting for devotees to show up for *satsang*. I was thinking about our relationship.

"What are you thinking?" he said, surprisingly, as it was the only time he ever asked such a question.

"About the *guru*-disciple relationship, Swamiji."

"Yes, what about it? I do not read minds," he said almost testily. I could sense a lecture coming on.

"Would you say I was your disciple?" I said.

Often, when a conversation seemed headed toward the personal dimension, he would conveniently fail to understand and go off on a tangent or dissemble. But he looked directly at me and, in a deadly serious tone, obliquely replied, "Well, Ram, the disciple gives ninety percent and the *guru* ten. Is that understood?"

It took me a minute to get it because a business deal was such an indirect way to respond, but when I did get it I was ecstatic. Doing ninety percent or more of the work did not scare me, because I was capable of anything. My heart was going to have its way.

When we were in Bombay the Swami had agreed to facilitate the renewal of my visa. As the deadline approached I sat on my agitation because I felt it impolite to ask again. It was due to expire Tuesday, and by Monday nothing had been done, though I kept putting out the thought, hoping he would pick up on it.

About three o'clock Monday afternoon he was having *satsang* with two or three devotees, but my mind would not stay with the discussion. About four, a well-dressed, middle-aged man arrived, touched the Swami's feet and sat down. They talked for a few minutes, the Swami got up to leave, and I started experiencing intense anxiety. I came from a legal family and we always had our papers in order. When he reached the doorway, the Swami turned, pointed to me and said to the man, "Ram's visa is about to expire. Will you fix it up?"

The man, the chief of police, happily agreed, and we walked out together. I made it back in time for dinner, visa extension in hand. The Swami, sitting in the front room smiling as I entered, said, "You look like the cat that ate the canary."

"Thanks," I said, "I thought you had forgotten."

"Even if I had," he said mischievously, "you could have meditated in jail. It's nice and quiet there."

"So did you put them in your pocket?" he said after a brief pause.

"My pocket, Swamiji?"

"Did you give the cops *darshan?*"

"You bet, Swamiji, they all have liberation now. Tomorrow there will be a crime wave in the city."

Lunch with the Maharani

The Swami resumed his schedule, ten-day stints in various towns and cities. One day, after he spoke at a religious ceremony at the Ramakrishna Mission, the head monk was showing us around the *ashram* grounds when we came upon a small shrine with a radiant icon of Ramakrishna. I was immensely attracted to this image and broke ranks, leaving my place behind the Swami. As I stood in front of it I was overcome by a powerful energy and transported in the twinkling of an eye to a dimension known as *siddha loka*, where the subtle bodies of enlightened souls emanate from. Ramakrishna was sitting in full lotus, arms outstretched, welcoming me. I responded to his gesture and entered into his heart *chakra*, where I dissolved into the state of pure being, *nirvikalpa samadhi.*

A few minutes later I was called back to reality by a boy from the mission shaking my shoulder. Overwhelmed with ecstasy I opened my eyes and realized I had fallen to the ground.

Swamiji, looking mightily put out, was standing nearby, arms akimbo. By way of explanation, he said to the monk, "Ram just had *darshan* of Ramakrishna. He's very emotional. He has devotion for all the saints."

The monk smiled.

Then he turned and handed me a clean orange handkerchief, and pointing to the dust on my white *dhoti*, said, "Well, wipe it off. It won't do. We're taking *biksha* [having lunch] with the Maharani."

I interpreted the experience to mean that I was about to become a *siddha*, an accomplished one.

The Fish Eye

During this period many extraordinary inner experiences, most of which I have forgotten – which is how it should be – took place. All of them were bathed in a subtle radiance, a light that seemed to shrink and swell, and come in several subtle, ethereal colors, although it is clear and still today. And all were accompanied by a steady vibration in the center of the chest, which I recognized as love. As the days passed I found myself more and more absorbed in the light and less interested in the experiences generated out of it.

"Self-realization is not an experience," said the Swami one day in answer to a question. "It is the knowledge that you are the self, the light. In the self there is no you and no experience. It is an experienceless experience."

I did not make much of the experiences except to wonder at and enjoy them as they happened. Liberation means freedom from even this marvelous inner stuff. Psychedelia had supplied me with enough spiritual exotica to fill a dozen diaries, but except to point to the dimension beyond the physical, what use had it been?

Spiritual experiences happen to prepare the mind for knowledge, but my contemplation on Vedic culture's plethora of spiritual symbols, both visual and auditory, the so-called gods, also worked to purify my heart and mind. The gods can be taken as independent entities, but I took them as personifications of the formless, all-pervading self.

For example, self-realization is tantamount to pure love. Therefore you have Krishna, "the one who attracts," a divine lover, who according to legend had 16,283 wives, a symbol of the immense potency of love. Radha, Krishna's consort, embodies the passionate feeling of the creation for the creator, the love glue that holds all the worlds together.

Another self symbol, Vishnu, is the infinite all-pervading stillness, the peace that passeth understanding. Vishnu reclines on the coils of a serpent in the center of an infinite ocean of milk in the sleep of *yoga*, self-realization. Snakes, one of India's most common spiritual symbols, represent the hidden or unmanifest power of the self because they live unseen underground, just as the self lies hidden in the realm beneath the senses. Owing to their vastness, oceans have come to symbolize the limitless nature of the self, and nourishing milk represents love, the essence of the divine, which nurtures the soul like mother's milk nurtures the child.

India's talent for creating provocative symbols is nowhere more evident than in the name of the Meenakshi, or Fish Eye, Temple situated in Madurai in the state of Tamil Nadu. I puzzled long and hard how such a wondrous edifice could have been given such a bizarre and apparently profane name. One day I met a South Indian *pundit* who confirmed my suspicion; because it has no eyelids, a fish eye, like the self, never sleeps.

The deeper I plunged into my inner being the more I began to see everything as a symbol of the self, not just my *guru's* subtle qualities and the conventional symbols, but every aspect of Indian life. The earth itself, trodden by saints and sages since time immemorial, seemed permeated by consciousness. At nearly every bend where a river turns back to its source and on every other street corner one encounters a temple or shrine, the most pervasive reminder of the self. Cows garlanded as God in small morning rituals regularly wander the streets, sporting the sandalwood-paste third eye. India's version of our soulless tractor-trailers are decorated like the chariots of the gods and often named for one of the many aspects of the all-pervasive Power. Dashboards of countless buses and taxis invariably have altars adorned with plastic flowers and tiny colored lights, and worship is the first order of business before the trip begins. Nearly every proper name, or its root, refers to God. One is continually treated to the sight of orange-clad *sadhus*, wandering ascetics, whose lives, like our monks, are dedicated exclusively to the search for Truth.

The fire blazing in my heart saw its reflection everywhere.

One day a sandwich board cluttered with strange symbols advertising the services of a *tantric* palmist caught my eye as I was walking along a busy street in Trivandrum, Kerala, South India. Curiosity compelled me to climb a flight of worn, rickety stairs, at the top of which I entered what could fairly be called a necromancer's chamber, a darkened, incense-filled room decorated with occult symbols, pictures of gods, saints and bizarre totems. Behind a cluttered desk in the center of the room sat an intense bespectacled man in his early forties. Since I put no stock in the occult and the reading cost one thousand rupees, I opted for the fifty-rupee special just for fun. Before beginning I was instructed to approach an elaborate altar on one side of the room and extract a thick silk thread from one of two highly-polished brass bowls sitting beneath a picture of Sai Baba, the *avatar* whom I had seen vomiting the stone *lingam* in the movie at the Holy Man Jam some years before. I did as requested and returned to my chair in front of his desk, where I was instructed to place it in the palm of my right hand and make a fist.

"Now put your fist in the center of your chest, close your eyes and chant your *mantra*, twenty-one times," he said.

After one or two silent inner repetitions I was overcome by a strong supernatural energy. When I completed the chanting he instructed me to open my hand. To my surprise, twenty-one knots at evenly spaced intervals appeared in the string!

Demon Ego

As the date of Swami's third world tour approached I had to get my worldly ducks in line, so I went into the city to make reservations. On the way back I purchased ten rupees worth of hash from a street vendor and a few days later found myself sitting on the roof of the *ashram* dormitory furtively smoking in the dead of night! Had I been discovered I would have been shown the door without so much as a by-your-leave.

The incident was troubling because I realized I was not in charge, the charade seemingly unfolding on its own, as if I had been possessed by a malevolent, dark energy. And in spite of prayer and increased vigilance, subconscious forces would soon lure me into an even more humiliating situation.

Chapter VII

The Shining World *of* Knowledge

Nothing but the Best

WHEN WE GOT to Hong Kong I was prepared to go to the Sikh temple, but the Swami invited me to stay with him in the luxury flat. The invitation confirmed my suspicion that I was nearly as much an inspiration to him as he was to me.

One afternoon I was sitting in the living room writing in my diary when my pen broke. "Damn cheap Indian pens!" I groused, throwing it into the wastebasket.

The Swami glanced up, a look of amusement on his patrician countenance, and said, "What's the problem, Ram?"

"All due respect, sir, but India is a useless country. It can't even make a decent pen."

He got up and went to his room, returning a few minutes later with a brand-new, gold Cross pen in its box. "What were you doing with such a pen?" he asked.

"I don't know, Swamiji. It was just what the Lord sent at the time."

"That's not good enough. Forget the Lord," he replied, handing me the pen. "Nothing but the best for a spiritual man!"

A few months before, I had had my chart read by a retired astrologer living in the *ashram*. Before the reading he revealed half a dozen small facts about my parents and early family life that had not been communicated to him by me.

"You see," he said, "I'm not telling you these things to impress you, like the palmists on the street, but just to show you that this is your chart."

He proceeded with a reading, which over the years has proven to be exceptionally accurate.

"In conclusion," he said with a twinkle in his eye, "this chart shows that you are indeed a great king."

When I smiled he said, "Unfortunately, no one came to the coronation."

When the Swami handed me the pen I felt as if the only person who mattered had placed the crown on my head.

A Crippled Limb

The day before the flight to Hawaii I came across the small flat packet of hash, not more than a couple of grams, sandwiched between the pages of a scriptural text, and realized I had unknowingly carried it through Hong Kong customs. The obvious response was to dispose of it, not only because it was third-rate dope I did not want, but because its discovery by customs would have put an end to my relationship with the Swami and caused me no end of legal grief, perhaps even a short stint behind bars.

Incredibly, I could not let it go, as if it were a crippled limb or a scar. Instead I tucked it neatly between a stack of fresh one-hundred-dollar bills in my wallet.

When we boarded the flight for Honolulu the Swami invited me to sit with him in the first-class cabin.

"I don't have a first-class ticket, Swamiji. They'll ask me to leave."

"Don't worry about it, Ram. When they ask, you can leave," he said dispassionately.

My mind began to agitate as the flight attendant approached. The Swami just looked at her and her mind went totally blank.

She hesitated, as if trying to remember what she was thinking and said, "Time to fasten your seat belt, sir," handing me a pillow with a smile. "We're about to take off."

I turned and looked at the Swami, who rolled his eyes mischievously. "Remember, Ram, nothing but the best."

After takeoff he blew my mind a second time by ordering bourbon on the rocks and sipping it with great pleasure.

"If only the devotees could see him now," I thought.

Next, he decided to make small talk, another major departure from form. Perhaps he was trying his hand at being a regular guy. I felt honored. But as I thought about it I realized that he was saying that one should not get too wrapped up in one's idea of who one is; that even great *swamis* need to sin intelligently to keep their sanity.

We disembarked, cleared immigration and stood in line waiting for customs. I figured that as long as I was in his energy bubble there would be no trouble, but another counter opened and he moved over at the signal from an agent, leaving me behind clutching the oxygen bottle. When my turn came he had disappeared into the bowels of the terminal.

The long hair, Indian dress and oxygen bottle was a bit too much for the customs agents to process. They went through my luggage with a fine-toothed comb and took me to a special room where I was strip-searched. As I was dressing the agent asked to see my wallet, which I presented without betraying my agitation. He looked in it but did not examine the money, perhaps for fear he might be accused of theft, handing it back with a look of genuine disappointment.

After depositing the hash in a trash can, I called the contact person to find out where the Swami was staying. Ananda Ma, the *yagna* sponsor and a well-to-do Honolulu native, had put him up in a two-hundred-dollar-a-day suite on the top floor of one of Waikiki's best hotels. When I rang the bell I was confronted by a white, good-looking, well-dressed woman with graying hair, a pained expression and the psychology of a pit bull, the antithesis of her name, which translates as "The Blissful Mother."

"What do you want?" she said suspiciously, peering through the partially opened door like a housewife checking out a door-to-door salesman.

"Please tell Swamiji that Ram is here," I said, zapping her with a bolt of love, which withered and died the minute it hit her aura. I could see her wheels turning, figuring out how to brush me off.

"Who is it?" said the Swami, hip to her game.

"Ram," she said dejectedly.

"Show him in."

One of the scriptures says something to the effect that a person who lies to his or her *guru* will spend a thousand lifetimes in a fiery hell. So far I had not put myself in that position and this was as close as I would come.

"Have problems with the customs, Ram?" he said glancing up from his work.

"Yes, Swamiji. It was my clothing. They thought I was a freak," I said, handing him the oxygen bottle.

"No law against clothing. What did they want?"

"They have profiles, Swamiji. Means if they don't like the way you look they can hassle you."

"What did they want?" he repeated.

"They were looking for dope."

"Well, it's good you did not have any," he said in such a way I thought he knew. Perhaps guilt was making me project.

"They were disappointed. They actually made me strip. Did they give you any problems?" I said, moving the conversation on.

"It's not my *karma*," he said enigmatically, turning back to his work and motioning me to sit.

I couldn't tell what he was thinking. The way he said, "It's not my *karma*," made me think the statement had meaning other than the obvious. He was a master of the double entendre. I remember once after a lecture in America a small Indian *guru* came up to pay his respects, accompanied by four luscious young devotees. He introduced himself, and motioning toward the women in an attempt to impress the Swami, said, "And these are my devotees, Swamiji."

"What else?" the Swami replied inscrutably.

Perhaps I was just a bit paranoid, but it didn't matter, because that was the end of it. I took a seat on the sofa and began telling the beads, The Blissful Mother breathing fire nearby. After a few minutes I settled in and put my bare feet on the edge of the coffee table, decidedly an impolitic gesture.

"Take them off," she said with vehemence. "Who do you think you are?"

I looked at her disinterestedly and let them linger a couple of seconds too long, causing her to unleash a volley of verbal abuse that would have done a fishwife proud.

"Why don't you say something!" she said when it was clear I was not rising to the bait.

"What's to say?" I replied. "You obviously have it in for me. I won't be drawn into an argument, but if you want my opinion, I think you're not angry for the reason you think you are."

The Swami perked up.

"And what might that be?" she said with contempt.

"I don't know for sure, but it can't have anything to do with me. You don't even know me."

"I do not have to know you to know that you have bad manners," she shot back.

"That's a matter of opinion," I replied. "I just have the sense that such a small breach of etiquette should not evoke such anger. My feeling is that you're angry because you can't keep the Swami all to yourself."

I'd evidently hit the nail on the head because she turned and stormed out in a fury.

The Swami burst out laughing, and looking affectionately at me, said, "Very good, Ram. Never come down."

A Different Kind of Bliss

According to legend, the Buddha, like many illumined souls, struggled valiantly with a temptress called Mara, whom he defeated just before attaining enlightenment. I made it past the dope demon by the grace of God, but one more lesson, full of ironies, awaited. My Mara was a thirty-something woman named Marla, who had shown a decidedly unspiritual interest in me during the first Hawaii *yagna*.

This time around I had just taken my seat during the evening talk when she appeared, looking like a film star and pointedly took a seat next to mine.

"How are you, Ram?" she said, her voice full of love as she took my hand. "It's so good to see you."

"Very good, Marla," I replied, barely able to conceal my agitation.

"You're still with the Swami," she said, stating the obvious.

"Can't get enough," I replied. "I'm not leaving till I get *moksa*."

"You seem pretty liberated to me," she said, stroking the back of my hand affectionately.

"Yes, it's been fantastic, India with Swamiji," I replied. "But there's more."

"I'd love to hear about your trip," she said.

"Well, yes. Why not?"

"Perhaps we could meet after the lecture," she said.

"There's *satsang* at the hotel," I replied.

"My, you are dedicated. I like that. How about tomorrow?"

"About the only free time I have is in the afternoon."

"Let's have lunch."

We met for lunch at the Royal Hawaiian and sat outside under an umbrella on the veranda, overlooking the beach, enjoying a fine lunch. I told her of my spiritual experiences, hoping she would realize I was not in the market, but my spirituality seemed to turn her on even more.

"That's incredible," she said when finished. "And the way you tell it makes it come alive. Come on, let's take a walk."

Grabbing my hand, she pulled me onto the beach. She was an attractive woman, several years older, well-dressed and obviously rich. I wish I could report that my mind remained fixed at the feet of the Lord, but it immediately began contemplating a different kind of bliss. We walked down the beach arm in arm, making small talk, flirting.

"I've got to go now," I said after we'd walked to Diamond Head and back. "The Swami will be finished with his nap and *satsang* will start in a few minutes."

"Skip it today, Ram," she cajoled. "Come over to my place for a cup of coffee. There's much more I want to know about you."

A totally different path opened up. I had to be clear. "Sorry, Marla. I'd love to, but I can't miss *satsang*. The Swami will be expecting me."

"Expecting you?" she said doubtfully. "I wouldn't think he would expect anybody."

"Well, you're right on one level," I replied. "But he has very traditional views. If I missed even a single event he'd ask what I'm doing. I don't want to have to tell him I'd been having coffee with a beautiful woman during *satsang*. It wouldn't go down too well."

"You've got to be kidding," she said, her voice full of disappointment. "What is he, your father?"

"Not exactly, Marla. But there's more going on here than lectures. He's a great *mahatma* and I'm his disciple. I have to do what he wants."

"That sounds pretty weird," she said.

"Don't get me wrong," I replied. "I want to do what he wants. I'm no dummy, Marla. I know what I want and I need him. And he wants for me what I want, so it's not like I'm just there out of duty or idle curiosity. He's done a lot for me. I wouldn't be where I am today without him. I can't disappoint him. He's taken me where I could never go on my own. There are certain rules that I have to follow or the whole thing goes down the drain."

"What whole thing?" she said.

"My *moksa*, the relationship with the Swami."

"You're incredible," she said.

"Why?"

"You really believe this liberation stuff!"

"I don't believe it, Marla. I know it. I've tasted it. I have it most of the time. There are just a few small doubts in the way. Why shouldn't I believe it?"

"You're incredible," she said, unable to conceal her irritation. "You're very grandiose. You actually think you can get what the Swami has. How can you even compare yourself to him!"

"The Swami was just a regular guy when he was my age, Marla. He didn't become like that overnight. He's worked hard on himself for over twenty-five years. It is possible. I know it. And I'm well on the way. I have to do it right. I'd be glad to meet you in the afternoons, but I cannot miss anything."

"I have to say I admire your spirit," she replied, the love returning to her voice. "Can I drop you off at the hotel?"

"I have to stop by my room and pick up my *Gita* for tonight," I replied.

"Never mind, I'll take you."

Not one to be denied, Marla realized I was vulnerable. Perhaps she liked a challenge. As soon as I took my seat for the evening talk she appeared and sat down. The Swami was sharp as a tack, not the innocent type, and would notice a pattern and draw conclusions. I did not want him getting ideas.

"Fancy meeting you here," she said in a sexy voice.

"Hi, Marla. How's it going?"

"Great! Absolutely great. I cannot say how much I enjoy sitting with you. You've got great energy," she said caressing the back of my hand, causing panic.

"Thanks for the compliment."

"Oh, it's not a compliment, Ram. It's the truth. You do have great energy," she replied, giving my ego the kind of strokes it loved.

"By the way," she continued. "What are you doing after the lecture?"

"The *satsang* as usual," I said.

"Oh," she said, "I just talked to Ma and she said the Swami needed rest and wouldn't be giving *satsang* tonight. He'll take his meal and sleep early. Why don't you come over and tell me more about your India trip? I'm thinking of going."

"Let's see how I feel after the talk," I said removing my hand. "Right now it's time for my meditation," I lied, since I was already in meditation.

When we stepped into the warm tropical evening she took my arm and suggested a walk on the beach. Too overwhelmed to resist, I agreed. Caught with the dope, I would have been taken into custody and I would have had the sense never to show my face again. But this was different. If I slept with her the word was bound to get out and I would be ruined. And things were progressing to the point where if I did not sleep with her she might spitefully tell The Blissful Mother I had, handing her a tailor-made opportunity for revenge. I felt trapped. And disappointed that I was not as far beyond my sexuality as I thought.

Suddenly I longed to be back in India, the land that gave birth to the *Kama Sutra*, where ironically temptation had not been a problem. A woman would never make her feelings known to a man outside marriage. And the Swami's views on sexuality were decidedly unsuited to the have-your-cake-and-eat-it-too philosophy. He was treating me like a man, master of my senses. To his mind God was God and sex was sex, a "stinking cesspool of sensuality." But I was in the prime of life and back in America, where the sexual revolution was in full swing, and in the attractive position as the disciple of a spiritual master.

I managed to keep her at bay with inspired talk on higher subjects for the rest of the evening, but when we parted she kissed me with such passion my body was shaking like a leaf in the breeze as I climbed the stairs to my room.

If I had loved my teacher as much as I loved myself I would not have given Marla the time of day. Not that I shared his rather primitive but understandable views on sex, but because sex was not in my contract. And secondly, the attraction had nothing to do with real love. In his heart of hearts I do not think the Swami gave a damn one way or the other either, but he was a spiritual master, a public figure, a conservative Hindu who lived an impeccably moral life, and anything I did reflected back on him, so I should not have even considered it.

The verse for the morning class came from an ancient text entitled *Narada Bhakti Sutra*, which loosely translates as "A Train of Thought on Divine Love." The text distinguishes between the love of God and the love of a paramour. Even in my confused state, the irony was hard to miss. Afterwards, struggling with my lust, I went for a walk along the beach. True to form, the ego childishly tried to convince me I could give Marla what she wanted without suffering any untoward consequences.

I turned off the beach, and for old time's sake, entered the International Market Place, which was just opening for business. The lovely, cool morning with the sun slanting through the palms, illumining the drops of rain that still clung to the flat green leaves of the tropical plants, reminded me of the morning the Lord had broken through my misery and taken over my life in front of the post office, a scant two blocks away.

About twenty yards ahead I noticed a young woman coming in my direction. As she approached I could feel the sexual energy concentrate itself to such a degree that I thought I might have an orgasm. Then suddenly, when she was about fifteen feet away, it moved up the spine and became finer and finer until it came to rest in the brow *chakra*, where it transformed into a powerful radiant light and lingered for a split second. Then just as we were about to pass, my mind tuned to her mind and the light, like a laser, pierced her brow *chakra*. She immediately broke out in a radiant smile and ran up to me gasping, "You! You! You did this!"

"I didn't do it," I replied. "It just happened."

"But it came from you. I could feel it. My God, what's happening to me?" she said, caught up in a wonderful inner experience! "Who are you? Who are you! What's going on?"

I invited her to sit on a nearby bench.

"This is wonderful," she said. "Fantastic. What is it?"

"The experience of the inner self," I replied.

"The inner self?"

"Yes, just like you have an outer self, a body and mind, you have an inner, spiritual self."

"This is unbelievable, absolutely unbelievable. I've never felt so good."

"We call it bliss, the joy of the self," I replied.

"We? What religion are you?"

"No religion. I'm the disciple of an Indian *swami* and follow the path of self-knowledge."

"But how did you do it?" she asked.

"I didn't do anything. It was as much a surprise to me as it was to you. I was just walking along, thinking about things, when I felt this strong energy rise up and concentrate itself. Before I could even understand what was happening it was passing into you. It was entirely the will of God."

"God? I don't believe in God," she replied.

"It doesn't matter. God believes in you. He wanted you to experience Him."

"Are you crazy? Nobody experiences God. It's just a belief some people have."

"It doesn't really matter what you call it," I said. "Perhaps 'God' is not the best word. We call it the self. It's a kind of dynamic, formless spiritual energy. I wouldn't have believed it either, but it has happened to me too many times to doubt it."

"Your *guru*?" she said doubtfully.

"Yes. When the inner self is awakened many strange things happen, things that can cause a lot of confusion. So it's good to be around someone who knows about the inner world, who can help you to sort out what's going on, a guide."

"I think you must be my *guru*," she said.

"No," I replied. "I'm not a *guru*. I still have a lot to learn. This kind of thing happens when the mind gets concentrated. It is not something I control. I'm just a student."

"So where is your *guru*? Maybe I could see him."

I told her about the talks, hugged her and continued on my walk full of wonder. It was not until late afternoon that I thought about Marla. The lust was completely gone.

The evening class consisted of a lecture by the Swami on the following verses from the *Gita*: "When the mind dwells on the objects of sense, attachment arises. From attachment comes desire, which leads to anger. Anger engenders confusion, which results in loss of memory. Loss of memory destroys the intelligence and the soul perishes. But the one who maintains discipline, moving among the sense objects with the senses free of attraction and repulsion and under control of the self, attains the highest state."

When the talk was over, Karen, the woman from the market, came up and said, "I don't know what's happening, but it sure is wonderful. It's still going on. Do you think I could talk with the Swami?"

"There's a small meeting tonight after the talk. I'll take you along. People can ask questions."

"I don't know how to thank you," she said with real feeling.

"Don't thank me. Thank the Lord."

As we walked out Marla came up, dressed to the nines, looking positively edible.

"This is Karen," I said. "We're going to the *satsang*. Would you like to come?"

"No thanks, Ram," she said with obvious disappointment. "I had hoped we could go for a walk."

"How about lunch tomorrow at the Royal Hawaiian?" I said.

"Yes, that's good," she replied perking up. "At noon?"

"Noon's fine. See you then."

"Who's that?" said Karen with interest.

"A lady who has the hots for me," I replied. "I have to give her the brush-off, but I hate to hurt people's feelings. I'll take care of it tomorrow."

"So being a disciple means you have your fill of gorgeous women," she said.

"I need gorgeous women like I need a hole in the head. I'm no saint."

Karen's interest transferred to the Swami during the *satsang*, and I breathed easier.

The next day as we sipped coffee after lunch, Marla said, "You know, Ram, I think I owe you an apology."

"What for?" I replied with surprise.

"For not appreciating how into your spirituality you are. I've never met anyone so focused."

"I can't be that focused, Marla," I replied. "Until yesterday I really had it bad for you."

"You did? I couldn't tell. It's hard to know just where you're at. Why until yesterday?"

"The night before last I put it in the hands of the Lord and yesterday the weight lifted off."

"The weight?" she asked.

"The conflict between my spiritual path and the love of a woman."

"Does there have to be conflict?" she replied.

"On some level, I suppose not. But I'm at the place where I have to make certain I have enough self-love to last forever. I can't be trying to get it from the outside, from someone else. When I'm one hundred percent sure that I am love, that it can never leave, I'll be able to love someone else purely."

"I don't like what I'm hearing," she said with emotion, "but I appreciate your honesty. I have it bad for you too, but you're right. It will never work. We're not even close to the same place. I like the spiritual idea, but I'm not ready to live it like you and the Swami. I still have my desires. I hope you get what you want."

From that point on I didn't look twice at a woman until I got what I wanted.

Breathless

After the San Francisco *yagna*, which was like a homecoming, I visited my parents just to reassure them I had not "gone off the deep end," as Mother expressed it. The Swami did not bat an eye when I informed him I was leaving; he just glanced up from his writing for a second.

She did think I had gone off the deep end but loved me anyway. I had been a problem for her all my life. I tried to get her interested in a spiritual path but she was not having any.

"I am not dissatisfied with who I am and my life, James. This spiritual business is all well and good, but the Lord doesn't bring home the bacon."

Ever one to have the last word, I replied, "The Lord is the bacon, Mom."

On another occasion she nearly broke into tears when she found me in the TV room in a *dhoti* with a sandalwood-paste third eye, sitting in meditation pose, chanting a Sanskrit *mantra*.

"I don't get it, James. What's wrong with your own religion?" This from a woman who claimed she had serious doubts about the divinity of Christ.

I could understand her views. Having failed at everything important in her eyes, I had committed the ultimate rebellion, transforming from a WASP – a white, Anglo-Saxon Protestant – into a WASH – a white, Anglo-Saxon Hindu. I would have to wait twelve long years for understanding, when, a few months before her death, she said, "Perhaps I was wrong, expecting what I did from you. I realize now that everyone has to find his own way. I think you've done a good job getting yourself together, James."

Dad, always a decent guy, who loved me no matter what, thought I should be worrying about my future, but did not nag me like Mom. And when the time to leave came he slipped me a couple of hundred on the sly.

Because I was forced to rely completely on the self, the separation from the Swami strengthened my meditation. During this visit I found myself in the state of *nirvikalpa samadhi* often.

Vedic culture has systematically identified and catalogued all states of consciousness. *Samadhi* is a term describing a state of mind in which all experienced objects have equal value. A quaint example from scripture says that a person in *samadhi* sees no difference between a lump of gold and the excreta of a crow.

Samadhi is classified as *savikalpa* and *nirvikalpa*. *Savi* means "with," and *vikalpa* roughly means "mental activity," i.e. thought or feeling. So *savikalpa samadhi* is a state of meditation in which mental activity is witnessed from the self's platform, as if one were the sun shining down on a turbulent ocean. Self-realized souls see everything equally and treat everything and everyone the same.

Nir means "without." So *nirvikalpa samadhi* is a state where the mind has stopped putting out thought and merged into the self, like an ocean without waves. In this state the outside world and the mind are not experienced, so there is nothing to treat equally to anything else. Because language is dualistic, this non-dual state cannot be described. The experience reported in the last chapter, when I found myself living without breathing, is the best I can do to describe it.

By this time I was in *savikalpa samadhi*, which is the only *samadhi* suitable for self-realization, ninety-five percent of the time. Only on rare occasions would I get identified with the mind for a few hours. But the intense *sadhana* I had been doing had burned out some unconscious tendencies, which in turn opened up a bit of space and took a little pressure off the mind so that occasionally it just dissolved into its source, awareness.

Sometime in the 1950s a *yogi* came to a small village in eastern India, had a hut constructed, went in and sat down. Twenty-five years later he had not moved, eaten or slept, the only observable change being the length of his hair and nails. After he had been sitting for ten years, another *yogi* appeared and took up a seat nearby. As time passed their fame spread and they became known as the Brother Yogis, attained the status of gods and became objects of worship. Eventually declared national treasures, they were kept under lock and key, and once a year on Shiva's birthday a government official unlocked the door, permitting pilgrims, who come in the thousands from all over India, to file respectfully past for their *darshan*.

Not that I was at that stage or even wanted to be, but life with Mom and Pop made this *samadhi* possible because, except for dishes, there was nothing to do. I would drive out to the rolling hills on the edge of town where I used to roam with my dog as a child, sit on a rock and disappear.

Meditation

The Swami actually did a double-take when he entered the lecture hall and found me sitting in my usual place. I could see he was tickled pink that I had shown up for the last dance.

"Ram, Ram," he said with great affection. "You're here!"

When Buddha attained enlightenment they say flowers showered from heaven. I think this means that since the universe is a temporarily self-forgetful extension of the self in time and space, it becomes happy when some small part, a human being, crosses the threshold and remembers who it is. Maybe a better way to put it is to say that as you approach the center of existence you start to vibrate with the vibration of the whole cosmos, like a tuning fork. Up until this moment, with a few duly noted exceptions, a sense of watching things, witnessing them from a hidden dimension, had characterized my experience, but when I arrived in India the third time, that fine spiritual sense of separation began to dissolve and an oceanic feeling of identity with everyone and everything arose.

Several weeks after my arrival, the Swami called me to his room. He sat on the edge of his bed, and I stood in front of him in the manner of a devotee. The room was suffused with light, and time stopped. I could hear my heart beat and see each and every thought with crystalline clarity as it arose and subsided in the mind. A crow lit on a nearby branch, made a few desultory squawks and peered intently into the room. The Swami sat in silence for a long time as the sun dropped behind the mango trees and the heat of the day began to dissipate. I noticed how tired and old he was, how frail and delicate, bound to life by the thinnest thread. I understood his heroism, willingly crucifying himself day in and day out on the cross of the world's ignorance. I felt a great wave of tenderness, followed by the thought that I had to finish my *sadhana* before he died. I loved these moments more than anything: just the two of us, totally self-aware, totally one, participating in an ageless ritual, the passing of the torch.

He looked up and said, "I want you to meditate."

"Swamiji?" I said, completely surprised. "I've been in meditation since we met, give or take a few days here and there."

"That's true, Ram, but that's been my glory," he said without a trace of egoism. "You've figured out how to tune in, but now I want you to find this state on your own, using the knowledge you've been given. These states you've been experiencing have just happened. It is important to know exactly how to get there, not just for you, but so you can show others."

I nodded.

He continued. "I won't always be around. You cannot rely on your relationship with me. Access to the self should not be dependent on the *guru*. You have to find it yourself."

I nodded. "The way I understand it, Swamiji, is that I'll just stay in this state until my tendencies burn out and then there won't be any need to get here ever again. I often sit and meditate."

"That's not meditation," he said, "but just a small calming of the mind. You have to go beyond the mind altogether. You have to evolve your own *yoga*."

The discussion was over. He looked up, his eyes brimming with love. I realized I had known him in many births and that this was nearly the last time we would meet.

"You can go now, Ram," he said, dismissing me so I would not see his feelings.

***

A bit confused, I returned to my room to think. The Swami was a Vedantin, not a meditation master. A day later, during an informal *satsang*, a newcomer, overwhelmed by the powerful meditation, asked, "What is your meditation technique, Swamiji?"

Surprised and amused, the Swami said, "Technique? I have no technique. I am the technique," an idea totally consistent with Vedanta, where meditation is the result of self-knowledge. Now he was talking *yoga*, self-knowledge through meditation. It seemed odd.

But he was right. I was not a master of my mind. I had never tried to reach the self with a meditation technique, unless you call love of God a technique. Until this moment I simply accepted my meditation as the grace of God. Since the initiation in the shower at Redwood City, things had happened so effortlessly I just went along with them, assuming that in the fullness of time all would be revealed. Evidently the fullness of time was now. His instructions of course were completely in keeping with his teaching in another sense: spirituality was a science, one performed experiments to achieve certain results. Meditation was the next experiment.

"Meditation," he said the following afternoon, looking squarely at me, "depends on knowledge. It is true you can just follow a technique and things will happen, but without the knowledge of the self, how can you know what the final state is? Many people get peace or bliss from calming the mind and assume that is all there is to meditation. So they stop short of the final goal. The *Upanishad* gives a very clear definition of what we are seeking. If you come upon an inner experience or state you can check it against your knowledge. In this way you discriminate the mind from the self. Meditation practice is only a temporary situation, a technique that shows you the self. Once you have experienced It and identified it as yourself, what need is there to meditate? Meditation is your nature."

I knew all that, but got what I was looking for in the idea that followed.

"All techniques have common elements because the body-mind-ego complex is universal. All involve working with the breath, synchronizing it with the mind, withdrawal of attention from the material sheaths, concentration on the self and so on. Though there are many techniques, the seeker has to be ready to experiment on his own. He should work with the breath and the mind based on the idea that where the flow of thought has ended the mind merges into its source, the self."

The hints were useful. The first time I tried, the next day after the morning class, the doorway to the self opened. I felt empowered because I understood that I was no longer tied to an outer path. I had no intention of abandoning our relationship or the Vedanta, because something in me knew that there was something beyond meditation, something that needed to come through the *guru*. And by this time I loved him so much I would have been willing to hang around forever, enjoying his presence. Nonetheless, I was overjoyed that I had successfully used my own knowledge of the body and mind to attain transcendence.

"What is the point of practicing all your life?" the Swami often said. "Religion can become as confining as worldly life. Once upon a time a man came upon a lion that had stepped on a thorn and was suffering immensely. He took compassion, offered to remove the thorn, and the lion agreed.

"'One thing I neglected to tell you,' said the man. 'This is going to hurt.'

"'Never mind,' said the lion, 'if I cannot walk I'll die.'

"The man took another sharp thorn, pushed it into the wound and popped out the first, much to the relief of the lion.

"So what did he do with the second thorn? He threw it away. Similarly, religion removes the thorn of worldly suffering. Then you are free to live. What use is it once you know who you are?"

I was now so close to what I was seeking I could almost taste it. It was not a knowledge that could be imparted verbally or understood intellectually. I had enough self-experience to know what It was. In fact my soul was humbly and expectantly standing before the Lord just as I stood in front of the Swami when he gave instructions.

That I saw the self more or less constantly and experienced its unalloyed mercy was not enough, however. One essential bit of information was missing. Meditation was an exciting, playful sport. As I probed deeper into the causal layers of the mind I came upon extraordinary *lokas*, fields of experience where the seeds of the soul's destiny lay dormant, ready to sprout when activated by *karma* – worlds of indescribable beauty on the one hand, the realm of the gods, and worlds of damnation and torment on the other, the hell realms.

During one session I re-revisited *siddha loka*, where I had experienced Ramakrishna, a plane peopled with the subtle forms of realized souls, many of whom I had met in past lives. A feeling of gratitude arose when I realized that without them I would never have come to this point in my evolution.

On another occasion I entered a hellish, protean, elemental world irradiated by a strange arc light and populated by shadowy souls emitting bizarre, tortured sounds. These beings, endowed with long, stringy plasmic bodies, sped about in torment, seeking release from their scorching, narrow universe.

The more I observed the mind, the more I became aware of the observer, the self. And invariably a merger would take place, a subtle "click" as I passed out of time and space into the timeless, spaceless reality and began witnessing as the self.

I learned how to stop the mind by turning my attention away from it and putting it in the self. A verse in scripture, "When pure awareness blends with a thought in the intellect, the experience of knowing is produced," confirmed what was happening. When I withdrew my awareness from the mind it died, leaving only pure awareness, the self, shining in great splendor. Returning attention to the mind caused the world to appear like a movie on a screen!

Mind control brought cornucopias of bliss, ecstasy so powerful I would lie for hours without moving. Life, the *guru* and my quest suddenly became supremely uninteresting and I found attending class difficult. Playing hooky, however, was unthinkable. Though he called himself a "modern" *swami*, Chinmaya was about as modern as Moses. Except for the brief family visit, I had not missed a single class, *satsang* or official function of any kind. He soldiered on. Therefore I soldiered on.

One night during an outdoor lecture in Bombay at the oval near Churchgate Station, attended by thousands, he was unable to come up with a quote to illustrate the meaning of a verse and appealed to the audience for the answer, but no one seemed to know. Though I knew, I was sitting too far away for him to hear. He shrugged it off and went on.

The next morning, I was simply too exhausted to get out of bed and missed my first meditation. Prepared for a taste of the lash, I wandered over to his hut where he was giving *darshan*. When I came in he stopped everything, looked at me with a baleful eye and inquired of my whereabouts.

"Remember the quote you were looking for last night in Bombay, Swami-ji?" I said.

"Yes, so what?" he said with obvious irritation.

"Well, it applies to my case," I said. "Do you want to hear it?"

"Okay, Ram. This better be good."

"It is, Swamiji."

The devotees shuffled because speaking with familiarity to the *guru* was a violation of custom.

"The spirit was willing but the flesh was weak," I said.

He burst out laughing. "Very good, Ram!" he said heartily. "You're forgiven."

Doormat *Sadhana*

One afternoon, during siesta, in a terribly exalted state of God-consciousness, I was walking around the gardens telling the beads. The sun was extremely hot, so I decided to go to a refreshment stand in the park next to the *ashram* for a cold drink. The grounds were deserted – "only mad dogs and Englishmen go out in the noonday sun" – so I made my way down the path to the park where I sat in the shade sipping a Limca, a carcinogenic version of lime soda. I returned about fifteen minutes later, apparently unobserved.

The next day, Sunday, during *satsang* in the temple, which was large enough to accommodate the weekend crowd from Bombay, a man asked for an explanation of the concept of ego.

"Ego is the need to be different, to think you're special," said the Swami, looking pointedly at me. Suddenly I felt the sinking sensation that accompanies the knowledge that you are about to be royally exposed, vainly hoping he would not humiliate me in front of the crowd. I had tasted the lash before and took it like a man, but this attack was notable for its ferocity. And to this day, though there was truth in it, I do not think it was fair. There was something personal in it, something that signaled a change.

I was not unaware of my ego and its arrogant tendencies. I would have suffered almost anything to rid myself of it once and for all, but that is not how it is. Ego is a superimposition on the self, a false personality built up over lifetimes, a carefully constructed edifice of fear and desire designed to protect oneself from the aggressions and cruelties of the world. No spiritual dynamite can reduce it to rubble in a matter of seconds. And if it is reduced to rubble, it miraculously reconstitutes itself. Unlike an atrophied limb, it cannot be surgically removed but has to be patiently dismantled thought by thought over a long time.

"Ram thinks he's special," he said with great scorn as two hundred fifty heads turned in my direction. "He thinks he's beyond the rules. He's convinced he's not a human being. He dresses up like a *yogi* and prances off in the middle of the afternoon to the tea shop with his *mala* conspicuously twirling. He wants the world to know he's spiritual."

In fact I was just thirsty and certain no one was about. He paused to let it sink in. I sat still, completely detached, listening carefully, discounting his anger.

"Just who do you think you are?" he said rhetorically with scathing contempt. "You think you're God's gift to the human race. You believe there has never been anyone as wonderful as you. Your idea is that the world should beat a path to your feet and worship you! What nonsense! Spirituality's not about building ego, it's about destroying ego. You were a big sinner and now you fancy yourself as a saint and you want the world to recognize you."

He paused to let it sink in and continued, "You're nobody. You're nothing. You know how you should be thinking? You should think that you're a doormat! A doormat! Do you hear?" He was shouting at the top of his voice.

"You should let the world walk over you every minute of the day, wipe its feet on you, grind you into the dirt. This is not spirituality. You think you're so clever, so wonderful, but you're wrong. You're nothing but a doormat, do you understand! A doormat!"

I nodded.

The storm abated and he continued talking in a calm voice.

I should have been devastated but, oddly, I felt quite good. Not, I think, because his point was well-taken, which it was more or less, or because the barrage of energy lifted me higher, which it did, but because I realized he was projecting, sharing his personal solution to the ego problem. He had a similar kind of ego and kept it in check by serving the world – doormat *sadhana*, if you will. It was a good lesson.

But it was the beginning of the end of our relationship and my spiritual quest. The change was inevitable because I had learned the fundamentals of self-inquiry, so I did not need to be there anymore. Secondly, there was no danger that I would ever go back to the old way of life. And finally, I think he felt uncomfortable that I was getting to know him a little too well on the relative plane.

I do not say this because I fancy myself a profoundly insightful person, but simply because I was probably the only non-attached person who consistently observed him every day in every situation from dawn till dusk. Most saw him in tightly regimented public situations, the classes or the *satsangs*, or in short interviews. In addition, the Indian *guru*-disciple relationship is practiced across a wide gulf of respect, superstition, fear and need. The *guru* is a kind of absolute monarch, always partly concealed in a cloud of mystery. So you are never dealing with a real person. He was, by his own admission, "an institution." This is not to say that there was not a real person there, but that that person was faithfully serving the teaching tradition and could not afford to be a normal person. It would have been too confusing. So some things that he probably needed to look at were not getting looked at because of his position. It is always the case when you are so involved in the world.

I was not looking for weaknesses or inconsistencies, but my mind was open, so I saw everything. I am not suggesting he had anything to conceal. He was not an uncultured, small-minded *guru* chasing power, wealth, fame or pleasure. He was a very classy, dignified guy. But, odd as it sounds, I think the intense awareness I focused on him brought up things he was ill-prepared to deal with.

One day, a month or so before the end, I was sitting in class in an extraordinary state. The body was automatically assuming complex yogic postures, the mind was so radiant with consciousness it was subtly affecting the other students. Gradually, in response to the energy, the students in my vicinity moved away until there was a noticeable ring of empty space around me. I think they must have unconsciously felt someone was spying on them. Such is the power of consciousness. I came out of my absorption for a minute and noticed that the Swami was looking at me in an unkind way, as if I had consciously done something to mess with the classroom energy, about which he was very possessive. At the same time I had the sense that he was drawn to me (perhaps momentarily envious?). Whatever it was, I understood that I did not belong there anymore; I was simply becoming too powerful.

I say "momentarily envious" because I think seeing me like that, more a god than a human being, must have called attention to the negative side of his own situation. His *karma* as a famous, jet-setting *mahatma* put such heavy demands on his mind that it often pulled him down, making him cranky and irritable, sometimes downright unpleasant. His body was not well and required a good deal of mental energy to sustain, energy he probably should have invested elsewhere. My body was young and strong, an asset, not a liability. He was an upper-caste Hindu born around the turn of the last century in a terribly conservative culture, who followed *sannyasi dharma*, the rules of renunciation, strictly.

I was free to do what I wanted, as if I were a ghost, transparent and unreal, unaffected by physical reality. I did not have to lift a finger and I spoke infrequently. I could fly and soar in the transcendental sky, dissolve into the emptiness and experiment all day long as I saw fit. While he squandered his capital at an alarming rate helping others, I husbanded mine, selfishly investing it in pure meditation. And finally, he had to live with the knowledge that he was nearing the end of his incarnation, whereas I was being reborn into a brand new life.

Maybe my speculations are off the mark, but my perception was accurate; our relationship was starting to become all too human. No doubt I was fulfilling him in a very deep way, but I was also starting to be a problem. Yet when the time came to deliver the coup de grâce, he played his part with consummate class, like the truly great man he was.

A Dip in the Ganges

After lunch one day I sat on my bunk and fell effortlessly into deep meditation. By this time the unconscious had been so heavily programmed by meditation impressions it was only a matter of minutes, sometimes seconds, before I achieved transcendence. I experienced all the usual effects: deep peace, radiant light, intense bliss, loss of self. The body, which had been purified by two years of austerities, was more spirit than flesh.

The *chakras* appeared, vibrating in inner space. Many believe the *chakras* are situated in the physical, but the physical body actually exists in the subtle body, which is made of subtle matter, *chitta*, and the *chakras* are vortices, energy centers, in the *chitta*. Suddenly, without warning, a powerful force, which I would later realize was the subtle body of a *yogi*, broke into my consciousness through the root *chakra*, awakening an overwhelming feeling of desire, illumining the meditation with redness. In a fraction of a second his consciousness pierced the root *chakra* and entered the Heart, lingering for a few seconds as if gathering momentum. A golden color accompanied by an unbelievable feeling of love flooded my consciousness. The energy continued its ascent, piercing the throat and brow *chakras*, and dissolving into white light as it passed out of the subtle body and into the thousand-petaled lotus, known as the *sahasrar*, the self. At this point consciousness of inner and outer disappeared, and only pure consciousness, me, remained.

By this time the experience of the self did not evoke great wonder as it once had. It was a natural, familiar state. But the piercing of the *chakras* was truly extraordinary, a *kundalini* experience with a twist. Instead of an impersonal kinetic force at the base of the spine as the texts portray it, in my case it was the subtle body of a Himalayan *yogi*. Who could it be? Two strong clues puzzled me for days. My body gave off the unmistakable stink of tobacco for days and the mind was permeated with an image of the Ganges and the Himalayan foot-hills.

A couple of weeks later we set off on a trip to Swami's *ashram* in Uttar-kashi, one of the holiest spots in India, high in the Himalayas. Since the region was off-limits to foreigners, I was to accompany him as far as Rishikesh. We flew to Delhi, stayed a week while he blessed the eager devotees, and left by car for Haridwar.

Because India's handmade roads are jammed with every imaginable mov-ing object, the ride from Delhi to the Ganges, about one hundred fifty miles, takes six bone-crunching hours. To beat the traffic and knock a couple of hours off the total, the trip should begin by three or four a.m.

Observed by a couple of ravens sitting idly on a nearby branch, I joined the group of devotees shivering in the cold, hazy morning, the silence of our meditation punctuated by the sounds of the waking city. The Swami came out wrapped in a shawl, looking very severe, a wondrous golden aura surrounding his elegant form. The devotees approached and took the dust of his lotus feet with great feeling. He waited patiently as they finished the ritual, occasion-ally touching a bent back and uttering, "Narayana, Narayana," in a deep, other-worldly way, each repetition bringing sweet ecstasies to the mind. When they had finished they formed a circle around him, their clasped hands pointing heavenward like cathedral spires. He stepped forward and the circle broke to let him pass. I opened the car door, he seemed to float in, and we drove off down the deserted streets in silence.

After a couple of hours, during which not more than half a dozen words were spoken, we pulled up at a roadside tea stall somewhere in the flat fertile farmlands to the north. Everyone but the Swami got out and ordered breakfast. He sent me for *chai* on the sly because the devotees had been instructed by the doctors not to accede to his requests. I sneaked it back and he sipped it with relish. A disgusting, sweet, excessively boiled concoction, *chai* is as much a part of India as the great god Shiva.

Within minutes people started showing up and before he could finish his tea we were surrounded by onlookers. As we were about to leave a peasant woman came rushing up holding her baby high over the crowd to give him *darshan* of the Swami.

Haridwar is often called the Benaras of the north and is mentioned in the notes of a Chinese traveler over two thousand years ago. It is situated at the spot where the Himalayan foothills give way to the vast Gangetic plain. Looking upriver from the *ghats,* one has the sense that a profound mystery begins here. A trek upstream would eventually lead to Mount Kailash, the source of the Ganges and the abode of the ascetic god Shiva, from whose matted locks the Ganges cascades.

It is not a large city by Indian standards; one could easily walk from end to end in thirty minutes. In addition to a noisy, dusty, chaotic main street, hundreds of small shops served by a maze of narrow alleys cluster next to the river. Many sell religious items: statues and pictures of the gods and goddesses, incense, *kumkum* (brightly colored powder for the third eye decoration), sacred ash, yogic paraphernalia and spiritual books. These are interspersed with yogurt shops sporting huge iron woks with piping hot milk cooking slowly over gas fires, fly- and bee-infested sweet stalls purveying an unholy array of sugar products (diabetes is one of India's most serious health problems), *dharmshalas* (cheap accommodation for pilgrims), music shops, restaurants, small shrines, bangle and *sari* shops. The narrow lanes teem with colorfully attired Punjabis, Rajasthanis, Gujaratis, Bengalis and Western-dressed, middle-class office types from Delhi, who compete with dogs, cows, goats, monkeys and beggars for precious space as they wend their way toward the *ghats.*

Emerging from the warren of streets, there is an old temple on top of the last small Himalayan foothill on the left and the Hari Ki Pyari (Light of the Lord) *ghat,* the city's claim to fame and one of the holiest spots in India, on the right.

According to legend, a long time ago the gods learned of a chalice of nectar, symbol of the self, sitting on the bottom of a deep ocean, the mind. The one who retrieves this chalice and drinks its contents attains immortality. The gods tried to find the chalice but were unsuccessful. Dejected, they went to Vishnu, the omniscient, all-pervading Supreme Being, and told him of their desire. Moved by compassion, Vishnu agreed to help.

"Churn the ocean until the chalice comes to the surface," he said.

"Churn the ocean? It cannot be done," they said.

"Sorry," said the Lord, "it's the only way. Think about it. Maybe you will come up with something."

In those days mountains had wings and flew around doing what mountains do when they have time on their hands. Indra, king of the gods, saw a holy mountain flying around and had an idea. "Hey," he called, "Mount Mandara, please come down here. We want to talk with you."

The mountain, always eager to chat with the king of the gods, flew over and landed nearby.

After explaining the situation, Indra said, "So you see, you would make a perfect churn. You could sit down in the middle of the ocean and enough of you would stick out so we could wrap a rope around your neck and pull. What do you say?" he said, pleased with his idea.

"Why not?" said the mountain affably. "As long as it does not take too long. I have things to do next week."

"No time at all," said Indra, who had no idea what time was because he lived in a timeless world. "We'll have you out of here as soon as we get the treasure. Not to worry."

The day was hot and Mandara had been flying around all morning, so the idea of cooling off in the ocean of milk seemed attractive. He flew out to the center and settled in.

"So far so good," said Indra. "Now we need a rope."

"There's no rope in heaven that long," said the gods in unison. "Not a chance. Forget it."

"I hate to admit it, but I think you're right," said Indra sitting down in despair.

Just then Vasuki, the cosmic serpent, slithered by and Indra was struck with another idea.

"Hey, Vasuki," said Indra, motioning him over. "I want to talk with you."

"Okay," said Vasuki, "what's up?"

Once Indra had explained the situation Vasuki agreed, swam out and wrapped himself around the top of the protruding mountain, his head resting on one shore and his tail on the other. One group of gods took the head, another the tail. They pulled and pulled, but nothing happened. Dejected, they approached Vishnu, who suggested enlisting the help of the demons, who were very strong – an idea they found distasteful but eventually accepted.

Indra instructed the demons to pull on the tail.

They felt insulted and refused. "You pull it," they said. "We want the head."

The gods did not want the tail either and a furious altercation broke out.

To resolve it Vishnu suggested flipping a coin. The gods got the head, so the demons unhappily agreed to pull on the tail.

After they churned enthusiastically for a long time, an emerald-green chalice, glowing with an ethereal light, arose from the depths to the cheers of the participants.

During the discussion about division of the spoils, the demons grabbed the chalice and ran off, the gods in hot pursuit. Eventually, somewhere over India they caught up and grabbed the chalice, and in the ensuing struggle four drops of nectar fell to earth, landing on holy rivers at Haridwar, Nasik, Allahabad and Ujain.

These places are therefore considered to be extremely sacred, and in addition to serving as pilgrimage centers, host the Kumba Mela, a celebration of immense importance that attracts millions. Astrologers have calculated to the minute the moment when each drop landed at each spot, and it is believed that to bathe in the river at that time washes away all sins. Although carefully organized, occasionally at the most auspicious moment the crowds stampede into the river and many die. Death in these circumstances is considered fortunate, however, because it is thought to release the soul from bondage to the eternal wheel of birth and death. Because of this legend hundreds of temples and *ashrams* have sprung up in Hardiwar, and many *mahatmas* and *yogis* reside there, contributing to an already charged atmosphere.

Although I sat on a *ghat* on the Ganges and spoke with the USA on the cell phone two years ago, in those days there was no information superhighway. TV was non-existent, the phones barely worked, and the mails were notoriously slow, but the grapevine made the fiber optics of today seem Byzantine. So by mid-afternoon devotees started showing up like ants attracted to sugar.

About four the following afternoon, the Swami came to my room and said conspiratorially, "Come with me, Ram."

We quickly slipped out of the bungalow and got in the car after waking up the driver sleeping on the back seat. In ten minutes we were standing on the banks of the Ganges.

"We'll take our bath here," he said with great love.

I had never seen him outdoors, alone, away from the devotees. We were always in university lecture halls, hotel conference rooms, devotees' homes, jet planes or automobiles going to and fro, surrounded by hundreds of people. How absurd, almost comic, to see him standing alone on the banks of the river without all the spiritual hoopla, an ordinary human being, indistinguishable from the hundreds of thousands of *sadhus* wandering India. I touched his feet.

We undressed and stepped into the icy, swift river. I took the downstream side lest he lose his footing in the current. I would never be forgiven were he to drown, not, I think, that he would have minded. Tradition dictates that *mahatmas* be immersed in the Ganges when they die.

After the bath we sat in meditation, and being downwind of the Swami I caught the smell of his snuff. The *chakra*-piercing incident flashed back! So he was my secret benefactor! By some incredible *yoga* he had pierced my *chakras*, a kind of mystic initiation, setting me up for what was to come.

I suddenly saw his past, the years of struggle to find the self, his discipleship and release from the round of births and deaths. I realized what it must have meant for him to disregard his *guru's* advice and descend from the Himalayas into the madness of Indian life to bring self-knowledge to the people. And how could it be that I had successfully negotiated my way through such a chaotic and apparently misdirected life to sit on the banks of the Ganges with this South Indian man, who would shortly set me free? The full significance of what was happening hit me with the force of a ton of bricks as we sat in deep meditation, serenaded by the sounds of the river.

The meditation could have lasted forever, but was broken by the sound of a car. I looked downriver and spied a white Ambassador, packed with devotees, racing exuberantly up the road next to the river in a cloud of dust.

He looked at me with a weary face, rolled his eyes, shrugged his shoulders, his palms up in a gesture of resignation. "What to do? he said, smiling.

Letting Go

The next morning I was up at three a.m., ready for the ride to Rishikesh. At ten to four the Swami appeared, looked at his watch, scanned the yard and said with impatience, "Where are the drivers?"

"Out back, Swamiji, taking *chai*. They should be here any minute," I replied.

"That's not good enough," he said with anger. "GET THEM NOW!" he shouted with incredible force.

I cannot recall ever being yelled at like that. My first thought was that my sense of surrender was imperfect. Perhaps I should have seen to it that the vehicles were parked out front when he emerged. But as I ran around back I realized he was just in a bad mood, a spoiled child who was afraid of not getting what he wanted when he wanted it. A great sense of love flooded over me and I found it charming to be reminded once more that my god had feet of clay.

We left at four on the dot. Thirty minutes later I was standing beside the road in the early morning light, a beautiful Vedic chant, the Ganesha Suprabhatam, wafting from a nearby temple, pervading the chill morning air. My mind turned inward, entered the cave of the Heart and exploded into meditation.

I went to the *ashram* of the Swami's number one disciple, the third *mahatma* I had met. Each *mahatma* was different on the surface, each had his own personality and unique *karma*, but something about them all was very much the same. And that sameness came into clear focus during my stay, a sameness that I could now see in myself. This realization, which was simply knowledge, helped to dissolve my attachment to the Swami.

Letting go of the spiritual path, a gilded crutch, was difficult – but attachment is attachment. It would be incorrect to say that I renounced the *guru*, the good times, the romance of India, the quest and the teachings. But attachment to these things began to drop away naturally at this time. They were a means to an end, not the end. Seeing myself as a seeker meant that I was not the sought. Being a lover meant I was not the beloved. All limitations had to go, particularly the sense that part of me was not included in my experience of God, the part that longed for union and was attached to the Swami and the "spiritual" life.

As the train sped across the Deccan plateau on the way to Bombay, I realized that letting go of outer stuff was still not enough. I had come to the subtle point where, like anybody driven by a dream, I had to not only let go of the dream, I had to let the dreamer itself go.

Contemplating a life without the questing, needy self induced a wave of doubt, and I momentarily lost heart. Though he had been a big fool and made many mistakes, I felt a great affection for him, even though he was little more than a tacky image stuck together by an ignorant child from bits and pieces of memory. Still, he had been "me" for so long I could not imagine life without him.

These were my thoughts when the train pulled into a station and the usual commotion ensued. Passengers struggled on and off. Beggars and kids swarmed through the cars with outstretched hands. Porters shouted, muscling their way through the crowd. A couple of goats appeared on the platform and a family of monkeys raced helter-skelter through the iron girders supporting the roof.

Suddenly, in the hustle and bustle of the moment the mind emptied and my vision shifted. Everyone and everything became transparent and ghostlike, and I realized that once again the self was reminding me how insubstantial life really was. And, as I had seen so many times, my reality was not reality at all but merely a momentary play of ideas in consciousness! I looked at myself, the person to whom I had been so attached just minutes before, and rediscovered that he was only a shadow of a shadow.

I broke into a deep, hearty laugh, attracting a beggar into whose hand I stuffed every rupee in my pocket, a king's ransom to him. "Take it," I thought, "you are taking me. I am yours. I am you. Take it all." He looked confused, as if maybe it were not really money, causing me to roar again with laughter.

What a joke the whole spiritual business had been! What a lot of serious striving. How could I get so sentimental and clingy about a mere thought, a phantom appearing in consciousness? What use was all the study, meditation and discipline? What had been gained? Was I any different for it all?

He stood before me, frozen in time, his outstretched hand overflowing with rupees, an image of life reaching for a blessing it already had, a manifestation of God shot through with a fine radiance, an eternal shiningness, which I recognized as myself. I was that endlessly blissful, self-generating light projecting from the center of the mind, not the poverty-stricken, hungry, little, dreamlike self illumined by It. There was nothing to give up, nothing to understand. As this Light I had everything – and nothing. As this Light I knew everything that needed to be known – and nothing. As this Light I would shine forever.

A family, little bundles of Light, entered the compartment. I nodded, welcoming them as my self. As the train pulled out of the station I knew I was nearing the end of a very long journey.

The Kingdom of Heaven

When I arrived at the *ashram* I went immediately to pay my respects to the Swami, but he was no longer the big *guru*. The mask was gone. The only way to describe it was that he was me, the Light.

"Ram, Ram," he said, with great love.

"*Hari Om*, Swamiji," I said, talking to myself.

As I took my place in one corner of the crowded room, my whole life flashed before my eyes, every experience superimposed on this eternal radiant Light.

If my quest had been exciting up to this point, it was nothing compared to what happened next; I was literally lifted up into a state so far beyond my equipment, as the Swami called the body and mind, that I honestly cannot remember what went on in the physical world, because the experiencer, me, was coming apart at the seams, a salt doll sinking into the ocean.

For three days an incessant rain of radiant golden light poured out from an unseen inner heaven, sweeping away every trace of self, every thought, feeling and emotion, until there was nothing left.

When the body lay down to sleep the experience continued, sheets of cascading light, seemingly without end. When the body got up and went about its business the light was unaffected. It rained and rained and rained. Unable to contain the ocean, the body, a small cup, poured the light into the world, blessing the table, the chair, the walkway, the souls sitting woodenly, comically, in front of the Swami, trying to grasp the truth. "It's you!" I wanted to scream. "It's you!" But I knew better.

On the third day the golden rain stopped. There was a knock at the door. One of the boys, dressed in white, an angel really, said, "Swamiji wants to see you."

This was it, my last instruction.

I walked up the path to his hut and entered his room, the silence so overwhelming I could hear my heart beat, the blood coursing through my veins.

An ocean of mercy, he looked up, smiled and showed me a chair. "How much food do you take every day?" he said.

I looked in disbelief and thought, "How absurd! What is this talk about food?" Under my shawl my ribs were showing. I was every inch an ascetic. That vice had been mastered, at least for the time being.

A smile appeared on His face as he observed my reaction.

"I don't know, Swamiji, whatever they give. I go in with the boys, take my place and eat whatever is put on the plate." The answer seemed irrelevant.

He paused for a minute, looked out the window, turned to me, cupping His hands and said, "From now on you will take no more than you can hold in your hands."

"What an odd request," I thought.

"Swamiji?" I said.

After a long pause He spoke the words I had been waiting lifetimes to hear. "I'm returning you to your original form."

An intense shudder passed over me and my body filled with a wild ecstasy. I felt like jumping up and dancing a jig. I had come to the end of the road.

"You can go now," he said.

I got up, touched his feet and left.

Three days later, about one in the afternoon as I was sitting on my bed, it happened.

The logic of my crazy life, all the dramatic inner and outer experiences chronicled here point to a dramatic crescendo, the heavenly host singing hosanna to the highest, a cosmic explosion – another incredible something! But, thank God, it was not like that. It was the simplest, sanest, most undramatic, anti-climactic non-event in my life, one that has continued unabated to this day, one that will never increase, diminish or stop.

I woke up in a timeless world where only I existed, the still-point of existence. I looked around and everything was as it had always been: the wall just a wall, the bed, a bed, and me, me. Nothing was hidden or missing. I knew without a shadow of a doubt that it was no longer necessary to do anything, go anywhere, search for anything. Everything desirable was in me: infinite peace, infinite love and unqualified freedom. I understood that I was whole and perfect and would never, could never, change.

Though words are never right, it was as if the light that blazed forth with every experience, good and bad, spiritual and worldly, throughout my short thirty years had coalesced into one simple consciousness and become a permanent feature of my experience. It would never leave, because it was me. I now inhabited a hermetically-sealed capsule, a state of total security and certainty. Untrue. I was the capsule. I would no longer be the "me" looking into the heart at the self, subject to the fluctuations of the mind. From now on I was the self looking out through the "me" at the world.

My *guru* had erased the veil.

I left the world of action and entered the shining world of self- knowledge, never to suffer the disease of ignorance again.

The body got up and walked out into the hot afternoon sun. The *ashram* was quiet, not a soul to be seen. A couple of ravens behind the cafeteria quarreled pointlessly over the leavings from the noon meal. I walked down the path to the park and came upon the body of a man who had just died, a look of perfect peace on his face. Recognizing him as myself, I continued on my way, appreciating the self's esthetics.

The boy at the tea shop was sitting out front listening to the radio. When he saw me coming he got up and began preparations for the sweetest cup of tea I have ever drunk.

Chapter VIII
After Enlightenment

AS FAR AS stories go, the quest for enlightenment was easy to chronicle, the plot with its peculiar twists and turns winding inexorably toward its climax. Now, from the top of my holy mountain a welcoming, light-filled landscape stretched endlessly before me, the boundaries that once defined – and confined – me having been obliterated by this secret knowing.

Knowing that you are limitless renders you fearless and reveals your desires to be as insubstantial as a mirage. What is there to do, knowing nothing can add to or subtract from your happiness in any way? You become lazy and satisfied. What can you say, knowing nothing important, meaning you, is going to change – forever? What words, no matter how eloquent, can hold a candle to the Word blazing eternally in everything you see?

Paradoxically, enlightenment's final ending is also a new beginning. I am pure and perfect, no doubt, and always will be, but some small part of me still needed the not always tender instructions life had to offer. Whether I come out looking good is up to you to decide. Or not. For me, evaluating outcomes is difficult. An acute appreciation of the unresolved is one of enlightenment's benefits. Life is vast. It carries our small vehicles to unknown destinations and incomprehensibly picks them up like a great wind and blows them on to places we could never imagine.

A Necessary Disgrace

A few weeks after the eternal moment on my bed, the Swami informed me that I would be enrolling in a two-year course in Vedanta, taught by his number one disciple, Swami Dayananda – information I received with mixed feelings. The idea of learning Sanskrit properly and systematically studying scripture was appealing, but I had attained everything the *Veda* reveals. Since nothing he did was uncalculated, I assumed he wanted me to become a Vedanta teacher in the West. The Chinmaya Mission is very exacting and turns out highly-qualified professional *gurus*, none of whom to my knowledge have been involved in the tawdry sex and money scandals that seem to perennially plague Hindu *swamis*. Not knowing or particularly caring what I wanted to do with the rest of my life and eager to please the person who had given me so much, I agreed. However,

I distinctly remember feeling sad as I walked along the path back to my room. If you do it right, discipleship happens only once.

The course began and I took my place among the boys, young, upper-caste Indians from middle-class families. Dayananda's teaching style was quite different from the Swami's, although the message was the same – you are everything that is. And over the years my ideas about the most effective way to communicate Vedanta have moved more or less in line with his. Not that Chinmaya was an ineffective communicator. Both his words, which rose spontaneously from the spiritual depths and were in harmony with scripture, and the extraordinary silence that permeated his whole being awakened and enlightened many.

Chinmaya billed himself as a modern *swami* for reasons that only became clear much later. I think he thought of himself as a reformer, a modern Shankara, whose mission it was to bring the stodgy, hidebound, conservative world of Hindu spirituality up to date by spearheading a Vedantic renaissance in post-colonial India. His teachings became known as modern Vedanta, perhaps to widen their appeal in a backward country struggling to enter the modern era. But on the doctrinal level modern Vedanta blurred the boundary between Yoga and Vedanta.

Dayananda saw the need to purge Vedanta of the yogic ideas that were trying to co-opt it, particularly the idea of enlightenment as a transcendental experience or an experience of the self. In the exuberant years immediately after my enlightenment I did not think about the teachings much, preferring instead to use them to awaken those who were attracted to my energy. Most who came were introductory-level people, and the teachings worked fine at that level. But as I cooled down and the light penetrated into the farthest reaches of my mind, I re-entered the ancient texts and realized that at the highest level of spiritual evolution Yoga and Vedanta need to part company.

In any case, I was impressed with Dayananda's teachings and decided to tape the talks. I did not know that taping was forbidden when apprised of this fact by one of the boys. I also do not know what got into me, because I gave the poor fellow quite a dressing down. Perhaps I felt justified criticizing the backward thinking that so much characterizes India's approach to life, but it was actually the Lord using my arrogance to move me on.

A few days later, after checking with the Swami, Dayananda gave me my walking papers. Though humiliated, I was secretly relieved. Something in me knew that I was not going to spend years in the Bombay suburbs studying ancient Sanskrit texts. Nevertheless, to save face I went to Chinmaya and asked to be reinstated. He looked at me with great love, and conveniently forgetting that the course was his idea in the first place, almost shouted, "No! You will explode upon the society with this knowledge! Go to California and sit under a tree in the park. They will come to you."

And that was it.

After paying her debt to me faithfully for three years, Magdalena pulled the plug, and I was soon to be dead broke. I had rights. I had it in writing. I could have made a fuss, but I did not care. Somehow it seemed right that I should start out all over again with nothing. I still had enough to stay in India for some time, so I decided to visit the *ashram* of Baba Muktananda, who lived nearby in a small Maharastran village called Ganeshpuri.

As the rickety bus huffed and puffed over the bumpy road that wound through the ancient beauty of the parched rural landscape a few miles from the *ashram*, I was hit with a bolt of transcendental energy from Baba that filled my body with such bliss I thought I would explode. As I got down twenty minutes later in front of the temple, the world seemed to be floating in space, magically manifested out of nothingness like the image of a distant city in a mirror. The *ashram* had a tentative, dreamlike quality, vaguely theatrical, as if patched together out of thought and feeling by a humorous and loving mind. And the whole scene was bathed in an effortless and gentle rain of pure blue pointillist light particles, *chitshakti*, that seemed to spontaneously dissolve and recreate themselves without reason.

I set my bag inside the gate, bowed at the altar and entered a small, shady marble courtyard behind the temple where a few people, mostly Westerners, were sitting in hushed silence. A small man in an orange silk *dhoti*, sitting cross-legged on a raised white marble dais, turned the moment I entered. Our eyes met, and I could feel his x-ray vision burn into my soul. A deep current of *prema*, divine love, flooded over me as I walked across the courtyard, bowed and touched his feet. He looked at me and with great love said, "Who are you?"

"The Infinite Self," I replied in Sanskrit with a smile.

He laughed, reached around behind him and unexpectedly crowned me with a lovely, hand-made, sequined, royal purple hat.

Knowing I could not have attained liberation without help, he asked who my *guru* was, nodding thoughtfully when I replied and readily assenting to my request to stay.

Swami Muktananda, Baba, as he was affectionately called, was the disciple of Bhagavan Nityananda, one of India's all-time spiritual giants, a strange, otherworldly *mahatma* known as an *avadhut*, a class of realized beings who live without possessions, often without clothing, wandering here and there, unaware of the physical universe, leaving a spate of miracles in their wake.

Baba, for whom I developed great affection until I found out about his sexual exploits many years later, was a *shaktipat guru* in the tradition of *bhakti yoga*. He rarely spoke, unlike Chinmaya, and effected miraculous changes through the transmission of divine energy, called *shakti*.

After several months, my visa was about to expire, so he sent me to the local magistrate. "Tell him Baba says to fix it up," he said.

The magistrate would not grant the visa extension until my health certificate was updated and sent me to the local clinic, a filthy, run-down shack, for an inoculation. The doctor asked me to sit in a chair near a small table on which was sitting a pocked porcelain dish containing a couple of used syringes and several bloody cotton balls. Before I realized what was going on he stabbed me with a used syringe from the dish! I awoke next day with a painful infection in my upper arm, which quickly swelled to an ungodly size.

Understandably, I was not bristling with confidence in the Indian medical system, so I did not return to the clinic for treatment, deciding instead to rely on The Big Doctor in the Sky. After the second day the infection showed no sign of abating and I began to reappraise my view, contemplating the arduous trip to Bombay, but, all things considered, decided to tough it out for another day.

I was sitting in the courtyard meditating the following afternoon when Baba came out and sat in front of a group of low-caste women who were hunkered down, lustfully glancing at a pile of *saris* that had been recently donated by a Bombay merchant. Never one to miss an opportunity to say a few words about the glories of God, he began to speak about the necessity of chanting the holy name.

A few minutes later a gust of wind blew my light, white cotton shawl up to expose the infection, the flash of white attracting his attention. He turned back and continued talking to the women, whose low state of consciousness and single-minded preoccupation with the *saris* provided a cover for what was about to happen. In a few minutes he again turned toward me, still speaking to the women, and made a syringe-like manipulation with his hand, which, coupled with a questioning look, made me understand that he was researching the cause of the infection like the Rishikesh *sadhu* had done two years before. I nodded and he turned back to his audience without disrupting his speech.

Then, as he talked, he turned his head slightly in my direction, and with my physical eyes I saw a ray of white light emerge from the space between his brows and strike on the swollen arm, which immediately began to deflate like a pricked balloon! A rush of warm, tingly energy flooded through me, relaxing the muscles. The skin tightened and the small scab where the needle had entered fell off. The arm was completely normal!

He spoke for another minute or two, passed out the *saris*, got up and disappeared into his rooms through a small door.

Baba liked me and gave me many gifts that would come in handy later on. Occasionally, when I was working on a particularly subtle problem, I knew it was about to be resolved when his little dog came waltzing into my room, followed by Baba. He would stand in my doorway, his aura filling the room, silently transmitting vital information. During my stay I had many interesting experiences and met three people who would later figure prominently in my life.

An Experiment

I arrived in San Francisco dead broke and called Jack, the merchant seaman I met in Morocco, India and Afghanistan. As fate would have it he was in town and invited me to stay. He let me sleep on the floor, and if memory serves, gave me an old Ford Fairlane. The Swami tried to set me up with an Indian importer, but I was unwilling to work for five dollars an hour. I drove the streets and dove into dumpsters instead, taking my booty to the Sausalito flea market, where I offloaded it for whatever it would bring. And I have to admit that I was not above ripping off the weekend overflow at Goodwill boxes, breaking into condemned Victorian flats in search of old furniture and fixtures or finessing foolish junk dealers out of their prized possessions. With food stamps I was able to make ends meet.

In a vacant lot south of Market Street I met a fiery flamenco dancer with a taste for the occult at a dance one Sunday afternoon. She was much affected by what I had to say and we soon became good friends and indifferent lovers. Scavenging was a long way from the big Waikiki bucks and the glamorous life with a jet-set export *guru*, but I spent some of the happiest days of my life cruising the streets looking for junk, Felicia at my side sipping coffee. I fondly recall sitting in an unholy assortment of Mexican restaurants listening to salsa, eating burritos and talking God or hanging out at the flamenco clubs in North Beach watching her dance. She was a bit crazy, but she had the eyes of God. One day, after casing an abandoned hotel in the Tenderloin, she observed me walking toward the truck. When I got in she said, "You're beautiful, a walking altar."

When we came upon an empty dumpster we marked it on a city map. On Saturday we would show up mid-morning before it was full, so I could meet the occupants of the house and gain access to the premises. I might offer to dispose of the contents for salvage rights or buy anything of value. One evening in Chinatown I came across a large assortment of valuable oriental antiques in a dumpster. Before long I had a consistently fat wad of cash in my pocket and a tidy little stash in the bank.

Tom, whom I had met at Muktananda Ashram, came back from India. We rented a flat on Cole Street in the Haight Ashbury. He was a smart, righteous young man, committed to his spiritual practice. I loved him dearly, but there was something menacing and unpredictable about him that occasionally made me uneasy and would eventually affect the outcome of the experiment. The experiment was my attempt to focus a number of minds so intently on the idea of self-realization that it just happened.

How ironic that three years after my psychedelic sojourn through the Haight Ashbury I wound up living in a large Victorian railroad flat just off Haight Street. By this time we had been joined by Terry, whom I also had met in the Muktananda Ashram in Ganeshpuri. Terry was a bright, honest, stand-up guy who faithfully served the experiment for many years. He had been an officer in Vietnam with a promising military career, but what he saw so disturbed him he did not renew his commission when his tour of duty ended. He must have been through a lot because he once showed me a picture of himself in full military regalia, standing next to a bright red restored Morgan, the picture of arrogance and entitlement. When I met him he was a shadow of his former self, a skinny, balding, ghostlike devotee, living off bananas in the *ashram* of a saint, doing penance and seeking enlightenment.

With Terry we got a bonus, a stunning Italian artist named Sophia, with a dark and unhappy past, who was ready to sand a lot of furniture to exorcise her demons. Jack's ex-girlfriend, Cindy, a ballerina, also joined up. She was a lovely person, the girl next door for whom the spiritual life did not come easy. Several others came and before long the flat was full.

It was just off the Park Panhandle, next to a three-storey Victorian inhabited by the White Panthers, a swaggering group of beastly, lower-class, bike-riding, drug-dealing, fornicating males – Hell's Angels with a political twist. My specialty is seeing the light in everyone, no matter how cleverly it is concealed beneath layers of sloth and stupidity, but I had to work long and hard to find the faintest glimmerings in any of them. The women were disgusting also, and the place was overrun with dogs and stinky, whiny, malnourished, half-naked brats – Appalachia on Ashbury.

While they slept in from wild parties inside their filthy, well-fortified bastion, their gleaming chrome hogs parked in a line out front, we sat quietly next door, meditating and chanting sacred *mantras*. Contrary to Transcendental Meditation's claims of meditation's wondrous power to change the world, to my knowledge not one holy vibration ever managed to find its way next door.

Once, about midnight, one of the Panthers decided to fix his car. He parked it in the middle of the street, jacked it up, turned on the radio full volume and crawled underneath with his tools and a six-pack of beer. By two a.m. I was fed up and shouted for him to turn down the radio. He ignored me, so I went to the pantry, got a big glass jar and hurled it at the pavement from a second-storey window, spraying him with shards of glass. I am the first to admit it was not enlightened behavior, but it got his attention. I told him if he did not turn it down I would call the cops, a foolhardy threat if I intended to go on living in the neighborhood. After a few counter-threats to save face he turned it down; there was probably an outstanding warrant for his arrest. We went in and out through the back door for a few days until the incident was swallowed by the dark haze in his drug-crazed mind.

I was driving home for lunch one day along the Park Panhandle when I had a vision of a woman sitting at a kitchen table. When we entered the flat, one of the most beautiful women I had ever seen was sitting in the kitchen in a very high state of consciousness. When she looked at me there was much more than a connection, there was a transmission. No, it was more than that: an understanding that she was the self arose in her, one that would never leave.

Marlena was a dancer who had been having many strange and wonderful inner experiences. Her friends and family, who had no idea what was happening, thought she was mad. One of the tragedies of materialist culture is its inability to distinguish madness from spiritual experience, although they are not always mutually exclusive. Instead of support and the counsel of wise elders, both lunatics and the awakened are often shunted off to shrinks and mental institutions. The world fears what it does not understand.

I spent the afternoon conversing with her, making sure she understood that her awakening was natural and instructing her how to live in the world with the fire of consciousness blazing in her heart. Six years later we would marry and embark on one of the most tragic, bizarre and rewarding experiences of my life.

The money kept rolling in and everyone was enjoying themselves, so we took a larger flat in a better neighborhood on Scott Street, near the ghetto. We turned the front room into a meditation hall, sat regularly every morning and worked twelve-hour days. We ate vegetarian food together and there was constant laughter and great camaraderie.

One day Terry asked if an Eastern European woman he had met in India could come and stay with us. I assumed that she was the spiritual type since she was connected to Maurice Frydman, a devotee of Nisargadatta Maharaj, who was responsible for the book *I Am That*, which is now considered a Vedantic classic. I said yes, not realizing that spirituality was hovering near the bottom on her list of priorities. All was not lost, however, because when Victoria showed up I knew I had found my next girlfriend. She was a beautiful young woman, bright, cultured and well-mannered, a petty aristocrat from an Iron Curtain country. The only problem: What to do about Felicia? After a bit of family *karma*, the good Lord solved the problem.

Shortly after Victoria arrived, my father called from Idaho and invited me to attend the World Series in Oakland. I had no interest in baseball anymore, but attending class B ball in Lewiston with him was one of my fondest childhood memories, so I readily assented. I put him up in a nice room next to the meditation hall. He must have thought we were all crazy, but he was unfailingly polite and friendly. In the morning he went out for bacon and eggs in one of the black eateries along Divisidero Street, since our spartan vegetarian gruel was not to his liking. I asked Felicia to tidy up his room and put flowers on the dresser. A few minutes later she was standing in the doorway, her eyes as big as saucers.

"What's happening?" I said.

"He's a dead man," she replied.

Three weeks later I got a call from Mom informing me of his death.

The Series went the full seven games, I think, and at the seventh inning stretch I could sense that he wanted to say something.

"Let me get you a hot dog, Jim," he said.

"Sure, Dad, whatever," I replied.

He returned in a few minutes and we sat contentedly munching the hot dogs to the dulcet strains of *Take Me out to the Ball Game*. When the song ended he put his arm around the back of my seat and said, "You know, son, I've been meaning to talk to you about something."

"Sure, Dad," I replied. "Shoot."

He hemmed and hawed a bit, and said, "You know, son, your mother and I have been thinking about your future."

"What have you been thinking?" I said, trying to make it easy for him.

"The post office, Jim. They got some very good jobs down at the post office."

It was all I could do to keep from laughing. "Oh, yeah, Dad, what they got?"

"Well, there's several grades, you know. Now the first ones aren't bad, about fifteen hundred a month, and you can work up. They've got an exam, but I figure you can pass it. You did pretty good in college. And they got good retirement packages too. You'd be surprised. What do you say?"

I reached in my pocket and extracted a wad of hundred-dollar bills, more than fifteen. "See this, Dad?" I said. "I made this on one deal a couple of days ago."

His jaw dropped. To my knowledge there had not been a businessman on either side of the family for generations, if ever. Everyone seemed to enjoy the security of working for wages.

"But you know, Dad, I like the idea. Perhaps when the money runs out I'll make an application. You never know, what with the economic uncertainty and all. Thanks for the suggestion."

A Recollection

That seemed to satisfy him, and as we watched the rest of the ball game in peace, my mind drifted back to the 1940s and Sunday afternoons in northern Idaho. After an idyllic weekend in the country camping and fishing, we would leisurely head home in our 1936 Plymouth sedan, my brother and I sitting in the back with the family dog on the plush brown mohair seats, staring out at the rich landscape, bubbling with good feelings, looking forward to Sunday evening. On arrival we would grab our bikes and disappear into the neighborhood for an evening of high jinks. Our inevitable late return would prompt a scolding and invite a sanction, usually an additional weekly chore. Then we would reluctantly practice the piano, do homework and stay up half the night reading adventure tales, *Robinson Crusoe* and the like, under the covers with a flashlight.

Wild goose chases ruined many a Sunday night though. We would be cruising along, Dad whistling sappy tunes like *My Darling Clementine* and Mom thinking her (always practical) thoughts, when the car would abruptly halt, usually forty or fifty yards beyond a narrow side road heading out tentatively into the wilderness. Dad would put it in reverse, steering with his left hand while he reached over to fumble through the jockey box (the "glove compartment" to Mom) and extract a local map. When we were strategically situated he would hit the brakes, spread the map on the space between them on the front seat and evaluate it with the dispassion of a sage. Mom, exercising Herculean self-control, would remain silent, fidgeting consciously to show her displeasure; she knew what he was thinking.

Totally absorbed in the map, seemingly unaware of her mood, Dad would mutter various snippets: "Cut-off to Superior, this neck of the woods, Sperry Grade, wonder if they fixed the…?"

Unable to contain herself, Mom would say, "You're not thinking of taking this road are you, Jim?"

Too involved to reply, he would look up the road and back down at the map several times, like a general plotting an attack. When he judged the time right, which of course it never was, he would scoot toward her side, ceremoniously place the map in her lap with great respect, as if he were consulting the Commander in Chief, and point meaningfully to a roadless section of wilderness. There would be a dramatic pause and then, in a conspiratorial tone, he would say, "What do you think? Doesn't this look like the cut-off that comes in just above Elk City? Carl said they fixed the bridge after the run-off. Take this and we save a good hour." "Save a good hour" was his response to her not taking this road.

Mom saw where this was heading and would firmly repeat herself, deleting "thinking of." "You're not taking this road, Jim!"

Dad was stubborn. With a massive muscular chest and shoulders, a big head and narrow hips, he somewhat resembled a bull. And Mom, born under the sign of the crab, could cling to her position like nobody's business. A civilized argument would begin but rapidly turn negative, a sign for my brother and me to start quarreling. When their war reached its crescendo the dog would bark uncontrollably.

Moments before breaking down and gushing her usually insincere torrent of tears, Mom would trundle out the heavy weapon in her formidable arsenal – guilt. "Must you subject me to this, Jim? It's simply not fair. Can't you see it's just another wild goose chase?"

But that was just the point. "Trust me," said Dad like a used car salesman, "we'll a save a good hour, hour-and-a-half."

An hour, maybe, an hour-and-a-half? Definitely not. The recently added half was meant to sweeten the pot. Given the nature of the road, sixty miles probably translated into two hours, eating up the lion's share of the alleged savings.

To be fair, Mom, who was uninterested in surprises, never wanted the extra good hour-and-a-half anyway. To her sensible Mid-Western mind, sticking to the tried and true, arriving on time without incident, was infinitely superior to taking an unmarked, obviously third-rate road late in the afternoon, solely out of curiosity.

In spite of her diminutive five feet, she was nobody's patsy. In the 1920s, long before the advent of feminism, she graduated from the University of Chicago with a master's degree and honors. Then, in the manner of an aristocrat, she did the grand tour of Europe, steamer trunks and her younger sister in tow, quite an accomplishment for a young farm woman from Fargo, North Dakota.

But Dad, who worked the mines in northern Idaho and loaded ships in the navy, was raised on a far-from-profitable dirt farm halfway up the side of a windswept Rocky Mountain foothill. Understandably, he was a tad macho. It did not look good to cave in to reason, not in front of his sons, so the car turned up the road and the wild goose chase began.

What percentage of these forays into the unknown actually accomplished their stated purpose and which were merely wild goose chases, I do not recall. On the one I am thinking about, the bridge north of Elk City that washed out during spring runoff had not been repaired, in spite of Uncle Carl's information to the contrary, and we were forced to backtrack. The good hour-and-a-half saved turned into a bad hour-and-a-half lost, making Mom right once again, a fact that did not impact strongly on Dad, who lived in a world where knowledge was king. The information that the bridge was still out somehow justified the wasted time, and indeed would crop up in all conversations with his peers for the next three weeks.

Sometimes the wild goose chase turned life-threatening. One Sunday afternoon on the way back from the woods we came upon a small branch road at a bridge approach that seemed to follow the Clearwater River across from the main highway.

"Betcha this cuts across behind Lapwai and comes out in the orchards just above the mill," he said with visionary conviction, wheeling the car off the highway.

The road innocently followed the river for a couple of miles and headed up the side of a barren mountain, becoming narrower and narrower as we ascended. Eventually we were crawling along at two miles an hour, treated to an unobstructed view of the river three hundred yards below. By this time the road narrowed to the point where Dad had to get out and remove fallen boulders to continue. "Don't you think that's a sign that this road is impassable?" said Mom, trying to conceal her irritation behind a façade of logic.

"Perfectly good road. It's the damn government," he groused. "Pay my taxes, they can't even maintain the roads. I'm going to write a letter to the editor. It's a scandal," he said, inching along at a snail's pace, to quote Mom.

Eventually, near the top it petered out into nothing and we could not turn around. In fact the passenger side was so close to the precipice that conventional egress was impossible.

"That's the last straw!" said Mom angrily, employing another of her quaint, old-timey metaphors. "How dare you put our lives in jeopardy! Get out! The kids and I are walking back." He squeezed out, the door unable to open more than a crack owing to the proximity of the mountainside, followed by Mom, who coaxed us out.

Dad, who was absolutely fearless, seemed surprised by her reaction. "Whatcha doing? No problem here. Wonder why they didn't punch it through to Lapwai," he said nonchalantly. "Guess I'll have to back up."

What had happened to that adventuresome and exciting man? Evidently even he could not remember, the intervening years having been swallowed by nine-to-fives too numerous to mention and postprandial nodding off in front of the tube until there was nothing left, just a nice old man who would have been overjoyed to see his son working at the post office.

The A's won the series, I think.

Onward and Upward

After several nightly sojourns down the hall to Victoria's room, it was abundantly clear that I had solved half the girlfriend problem. However, the other half, Felicia, was crying for a solution.

One morning at seven, everyone gathered in the meditation hall except Felicia. I waited before starting, thinking she would be along shortly, but after five minutes there was no sign of her.

"Where's Felicia?" I said.

Everyone shrugged.

"Please get her," I told Tom.

He returned a minute later. "She's not coming," he said.

"She's coming," I said. "Everyone sits."

He shrugged and sat down.

I got up and went down the hall to her room. She was lounging in bed, reading a book.

"Get your ass down the hall," I said. "Everyone sits."

"Fuck you, Ram. I'm not coming."

I had to admire her. She had spunk, as Mother used to say. "Any special reason?" I said, glancing down the hall, where several heads were sticking out, listening.

"I just don't feel like it. That's all."

"That's good. You don't feel like it. Now, what if everyone doesn't feel like it? Then do we have a meditation or not?"

"Guess not."

"And if we don't have a meditation, do we have any reason to be here in this house?"

"Fuck you, man. Don't give me any of your clever, intellectual bullshit."

"Okay. Let's put it this way. Either you come and sit with the rest of us or you pack your bags."

"You're not getting rid of me that easy," she said. "I'm not leaving."

I recalled that by her frequent admissions she had been a queen in at least a dozen past lives, and wondered if she was not a bit confused about her status in this one.

"Okay. This is your last chance. You sit and we'll talk about what's bothering you later. If you don't sit you're outta here."

"Who's going to throw me out?" she said. She reminded me of a cat I once had that thought it was a human being. If you messed with it in a certain way it attacked like a raging demon. She was not an inch taller than five feet and probably weighed ninety pounds soaking wet. I am nearly six feet and weigh in at two hundred.

"Come on, Felicia," I said, turning on the charm. "It's so easy to just get up and walk down the hall and sit for thirty minutes like the rest of us." It still did not dawn me that this was the perfect opportunity to get her out of my hair. I guess I really loved her.

"Fuck you, Ram."

I walked over, grabbed her and hauled her down the hall. She was kicking and scratching and screaming and biting. I could not believe the filth coming out of her mouth.

When I got her out on the porch I locked her out, went back to her room, gathered up her possessions, which took all of five minutes, and delivered them to her. Someone once called her the closet saint because she was so small and had so few possessions she could easily have lived in a closet. A rich kid from the East who was visiting took pity, drove her to the Muktananda Ashram in

Oakland and paid for her room. I saw her on and off over the years and tried to make amends, but she would not have any. Twenty years later, after dozens of attempts, I gave up. Fifteen years after that I was sitting in a coffee shop when she came in. I called her over and we had a nice chat. Time heals all wounds.

I know it is hard to believe, but it was only after she drove off that I realized I had just solved my problem. There would be no more furtive trips down darkened hallways in the dead of night. Guru Jim was getting respectable.

And although Victoria was not spiritual she had enough spiritual qualities to keep us together for the next few years – and our worldly needs dovetailed nicely. By spiritual I mean the understanding that there is an inner way to solve the need for security and love; that a green card, a cushy little job and the love of a man are not enough to satisfy the longings of the soul.

One day Tom told me that his mother, an attractive forty-something widow, was in a quandary about whether to marry a sexy gambler or a respectable lawyer. I told him to recommend the lawyer because I knew that she would only suffer with the gambler. The lawyer, on the other hand, was not much to look at and a bit short on style but he was a moral, decent, wealthy fellow who would make a nice companion in her sunset years. She picked the lawyer, and we fell into a nice house in the Sea Cliff belonging to Tom's mother.

The Sea Cliff, one of the most prestigious locations in San Francisco, was an unlikely place for a group of erstwhile spiritual types. We did not get one of the mansions along the ocean, but we did get a very nice two-storey, upper-middle-class home just inside the gates on 28th Avenue. If memory serves we did not have one unpleasant incident with the neighbors, a remarkable fact considering that we chanted every day and ran an antique furniture restoration workshop in the basement. I called the experiment normal *yoga* and ruthlessly screened misfits, freaks, slackers and rebels. Everyone was required to dress conservatively and behave decorously. The idea, one that I believe in strongly today, is captured in an old saying from the Zen tradition: "Next to good manners, enlightenment is the most important thing in the world."

Tom's mother gave us a deal on the rent and eventually sold us the house for a very fair price. We ate together, meditated in the morning, chanted often and worked like demons on the antiques. A real sense of community developed, and I do not think I have ever laughed so much in my life, except during my college days at Berkeley. Indeed there were occasional small problems, but the atmosphere was so unfailingly positive that they never developed into serious conflicts.

The consistent inspiration that flows in the mind when one knows who one is lifts a lot of boats, but working with people is difficult. Because I attained transcendence so quickly I was unable to completely clean my mind before-hand, so keeping selfish tendencies in check for the sake of the experiment in-volved additional effort. I do not regret a moment of this period of my life. But if I had to do it again, I would have ignored the Swami's instructions – as he did his *guru's* – and worn the hair shirt for at least ten years before even considering exploding on the society. He stayed with his *guru* in the Himalayas for seven years and could not wait to descend to the plains and begin teaching once he realized the self. The *guru*, however, a great sage of the old school, understand-ing his ambitions, the nature of his mind and the purpose of the tradition, told him to stay put. "If they are meant to get something," he said, "they will come to you." But he could not wait. He was a man on a mission.

I did not realize it at the time, but instead of finding my own voice, I was really just aping the Swami's dynamic missionary style. Fair enough because it was all I knew. But if I had to do it over, I would have taken time to grow a few gray hairs and see that my ambition to enlighten the world was a bit less keen before I set out.

At this point there were about ten of us living in fairly ritzy digs. One Saturday morning in 1972 I was cruising Fisherman's Wharf when I spied an empty dumpster. I parked across the street, walked over and peered inside. About twenty Art Nouveau picture frames in mint condition, worth about three hundred dollars, were scattered on the bottom. I boosted myself over the edge and squatted to examine them. As I appreciated their beauty and marveled at my good luck, another equally valuable batch came flying over the rim of the dumpster and rained down on my head. I jumped up and looked out to see an attractive blond woman walking toward a storefront. When I called to her she turned, surprised to see a strange head staring at her from the dumpster.

I hopped out and asked her what she was doing. She said her husband had died recently and that the landlord was insisting that she pay the rent on his shop or vacate immediately. I asked her if I could examine the shop, and she agreed. Her husband was a local character who in an earlier incarnation had been a merchant seaman with a penchant for oriental antiques. When I scanned the shop I realized that my ship had come in. I told her that she was a fool to throw it away and talked her into allowing me to fill the Ford and take it to the flea market. She agreed to a fifty-fifty split. I visited her at her home in the evening and gave her nine hundred dollars. I do not recall how much my share of the shop was, probably over twenty grand, but it was a big shot in the arm financially.

After liquidating the store I got a call from the woman inviting me for dinner one evening. She lived in a very large Victorian flat in North Beach with a view of the bay. The flat was filled from top to bottom with antiques. After a lovely, home-cooked Italian meal we repaired to the living room for a drink. Eventually she said, "I'll bet you're wondering what this is all about, aren't you?"

I nodded, expecting her to come up with a romantic proposal.

"Well, I'm very pleased with the way you helped me out and I've another deal, if you're interested.

"You bet," I said, surprised but interested.

"As you have undoubtedly noticed, this flat is stuffed with antiques. They were my husband's passion. I hated my husband and I hate antiques, and I'd like to offer them to you under the same terms."

I agreed, obviously, and asked how she was planning to decorate the apartment.

"Danish Modern," she said.

With more money I was able to buy better stuff and trade at a higher level. One day I was in the workshop sanding an oak dresser when a dealer friend came in and asked if I would be interested in a storefront. I told him I did not want the headache of dealing with the public six days a week.

"Come on, Sunny Jim, have a look. I think you'll like it," he said. I do not know why I agreed to look at it, perhaps I was tired of sanding furniture and wanted to get out of the shop for an hour, but I agreed. We drove down to Divisadero Street to a Victorian storefront, situated between the ghetto and Pacific Heights, and walked through the junk-filled rooms.

"So what do you think," my friend said.

"What do I think about what?" I replied.

"The shop. Do you want it?"

"I told you, Rhino, I don't want a shop. It's a pain in the ass."

"You want this one," he said.

"Why do I want this one?"

"Because I'm giving it to you."

"Come on, Rhino, what's the catch."

"No catch, Sunny Jim, no catch at all."

"Okay. Why?"

"Because the guy who's been running it is a flake and my shop on California Street is making big bucks (I would later learn that his dope business, for which the shop was a front, was making big bucks) and it's too much trouble to deal with anymore. So I give you the key and you pay the rent and the phone bill and it's yours, lock, stock and barrel."

"Why me, Rhino?"

"I like you, Sunny Jim."

"That's it?"

"That's it."

"Thanks. Okay, give me the key."

It was a nice Eastlake Victorian with great windows. The sign said "Old Stuff." There was a fading copy of a page from a sixties issue of *Time* magazine with an article on the store taped on the kitchen wall. I rented the ceiling to a friend I met tending the cows in the Muktananda Ashram in Ganeshpuri, an antique lighting restorer named Michael, and we filled the rooms with our best stuff. In a short time we had a classy antique store and real money started rolling in.

Slay the Buddha

For a few years nothing changed. Some new people came, until the house reached critical mass, a spiritual pressure cooker. Something was about to happen. I kept the energy ratcheted up and watched with interest. Either everyone was going to wake up or the whole thing was going to collapse like an imploding star. Or both.

The Swami came to town and said to back off on the business side. Before I had time to consider how to properly accomplish this, things started to unravel.

Success is a fickle and demanding mate. Because you generate it with skillful actions you are always tempted to think you are in control. And you are – up to a point. But a time comes when it takes on a life of its own and wrests control from your hands. And if you are attached to what it gives, from that point on you are as much its victim as its author. Either you succumb to its seductions or you look for a way out.

Although it seemed like I was locked in, I was ready to bag it. I gorged on success in Hawaii and still felt empty. And lest I needed to be reminded of its unremitting downside, all I had to do was contemplate the Swami's *karma*. Irrespective of all that, I had my ace in the hole, self-knowledge. It does not matter what happens to your little life. By dint of who you are, you are always free of everything. So I was not in love with what had been created. It would have been pointless. In fact I was sacrificing myself for the sake of a very abstract idea.

I hope I get the next sequence of events right because a lot of water has flowed under my bridge since then. My first mistake, which was not a mistake, was caused by my love of beauty. One weekday morning about nine, a man came to sell me a very elegant piece of antique stained glass at a reasonable price. When I saw it I immediately visualized it behind the altar in the meditation room. He seemed respectable and his story sounded right, so I bought it.

Over the next year I purchased twenty or thirty pieces from him, none of which I sold. I do not recall at what point I started having suspicions about the source of the glass, but eventually I realized it was hot. My supplier was a very athletic junkie who removed it from public buildings in the early morning hours. I was in a quandary about what to do. I should have called the cops and turned it in, but I was attached, so I dithered. I decided to move my collection to a secure storage space, but before I could, the chickens came home to roost.

One morning Carlos, the junkie, brought an exceptionally rare and remarkably beautiful cut-glass Victorian lamp in mint condition that was easily worth thousands of dollars. In spite of my vow to wean myself, I was unable to resist. The next day I got a call from the store saying that two detectives wanted to talk to me. I had plenty of time to dispose of the lamp but decided to give it to them. When they asked if there were any other items I told them about the stained glass. They were taken aback by my confession; they had not connected the lamp and the stained glass. In fact I suspect that very few of the windows were ever reported since they came from once elegant but run-down apartment buildings owned by absentee slum lords. They booked me, I posted bail and we got Tom's stepfather to get us a good lawyer. I cut a deal with the cops to deliver the junkie, plead guilty to a misdemeanor count of receiving stolen property, and that was that.

Coming clean was not an act of courage. I made two quick calculations while the detectives were on their way. First, I had a spotless record and was unlikely to get more than a slap on the wrist. Second, even though Tom was in on it, the store was registered in his name and the experiment would have been in jeopardy had he been charged because our business license would not have been renewed. Additionally, he probably would never have flirted with the dark side had he not been associated with me, so I did not want to involve him in it.

The incident had a silver lining. Since most of the stained glass had gone unreported, after the proper waiting period the police held an auction and made some decent money for their war on crime. And as it turned out, the junkie got a chance to go into a drug treatment program. When I looked at him in court he smiled.

Did I regret it? Yes. Would I ever do such a stupid thing again? No.

Mistake number two. Well, there are no mistakes. Everything here serves a purpose. But let us assume the conventional point of view and call my next decision a mistake. The second mistake was attachment to pleasure. One of the great saints of the last century, Ramakrishna Paramahamsa, often said that there were two big obstacles on the road to enlightenment: women and gold. I can amend that to read "before and after enlightenment."

The Love Issue

This was an area where I needed a bit of work. Without putting too fine a point on it, as we all know, there are basically two kinds of love: conditional and unconditional. Conditional love is business: I have my special needs, you have yours. If they roughly coincide and we are needy enough, we agree to take care of each other's needs, and to make ourselves feel good, we call it love.

Unconditional love means that I love you for who you are, warts and all, no matter what happens. If you do not give me what I want, I still love you. I knew this intellectually at the time, but was victim of a slight confusion, one that resolved in the next chapter of my life.

The relationship with Victoria was perfect for who I was at the time. In addition to admiring her many good qualities and respecting her for the service she did on my behalf and on behalf of the group, I genuinely liked her. I also found her extremely attractive as a woman. My only complaint was her lack of interest in the spiritual life. There was nothing to be done about it. Spirituality, unlike religion, is not a matter of belief. Only through a proper evaluation of the limitations involved in seeking happiness in the world do you begin to look elsewhere.

Anyway, one day she told me that she needed to go home to take care of some family affairs. I asked her to postpone her visit because things were a bit dicey, but she said it was urgent, so I agreed.

The energy in the house was intense and it attracted one of the loveliest young women I have had the pleasure to know, the kind of open-minded, inno-cent, enthusiastic person that comes along once in a blue moon. Sandy took to the idea of enlightenment like a duck to water and within a month or two real-ized who she was. And, as fate would have it, we ended up lovers. How could I resist someone who had everything Victoria had – and knew who she was?

It does not take a genius to understand how these two developments might cause agitation in the minds of some of the group, although it turned out when all was said and done that Victoria had actually been unfaithful as well. But everyone was having such a good time no one was ready to kill the goose that laid the golden egg over a few misdemeanors – except Tom, who was young and self-righteous and plagued with strong feelings.

Perhaps because I live so unapologetically, I have periodically been the victim of envy. One day I heard him on the phone with someone who wanted to speak with me about a business deal. He offered to deal with it, but when the person insisted on speaking with me he angrily said, "What's the difference? I can handle it!"

I realized then how badly he wanted what he thought I had. To me the power was a burden, not a source of satisfaction.

As I think about it now, almost forty years later, he may have been just longing for more of my company. We had been very close in the beginning but as we became more successful I was spread increasingly thin. There simply was not time to put the same degree of care into my relationship with him.

The third mistake that was not a mistake was my attachment to compassion. Ever since I was a boy I've had deep sympathy for people with disabilities, mental or physical. Sophia arrived in the early days when we were living in the Haight and seemed quite normal. She was a slim, beautiful Mediterranean type with olive skin, refined features and a lovely, whimsical personality. I found her hopelessly charming. She fell in love with Terry and they are still together today. I do not know how she slipped under my radar because I was careful to avoid persons with psychological problems. Perhaps the symptoms did not develop until after she joined the group. Anyway, within a couple of years I had a full-fledged anorexic on my hands.

Because of the way things turned out, no one believed I had such a strong love for her, but I did. And I did what I did not just for me but for her. By this time we were about five years into the experiment and people were waking up. I do not want to get into details, but at a certain point they just started popping like popcorn. I cannot take credit, nor would I if I could, because it was really the power of an idea and the traditional method that brought it about. True, had it not been for my persistence, keeping the minds headed in the right direction, it would not have happened, but it was more will power and inspiration than skill.

It was a wonderful spiritual event, no doubt, but like everything in life, it brought changes. When you wake up you are not the same person who went to sleep, although your old tendencies remain for some time. And you no longer need what brought you to that point. In fact some of the outer spiritual stuff, the *guru* particularly, needs to be jettisoned if you are to reach your full spiritual potential. I had been the focus of their spirituality and I was no longer need-ed. The incident with Sophia, diverting my affections from Victoria, and the stained glass incident, coupled with Tom's envy, set the stage for the final act.

There is no need to detail the symptoms of anorexia, as they are well-known nowadays. It broke my heart to see such a beautiful young woman reduced to what might reasonably be called an ambulatory cadaver. I tried to figure out what was causing her bizarre behavior. In our talks it came out that the prob-lem had begun around puberty, and I surmised that perhaps she starved her-self to appear unattractive to her father, who had shown inappropriate sexual interest at that time. Unbeknownst to her I consulted several psychiatrists and psychologists but came up with nothing useful. Looking for understanding, I made calls to her family in Europe but got nowhere. I tried to reason with her, but she was too well-defended. Eventually, I realized that if nothing were done I might have a fatality on my hands and a huge legal mess. Can you imagine what an ambitious lawyer might have done with the cult idea? So I decided to resolve the issue one way or the other.

In front of everyone, I told her that if she were going to stay she had to eat. I told her that she would have to take a little bit every day and that as her body adjusted we would slowly increase the intake until she was back to normal. She reluctantly agreed and the program began. We all ate together and every day the food on her plate disappeared before my watchful eye. I was quite hopeful in the beginning but did not notice any change in her appearance or energy level as time passed. I puzzled long and hard about why this might be but was unable to come up with a reasonable explanation. Then one day as I lingered after the meal in conversation with a friend one of the women washing dishes said, "Yuck, what's this?" I looked up as she turned over a plate to reveal Sophia's masticated meal carefully packed inside the rim on the bottom! Why she had been unable to dispose of it is a mystery. Evidently it was time to get caught.

I called Marlena, who had a big house with a small group of theater people, and she reluctantly agreed to take in Sophia as a favor to me. This did nothing to enhance my reputation as an enlightened, compassionate person. It gave the faction gathering around Tom and Terry another issue in their campaign to bring me down.

What they did not know was that I was not up. I think perhaps they thought that the whole experiment was happening by some sort of magic and that, unchecked, I might screw it up. But the reality was that I got up at four every morning and worked non-stop, late into the night seven days a week, three hundred and sixty-five days a year for over five years. I was not sitting on a throne waving a peacock feather to bless the faithful. If I had a dollar for every time I gave impartial and sensible counsel, lifted someone out of the doldrums, made a clever business decision or headed off a problem before it had a chance to become a problem I would be a millionaire many times over.

Perhaps if I had insisted on being treated like royalty, like so many small-minded *gurus*, or shown them a taste of the lash, it would have generated more sympathy, not that I needed or wanted it. I had one small room to myself and three or four changes of clothes, and drove a beat-up, ancient Chevy pickup. I handled thousands of dollars a week and never took a dime for myself. One rumor I heard after the break-up was that I had embezzled one hundred and fifty thousand dollars! In fact when all was said and done I came out with three grand and a pickup full of antiques for my trouble. The prevailing view was that I was too big for my britches and needed to be reined in before a serious disaster happened. They wanted a saint and I was only a regular guy. It is always that way.

What a pity that I was unaware of the "crazy wisdom" idea that was about to appear in the American spiritual scene. Crazy wisdom says that *gurus* who are attached to their bad habits can turn vices into virtues by convincing their students that the *guru's* sins are compassionate teachings meant to shock stupid egos into enlightenment. Screw a devotee and you are raising the *kundalini* or balancing the *chakras*. Relieve them of hard-earned cash and you are breaking their attachment to the almighty dollar. For their own good.

I think the word in vogue then in spiritual circles was that I was "impure." I can understand their fears. I was not doing anything to look like the white knight except making it possible for them to live like gods. Mind you, I was not bothered about what they thought. I was not a politician, feeding on the opinions of others. And I had experienced this sort of thing throughout my life, some of it justified, most not. When you are a public figure you learn that you really only exist as a projection in the minds of others. The public has no way of knowing who you really are or understanding what is going on in your mind. So all I could do was stick to my path and take what came with a grain of salt. "Through the power of knowledge maintain perfect equanimity in the face of praise and blame, virtue and vice, likes and dislikes," said a great sage.

I do not remember if a specific incident precipitated the confrontation. I think not, but at one of our regular meetings Tom, who had the support of several members of the group, told me that things were going to change. Specifically, I would no longer be exclusively calling the shots; we were going to evolve a more democratic style of leadership.

One thing they did not know was that democracy and self-realization have nothing to do with each other. The reason things worked so well for so long was that a high ideal was working behind all our activities and I was able to show it to other minds and inspire them to reach for it. If the mind does not have a noble goal it becomes drowned in myriad unfulfilling rituals. Self-realization is not achieved through consensus but through knowledge born of experience. It was handed down to me in traditional fashion by the Swami. Tradition means that a workable path has evolved over a long time. It is never a question of inventing something new, in which case a wide range of opinions could be profitably solicited and new paths tested, but of applying a time-tested means.

There is no better way. There may be other ways that work, but there is no better, modern way. I've always felt a bit sorry for those who claim to have attained enlightenment outside of a tradition, because with nothing to guide them, they are often forced to invent their own spiritual teachings.

When this happens you invariably end up with *gurus* with huge distorted egos who fancy themselves world saviors but who, in the fullness of time, will not rate even a footnote in spiritual history.

I learned an ancient and effective means by observing the Swami work it on me and on others. It is such a simple, elegant method of enlightenment that it passes under the radar of many supposedly highly-evolved types. I invented nothing, added nothing, except my own enthusiasm. And that enthusiasm came directly from within, from knowing how completely it had transformed my life, not because people were impressed with my brilliant teachings.

And secondly, they did not know I was suffering enlightenment fatigue and was fed up with the whole *guru* business and the self-obsessed spiritual world. The experiment was successful beyond my wildest expectations, and I needed to live a different life. So I told them they could continue without me.

Chapter VIII

A Comfortable Hair Shirt

IN 1948 MY father purchased a hand-hewn log cabin and bunkhouse on the south side of the Big Blackfoot River in the foothills of the Rocky Mountains, fifteen miles upstream from Missoula, Montana. The Big Blackfoot, a blue-ribbon trout stream, attained fame in literary and fishing circles many years ago through Norman Maclean's novel *A River Runs Through It*. Recently a movie with the same name introduced it to the general public.

To access the cabin, one parked on the north side of the river and walked across a charming swinging bridge. It was nestled in an old-growth forest at the foot of a mountain, in a stand of magnificent ponderosas on a pristine stream, which is so pure that to this day one can confidently drink from it. Ours was the only dwelling on the south side of the river for several miles. Deer, elk, moose, lynx, cougars, bears and many smaller critters – marmots, skunks, coyotes, squirrels, flying squirrels, porcupines and pack rats – were our only neighbors. Eagles, osprey, woodpeckers, kingfishers, cedar waxwings, grouse and hummingbirds ruled the skies.

I spent at least a third of my sixty years there, and it would be impossible to express in words the love I have for it. The cabin's chief virtue, in addition to the natural glories surrounding it, was isolation. Electricity came in the 1950s. The bridge washed out in a huge spring runoff in the late sixties and was replaced by a primitive cable car. I did not install a telephone until the mid-eighties. By the nineties economic and demographic forces caused us to lose the cable car, leaving only boat access. Family and friends came for a few weeks in the summer, but most of the year I was alone with my fishing rod, chain saw and my own mind. When the weather turned cold in October I left for India and returned after spring runoff for the salmon fly hatch, a pattern that lasted more than twenty years. During one nineteen-day stretch I did not speak to a human being.

At age thirty-six it was time to come to terms with a neglected part of myself. Shorn of the stress created by my ambitions, worldly and spiritual, I found in the cabin a comfortable hair shirt and a simple, purifying life, one that naturally turns the mind back on itself. What had been achieved so far with great effort was quite enough: the distracting and extravagant forays into passionate love, business, psychedelics, world travel and gurudom. I was deeply content. But as I fished up and down the river, chopped wood and carried water, my attention came to rest on a tiny grain of sand that was irritating the tissues of my mind.

I am clear on one point – the mind is me, but I am not the mind. The awareness that I am illumines it across an invisible but secure boundary. In the years since my enlightenment I more or less ignored the mind, reveling instead in the limitless bliss of the self. When one lives in the self as the self, one's actions are motivated by a pure force, a power that gradually creates a luminous new mind. More often than not, a few tendencies left over from one's previous life in the shadow of beginningless ignorance, and known only to oneself, persist. They will not create *karma* in the world, because the buffer between you and them, the dispassion that is the hallmark of self-realization, allows you the luxury of examining them and renouncing them before you act on them. For all intents and purposes you need do nothing about them. It is only between you and yourself. But because I like challenges, am a thorough person and had nothing better to do, I set out to eliminate them – as a kind of entertainment, a hobby, really.

The mind is remarkably resistant to change, yet it wants to change if what it is experiencing is less than perfect happiness. If it wants to change, it will listen to reason. Will power is not enough. Prayer is always helpful. But as far as my mind is concerned, understanding is king. If I can demonstrate, based on experience, how thinking creates problems, my mind will attempt the cure.

The cure is straightforward. Be there with it every minute as a commentator, coach and friend. Patiently teach it to think from the self's point of view. Eventually it will completely harmonize with its source. Purifying the mind, although punctuated by entertaining moments, is the drudgery of spiritual life, and I will not bore you with my efforts. The work went on continuously for many years when an unlikely and remarkable process purified the irritating tendencies altogether.

Meanwhile, a rich outer life provided entertainments aplenty.

The Divine Marlena

After several months in the cabin I returned to San Francisco for a few weeks to make some fast and easy money. When the job was done I inquired about Marlena, the dancer I had met in the flat in the Haight Ashbury five years before, and was sent to a large flat in the Mission District inhabited by a gay, transvestite prostitute, a couple of Chicano junkies, and a down-and-out hippie couple. The transvestite led me to a small room at the back of the flat. Marlena was lying on a small cot about two feet from the wall, her body surrounded by a remarkable white aura. She seemed unaware of my presence. As I approached I noticed that she was in an altered state – to say the least. Her body was convulsing rhythmically. I could hear the bones crunching against each other and her face was changing in the most extraordinary fashion. The flesh was no longer flesh but had become a luminous river of energy, and out of that river personality after personality emerged, lived a second and dissolved back into it. In the space of a few minutes she became scores of entities: some benign, some horrific, some of which I recognized and some from worlds beyond human understanding. The energy was so intense that I thought I might lose consciousness. Then, miraculously, her body floated off the bed and fell to the floor when it encountered the nearby wall!

Seeing her in such squalor, suffering such a terrible fate, I forgot myself and decided to look after her. I gathered a few of her clothes, scooped her off the bed, put her in the van and drove to Montana.

"What's going on?" I said one day when we were settled in the cabin and she experienced another episode.

"I have the wrong body," she said.

"The wrong body?"

"Yes, this one belongs to someone else. It's not mine. This is why it's changing. It's being completely rebuilt cell by cell. It will soon match my soul."

I tried to argue with her, but eventually came to the conclusion that her explanation was as good as any and let it slide. Five years later I would discover the truth. In the meantime, we fell deeply in love and tied the knot.

"Why do you love me?" I said one day.

"Because you are me," she replied.

I am not the marrying type, but marriage suited me and I would still be married today had things turned out differently. Why did I do it? I thought my love would help her heal. I wanted to please my aging mother. And I was powerless not to passionately love someone whose vision of the self was as pure and intense as my own.

On another occasion, she said, "You love me just like you love everyone, don't you?"

"Yes," I said. "How do you feel about that?"

"It's good," she replied. "If it was special, it would only feed my ego and would not last."

For the first two years the episodes, which were always a variation of the first one I witnessed, were infrequent, although they might last for several days. I tried to persuade her to see mental health professionals, but she would have none of it. Even when I did finally get her to see a psychologist she completely concealed her condition, and the psychologist implied that perhaps I was the one who needed some help. After the third attempt, I decided to deal with her condition as if it were normal – so we went about our lives as if nothing were happening.

She was not only a great spiritual presence but an accomplished artist and poet as well. When we met six years before she was teaching a class at the University of San Francisco and dancing with a local company, Dance Spectrum. Later, to express the creativity her awakening inspired, she started a small experimental dance theater company. One day she said she wanted to contribute to our financial situation and offered to put together a nightclub act. We went to Las Vegas, where she worked on the routines and the music while I designed and constructed the costumes. When everything was ready we invited a big agent to see the act and he hired her on the spot, booking her in top clubs around the world.

So we spent the glorious Rocky Mountain summers at the cabin, booked shows for six or eight weeks in spring and fall, and spent winters in India. I secretly hoped that we might come across someone who could heal her, but it never happened. Nonetheless, she loved India and was unfailingly polite and loving toward me.

During this period we attracted many people, but nothing worked because her bizarre episodes drove people away. Eventually, I started to hear the view that somehow I was responsible for her condition! On one level it was understandable because anyone with the slightest sensitivity could see that she was an extraordinary being. Her beauty, purity, intelligence, compassion and selflessness were natural and obvious. It seemed impossible that such an exalted soul could be afflicted by an inexplicable madness. Additionally, I am not the type to attract sympathy. This, coupled with the shadowy tendencies that I was purifying, made it possible for a certain kind of mind to draw the conclusion that I was some sort of black magician who had put a spell on her.

In the fourth year things started to go downhill. The episodes intensified and lengthened. There is a voluminous literature of fear, but I was never drawn to it, so I am ill-equipped to describe what I experienced when the madness erupted. I suppose a crude diagnosis might be demon possession, which is just a way of speaking of primal fears. But she was always above the mind, so it was more accurate to say the mind was possessed. It's a fine point, but there is a world of difference.

Nonetheless, during these episodes, many strange things happened. The elements seemed confused. Clocks stopped and started inexplicably. Objects moved from one place to another under their own power. One day she was lying on a chaise lounge in the field when a violent storm came up the river. I watched from the cabin, expecting her to get up and come indoors, but she did not move. The sky emptied buckets and the wind whipped the rain with great force. But not one drop of rain fell on her, nor was a single hair moved by the gale! When I mentioned the storm at dinner, she said, "What storm?"

These events were a source of interest to me. From my state, nothing is strange. Also, my experience with psychedelics helped me cultivate an appreciation of the bizarre. Some years later when I saw the movie *Ghostbusters*, I recognized every one of the demons because, in a sense, they had been like household pets.

Then one day in the fifth year I realized that there was no hope. Throughout the relationship I persisted in discussing what was happening with her. I had always assumed that the episodes were happening involuntarily and that her strange explanations were attempts to justify them after the fact. But on this day she told me that she was actually causing the convulsions.

"You're causing them?" I said in disbelief. "Whatever for?"

"I'm making my new body. It can't wait."

"So just what are you doing?"

"I'm transforming it cell by cell. Before long it will perfectly match who I am."

"So you could stop then?" I asked.

"Oh, yes. But I won't stop, because it is absolutely necessary that I have the proper body."

"Necessary for whom?"

"For the world. When I have the right body, the world will know who I am and they will all become happy."

By this time the episodes had become normal life, and normal life an occasional episode. Her health declined and she was unable to work. But the saddest fact for me was the realization that my love was no longer helpful. From this point on her mind was in the grip of a force that would not be denied. Eventually she ended up in bed in a terrible state.

I asked her how she was feeling.

"I can't go on," she said. "I want to die. Please let me die."

"I understand," I said. "You can die. Nobody should suffer like this. But you have to think of me."

"What do you mean?" she said.

"If you die here in this isolated cabin without proper medical attention, I'll be charged with negligent homicide. I'm your husband. It's my duty to look after you. You have steadfastly resisted my attempts to get help. I have respected your wishes, but now you need to let me take you to the hospital so the society can take the responsibility for you. You can die there if that is what is meant to be."

"Please take me," she said. "I can't live any longer."

I put her in the hospital in California and waited to see what would happen. The doctors removed her intestine, which had been destroyed by Crohne's disease, and when it was clear she was out of the woods I went to India. When I returned in the spring, she had disappeared. I went to see her mother, but she had moved. On an outside chance I decided to call on her uncle. Her cousin opened the door.

"I'm looking for Marlena," I said.

"Come in," she said cordially. At some point in the conversation the cousin said, "So you didn't know?"

"Didn't know what?" I said.

"Why she is like that."

"No. What was it?"

"Ours is a big, old, ingrown Italian family. It goes way back. There are many tragedies and skeletons in the closet. The whole family was against it."

"Against what?"

"Against the marriage of Stefano and Maureen."

"Why?"

"They are first cousins. It's the same as incest. Children born in that situation are often hemophiliacs or develop madness later in life. Marlena started to lose it when she was about twenty-seven."

A Real Mahatma

My mother died a few months before my marriage to Marlena ended and left me a small inheritance, one that made it possible for me not to work, particularly considering the fact that the lease on the cabin cost one hundred fifty dollars a year, and India was not much more expensive. The following summer I met the Swami on one of his annual tours to the West and asked him to recommend a *mahatma* in the *bhakti* tradition.

"So I'm not good enough anymore, eh, Ram?" the Swami joked.

"Don't be silly, Swamiji," I said, "you're always number one with me. But I have the time and money to get into India in a way I never have and I would like to know more about *bhakti*."

"Go to Trivandrum. There is a *mahatma* there. He has an *ashram* near the Padmanabha Swami temple. His name is Swami Abhedananda. You may think I'm somebody, but I tell you I'm a third-rate spiritual businessman compared to him. He is a real *mahatma* of the old school. Tell him I sent you."

When the frost came I boarded up the cabin and caught the plane to South India. I learned that the Swami was at his *ashram* in the country, about forty minutes from Trivandrum. About a mile from the *ashram* I noticed a wonderful feeling in my heart, as if the petals of a lotus were slowly opening in the first light of day. The vibrations were blissful, rhythmic and intense and continue to this day. When I entered the *ashram* grounds a *yagna* was taking place, a hundred or so fully-absorbed devotees clustered around the sacrificial fire as the priests chanted and offered the prescribed items to the gods. On one side I noticed a very dignified seventy-something man who was emitting such radiance I could hardly stand to look directly at him. When the sacrifice was completed a devotee brought me to the Swami. He asked who I was and what I wanted.

"Swami Chinmaya sent me," I said. He nodded and instructed the devotee to give me a room.

When you understand the nature of reality you know there are no real distinctions, only apparent distinctions. There are no enlightened beings, nor are there any unenlightened beings. Nonetheless, the shift in identity that is enlightenment does not miraculously eliminate the subconscious tendencies that define a person.

The personality has a peculiar ontological status; it is neither real, nor is it unreal. It is not real in the sense that you can never put your finger on it and say conclusively "this is what it is." It is just the notion of an "I" carelessly ascribed to a complex of ever-changing tendencies. So even though there is actually no one "there," except awareness, we seem to experience a distinct individual. In that sense the individual has a certain limited reality. It exists but it is not real, meaning substantial and enduring.

Much is made of the individual we call "I." One of the most salient features of individuals caught in the dream of duality is the need to distinguish themselves from each other on the basis of various criteria. One would hope it was not so, but the so-called spiritual world is as status-conscious as any petty racial, social, religious or political world.

As much as we would like to, we cannot summarily superimpose what belongs to reality on the apparent reality. Insofar as we find ourselves in the dream we need to function here according to the rules operating in the dream. Therefore it is often useful to make distinctions between apparently real things. If I have a particularly subtle or complex problem I need to go to an expert; it will not serve to approach the man next door, although both are nothing but awareness.

The generally accepted standard for evaluating the spirituality of human beings is related to the quality and quantity of their subconscious impressions. Not to put too fine a point on it, there is a direct relationship between the type and number of impressions and the level of evolution. A person like a saint with a few light and pure impressions would be at the upper end, and persons with many active and dull impressions would inhabit the lower reaches of the scale. And while there is a broad correlation between enlightenment and the upper end of the scale, it is possible for someone to attain enlightenment when there are still a few gross impressions because enlightenment is simply the hard and fast understanding "I am ordinary, actionless, limitless awareness." And it needs to be understood that saintly behavior does not necessarily indicate enlightenment.

Another argument says that the highest class of enlightened beings does not interfere with the operation of their tendencies, because their vision reveals the tendencies, whether pure or impure, to be nothing but non-dual awareness, which they would be if this is a non-dual reality – which it is. There is merit to this argument, but traditionally it has been the cause of great mischief because it is often used by the enlightened and unenlightened alike to justify unhealthy behavior, violations of *dharma* and the like, although an enlightened individual whose knowledge was firm would never violate *dharma*.

The non-elimination of the gross, subconscious impressions argument does not apply to non-gurugic individuals, because their behavior has no more effect than does that of any unenlightened person. But the question of purity becomes operative when one sets out to teach enlightenment to others. Therefore the best standard by which to evaluate individuals is related to the degree of purity of their minds and hearts, not whether or not they are enlightened. It is incomprehensible that people these days flock to gross, extroverted, self-obsessed, self-promoting, desire-ridden, arrogant *gurus* when such people can be found on any street corner.

Swami Chinmaya was correct. Swami Abhedananda, whose name, "the bliss of non-differentiation," says it all, was simply off the scale. In the best of all possible worlds one imagines there are such souls, but one never knows unless one is fortunate enough to meet one. We actually have no way of knowing, because all statements about spiritual attainment are suspect, owing to the tendency of unfulfilled minds to project their spiritual fantasies, but maybe the Buddha, Christ, Ramana Maharshi, Bhagavan Nityananda and others were at this level. Certainly they were not above it, because in terms of human evolution there simply is no "above."

To live in the *ashram* was to live in an ocean of unself-conscious love, not the smarmy, self-conscious love of spiritual doers. During my stays I did not witness a single argument or one raised voice. No one had problems. Every person I encountered was a pure soul of the highest moral character and completely aware of the tremendous good fortune that had been showered on them, by virtue of their association with the Swami.

When he came out in the morning and sat in the courtyard I swear the small bushes and plants near his seat gradually leaned toward him, as if to protect and embrace him. The *ashram* was almost completely silent, but it was not the precious, self-conscious, controlled silence one frequently finds in spiritual groups that cater to beginners trying to suppress their minds; it was the ever-free silence of pure awareness. The sense of no otherness that the Swami's presence invoked was so overwhelming that any mind that came near him immediately lay down like a contented puppy. Surrender was not optional; it happened without effort.

In the morning we read from the *Srimad Bhagavatam*, the "Bible of the *bhaktas*." A *bhakta* is a lover of God. Although I was the only foreigner and the text was in Malayalam, the Swami had every verse translated for me. The philosophy of *bhakti*, pure love, scoffs at liberation philosophies because it approaches the problem of suffering in a completely different way. It says that if you love yourself the idea that you need to be free of anything will never arise. And how do you love yourself? By loving God. When you love God you come to understand that God is everyone and everything, including yourself. So love of self is included in love of God. How can attachment to anything in the world be painful when everything is your beloved? Why would you want to be free of yourself if your nature is love? What kind of problems will you have with the world if everyone in it is you?

So the practice, if indeed it could be called that, was worship of God. Worship is quite different from prayer, in that one does not feel compelled to ask for anything; it is pure gratitude. This is so because one appreciates the fact that one is cast in God's image and as such always has everything one could ever need.

No one worships God like God. When the Swami sang we were transported into luminous fields of bliss. I have experienced many wonderful things in life, but chanting the name of God with that group of pure souls tops them all. The devotees claimed that he was an incarnation of Sri Chaitanya, a sixteenth-century Bengali whose love of and identity with God was so great that it awakened a love of God in millions of souls and revitalized an ancient lineage of God-realized devotees.

I am a practical, apparently cynical person who hates the glorification of human beings based on select criteria, but there is no doubt in my mind that there are a few rare souls who are purely divine. In India they are called incarnations, or *avatars*. These are not people who need to free themselves, because when they appear here they are already free. They do not need to learn anything, because they know everything that needs to be known. They have nothing to gain or lose.

They come to reveal the self through their presence and a particular talent. They are people of the highest moral character who are completely free of vanity. It is pity that the word *"avatar"* has been mightily defiled in recent times, having become the self-assigned spiritual status of many ambitious fools out to make a name for themselves. Today even pedophiles claim to be *avatars*.

Abhedananda's *guru* was a *yogi* named Chatambi Swami. Chatambi Swami was an extraordinary man who is still venerated today in South India. There are many stories about him. One day a devotee saw him walking on the street and invited him to lunch. It is considered a great honor to feed a *mahatma* in India. The Swami said, "Yes, I will come, but I will bring thirteen friends." The devotee's wife prepared a scrumptious feast and the devotee set fourteen banana leaves on the floor and waited for the Swami to appear. Banana leaves serve as plates in South India. When the Swami appeared he was followed by a single row of thirteen dogs that filed in and took their seats. When the food was served the Swami chanted the proper prayers. When he was finished the dogs began eating. When the meal was finished the dogs picked up their leaves and deposited them outside, as is the custom in *ashrams* in South India.

On another occasion a group of villagers caught a large Bengal tiger in a pit trap. They were arguing about what to do with it when the Swami arrived. "Leave it to me," the Swami said, fearing for the life of the tiger. He walked over to the pit and removed the logs. Then he pushed one log down into the pit so the tiger could climb out. When the tiger emerged it walked over and sat in front of the Swami, who began talking to it. After a short conversation the Swami headed off into the hills, the tiger following dutifully behind.

Abhedananda met Chatambi Swami only once and spent thirty minutes with him in a cave in the Western Ghats. One of the functions of an *avatar* is to blow new life into existing spiritual institutions. Therefore they engage in human rituals. The *guru*-disciple institution is of utmost importance to the world because it serves to awaken people to God. So even *avatars* often take *gurus*. Even if Abhedananda was not an incarnation, he was an *adhikari*, someone highly qualified for enlightenment, like Ramana Maharshi. This is why *diksha*, teaching, if that is what happened in the cave, took less than half an hour.

In the *bhatki* tradition there are many styles of worship and we practiced them all, but the favored style was passionate love of God. The chants, which were held in Trivandrum in the evening, were extraordinary spiritual events attended by scores of the Swami's devotees. Many were accomplished musicians who warmed up the crowd. When everyone was in a state of intense love the Swami would pick up the chant. It is impossible to describe the wild excitement, the rocking, transcendent joy, the overwhelming sanctity that his singing evoked. I do not think that one person, myself included, did not feel completely honored to have participated in those evenings. The energy was so pure and pervasive it rooted out every sense of duality and you did not leave the venue with the doubt that you were separate from God. When we stumbled silently out into the night the whole world was radiant and alive with *prema*, divine love.

On certain occasions we would leave the *ashram* on foot and proceed along the roads, chanting the names of God. One person would lead the chant for half an hour and then another. The energy was intense and attracted crowds of people who left their homes and their work to come for the *darshan* of the Swami. People would throw themselves at his feet and women brought their babies for blessing. We chanted continuously until noon, when we would stop at a village temple where food had been prepared. After lunch we would nap and then begin walking again in the afternoon, arriving around sunset at an ancient temple, where we would worship and take *prasad*, holy food. Often in the evenings a meeting was planned with chanting and sometimes a few words from the Swami, who rarely spoke. Words are basically superfluous in the presence of God. I was often asked to address the crowd and was treated with great respect because they appreciated my great love of their culture.

At other times we would take pilgrimages to various holy sites. One of the Swami's favorite places was Courtallam, at the foot of the Western Ghats near the Tamil Nadu-Kerala border. It was winter, meaning the temperatures were in the seventies, and the town was deserted. There were many empty hotels, so we had no trouble finding accommodations.

I found it very interesting that the Swami never made reservations for trains or hotels, no matter how many people went with him. We would just get on a train and there would be seats, and when we got to our destination somebody would always appear out of the blue and guide us to comfortable accommodations. One had the constant sense that there were magical little creatures hovering around in the air, that this was a benign and conscious universe, one dedicated to looking after our every need. Nor did he carry money. If we ran out of money we just stopped, and within a few minutes someone would come up and offer to get us what we needed. One day we were sitting in the courtyard when a white Ambassador came into the *ashram* compound. The driver got out and opened the door for a very dignified man, who walked up the path carrying a very large silver tray. He came right up to the Swami and offered him the tray, which had a huge mountain of bundled one-hundred-rupee notes stacked upon it.

He was completely unattached to his devotees, his *ashram* or his position at the pinnacle of Indian society. Maitli, a *sannyasi* who served him for many years, told me that one time he walked out of the *ashram* without anything except his stick and his shawl. The devotees assumed he was going for a walk and for some reason did not feel inclined to follow him. Six months later he had not returned and no one had heard a word from him. One day a devotee who was on a pilgrimage to Mount Kailash returned to Trivandrum and reported that he had seen the Swami sitting on the banks of the Ganges near Haridwar with a group of *sadhus*. He went up to him and said, "Swamiji, what are you doing here? Your devotees are distressed and worried about you. You must go back to your *ashram* and see them."

"Oh, I forgot," he said.

A few weeks later he appeared at the *ashram*.

Swami was a *guru's guru* and had many enlightened devotees. As many as eight or ten *mahatmas* came to see him every week. Often we would visit households where the whole family was awakened. I met many women, ordinary housewives, who were fully enlightened. He seemed to have a kind of sixth sense, one that could feel the longing of the heart, and he would always appear at the most fortuitous moment in a person's journey and move them on to the next level or set them free altogether. But no one ever talked about it. It was considered bad form. There was just a shared secret knowing, a very natural thing.

The falls at Courtallam are fed by a beautiful stream that runs out of the Western Ghats. The jungle is particularly pristine, even today. One day we took our bath in the falls and worshipped at the temple. When we finished, the Swami set out to climb a steep path near the falls. Because I was big and strong and energetic, it was my duty to stay close behind him and catch him if he started to fall. He was in such an exalted state most of the time that he had almost no body or earth consciousness. It was a great honor to have this duty because it meant that I was always directly in his energy field, which kept my mind tuned to his and allowed me to experience many incredible things.

At the top of the falls the path followed the stream into the mountains. The beauty of the place was overwhelming and we walked in silence as we moved slowly up the valley. Every fifteen minutes or so a *sadhu* would miraculously appear out of the jungle as we passed. I could tell by their vibrations and their bodies that these men were ascetics of the highest caliber living somewhere in the jungle and that the Swami was their *guru*. Each approached the Swami, touched his feet and stood silently for his *darshan*. When the transmission was over they melted back into the jungle without a word. After about an hour we came upon a small feeder stream and the Swami began walking carefully along it. In a few minutes we came to an enchanting grotto where one could sense the presence of *devas*, gods, hovering all around. On a rock in the stream was a picture of Sri Ram, one of India's most beloved deities (the Swami and his flock were Vaishnavites) and next to it a very old woman, perhaps more than ninety years old, worshipping the god with incense and beautiful *mantras*. When she saw the Swami she became overwhelmed with devotion. Tears streaming down her cheeks, she fell to the ground in front of him and grasped his feet. No words were exchanged but I had the feeling that she had just received her last instructions and could now end her incarnation, never to return. The situation reminded me of a story in the *Puranas* where Sri Ram returned after slaying Ravana to a place not far from this very spot to grant liberation to an aging woman devotee, Shabari.

Somewhat later we came across a clearing in the jungle at the foot of another large waterfall. At one end of the clearing was a small temple that had been locked for the winter season. The Swami walked resolutely toward it, and just as we entered the courtyard a priest came walking out of the jungle! To this day I am not sure if it was a flesh and blood priest or if it was a transcendental priest conjured up by God to please the Swami, who was intent on having the *darshan* of the deity. The priest unlocked the door and we entered for our *darshan*.

After Courtallam we drove to Papanasham, a small rural town perhaps fifty kilometers away. Instead of entering the town, whose tall *Gopurams* were visible in the distance, we turned and came to a fairly large *ashram* cum temple, situated on the banks of a beautiful stream coming from the mountains in the distance. Like the small temple near the waterfall, it had been shut up for the winter. The Swami sent someone to town to fetch the caretaker, who appeared an hour later with the keys and a group of devotees eager for the Swami's *darshan*. We spent several extremely enjoyable days there doing nothing in particular, mostly sitting in the mild sun on the banks of the river, reading scripture and chanting.

On a tiny island in the middle of the stream, which was perhaps forty feet wide, a small shrine had been constructed. Indian deities are treated as if they were living beings. They are fed, bathed, clothed and taken out of the temple to see the world and let themselves be worshipped. In many temple complexes in South India there is a small temple in the middle of the large bathing tank to which the deity is taken in a boat on certain important occasions for an outing. Evidently the gods become weary from constant worship and need a day off and a picnic near the water.

One day I dove into the river and swam to the shrine. The Swami was sitting nearby, watching with interest. I could see he wanted to join me, so I called to him, "Come on, Swamiji, the water is fine."

"But he doesn't know how to swim. He will drown," said Maitli, trying to dissuade the Swami who was walking down to the water's edge.

"I'll teach him," I said, and the devotees looked horrified.

"Okay, Swamiji," I said, "watch this." I dog-paddled a few meters and returned. "Now you try it."

Without a thought he entered the river and followed instructions to the letter, eventually ending up on the far bank of the river. When he arrived he sat at the water's edge beaming like a child at his accomplishment.

"How did I do, Ram? Good?"

"The best, Swami," I said, giving him the thumbs-up.

On another occasion we traveled to Rajapalayam, a large, dusty town on the plains east of the Ghats. We stayed with a wealthy family of devotees who were sponsoring an *archana*. An *archana* is a prolonged worship that involves chanting the name of God hundreds of thousands, sometimes millions, of times. The venue was a large, whitewashed, pillared hall in a temple complex that dated back to the eleventh century. The devotees, of which there were several hundred, sat in a long row in front of a tall brass oil lamp and offered a flower with every *mantra*. The lamp represents the self, God, and the flames represent the five elements that make up the cosmos. As the worship proceeds a small mountain of flowers grows in front of each devotee's lamp. Once a flower had been offered it could not be offered again. Every few hours a large truck, full of scores of wicker baskets of flowers, pulled up at the site. Young men and women would unload the baskets and work their way down the rows, clearing the used flowers and supplying the devotees with new ones. The chanting went on for three days. This kind of worship is exceptionally powerful because the atmosphere becomes intensely charged with *shakti*, spiritual energy. As the energy intensifies with the continued repetition of the *mantras*, the mind turns within and becomes purified in an inner rain of awareness.

One day as we were sitting with the Swami, someone brought me a telegram. The Swami told me to open it and asked what it said. "My mother just died, and I have to go the United States," I said. "Any advice?" He looked at me, smiled and raised his hand in *abaya mudra*, the gesture of fearlessness, and said, "Take it easy." It was a valuable instruction because it destroyed every bit of my spiritual ambition. When I returned some months later, he was dead. I asked Maitli about his passing.

"He wanted to be put in the Ganges. Everything went as planned, but one very strange thing happened. As you know, the body is made to sit in a yogic pose just before rigor mortis sets in, so it is stiff and can be carried through the streets for worship and on to the *ghats* or the cremation ground for the final rites. But in his case, rigor mortis did not set in. His body remained as flexible and limber as it was in life. We had to get some ropes and have a carpenter construct a mast on the cart and tie him to it so he could sit up. Then we took him to the Ganges and put him in."

His death did not sever our bond. A few years later when I was in the cabin in Montana working on a particularly subtle problem, I decided to ask the Swami if my conclusion was correct. I went to my dresser, where I kept an altar. His picture was on the wall behind the dresser, and there was a candle several inches below and in front of it. I invoked him, transmitted my idea and asked for a sign whether it was correct. The room became deathly silent, and my eyes became riveted on the candle. Instead of running down the side of the candle toward the dresser top, the wax started building up in an arc and growing toward his picture, defying the law of gravity. As I watched, it gracefully curved upward and stopped when it touched his heart.

***

I think it is almost time to stop my story. Because my life up to this point has been so interesting, people assume that the next thirty years were just as interesting, and since I wrote this I have had many requests to carry the tale forward. The last thirty-some years have been as interesting but in a very different way. Life is interesting if you are interested in it, and I love life, so the interest is always there.

The life chronicled here was the way it was because it could be no other way. I suffered the disease of ignorance and needed to learn my lessons. But once I graduated it had nothing to teach. Self-knowledge is "that knowledge that ends the quest for knowledge." No, I do not want to know each and every fact about existence, even if it is possible. God knows it all and I am quite happy to let God caretake and practice Its knowledge. Because of it, the worlds are born and die, and the creatures come and go in eternal cycles of time. I do not need to know, because I know it all without knowing all the facts. I know the essence, that which makes knowing possible. I know it because I am it.

Some people read my story and ask if it is true because it seems quite improbable. They usually think that I am a clever guy with the gift of gab and a hyperactive imagination who wants to impress people. It is natural to think this way if you have not been driven to know why we are here. We are all mystics by default, but if you operate your own life according to your own lights, the default setting may never kick in and you will never be led down this dangerous path to freedom. When you are swept up in the arms of existence, you no longer call the shots. Existence has its way with you, and when that happens truth is sometimes much stranger than fiction.

I wrote it years ago, when my memory of the events was still reasonably fresh. I wrote it because I became weary telling it when people asked. People think something is wrong if they cannot remember something, but usually there is nothing wrong. The self graciously wipes away the memories that no longer serve its purpose and leaves the mind free to gather more experience. I wrote my story because it was leaving me. I was happy to let it go. It means nothing to me. It is a leftover from a life well-lived. I saved it because it is a good story. I saved it for you. If it is too much to swallow as truth, see it as fiction. It is fine with me. Everything here, including what those lost in the dream of life think is true, is a fiction cooked up by the disease of ignorance. Whether it is truth or fiction, the message rings loud and clear.

All that is left to say is that when you know who you are, life flows unobstructed to its destination. It does not matter what happens, because you have the confidence to weather any storm. So I will finish it now after this: do not think that mystic experience is required for enlightenment. These experiences can be a great boon or a great curse. And because the self is always present, it can be realized by anyone at any time, assuming certain qualifications, none of which have to do with particular experiences.

I still go back and forth between India and the West, and keep a small apartment in Tiruvannamalai, at the foot of the holy mountain Arunachala in the state of Tamil Nadu. What do I do? I collect a little social security and sit patiently, waiting for my coronary or any other way life seems pleased to make room for another soul. While I wait, I sit in my favorite café, watching the passing show and chatting with friends. I talk Vedanta and comment on scripture. A few people come and listen to what I have to say and then go away. After some time, others come who have seen how Vedanta has transformed their friends. They too sit and listen and go away.

Made in the USA
Columbia, SC
23 July 2020